ESSAYS IN
POLITICAL AND INTELLECTUAL HISTORY

Essays in Political and Intellectual History

by

SAMUEL BERNSTEIN

Essay Index Reprint Series

 BOOKS FOR LIBRARIES PRESS
FREEPORT, NEW YORK

STANDARD BOOK NUMBER:

8369-1171-7

LIBRARY OF CONGRESS CATALOG CARD NUMBER:

73-86729

PRINTED IN THE UNITED STATES OF AMERICA

To Rose

FOREWORD

The present essays appeared in several journals over a period of more than eighteen years. Most of them first appeared in the quarterly, *Science and Society*. The others were originally published in *Società* and *Pensée*. "From Social Utopia to Social Science" was read at the meeting of the American Historical Association in December 1948. Two of the essays are now presented for the first time: "The First International in France, 1864-1871;" and "The American Press Views the Paris Commune." They have been included here to give greater unity to the selection. The essay on the American press and the Commune should be of special interest to students of American intellectual history.

The essays, here republished, have all been revised to a greater or less degree. The revisions in several of them have been more in the phrase than in the content. Others have been recast in the light of fresh research in libraries and archives. The method and argument, however, remain essentially unchanged. The essays serve to demonstrate the kinship of ideas and the mutual sympathies of peoples in matters concerning human betterment.

Without the assistance of Rose these essays might not have been written.

SAMUEL BERNSTEIN

May 1955

CONTENTS

I. Marat, Friend of the People 9

II. Robespierre and the Problem of War 26

III. British Jacobinism 38

IV. Jefferson on the French Revolution 57

V. Babeuf and Babouvism 77

VI. Saint-Simon's Philosophy of History 100

VII. From Social Utopia to Social Science 113

VIII. French Democracy and the American Civil War . . . 121

IX. The First International in France, 1864-1871 134

X. The Paris Commune 150

XI. The American Press Views the Commune 169

XII. The First International and a New Holy Alliance . . 183

Notes 200

Index 222

MARAT, FRIEND OF THE PEOPLE

POPULAR leaders make history and are made by it. They are sharp-eyed men, generous and human. They see through people and events like X-rays, dig beneath the surface to detect the relation of things, their movements and their consequences to individuals and the community. Their perspectives are large. If they at times look to the rear it is not to nourish on the promises of yesterday, but to learn from the past, its errors and its merits, its knavery and sublimity. They are like stalwart oaks, with roots deep down in their country. They are of the people, yet freed from common vices and conventions. That is perhaps why their visions are far and their judgments prophetic.

Robespierre and Marat were two such men. The first was a parliamentarian, legalistic, cautious and acute; the second was a journalist, relentless, trenchant and astute. Each valued the other's services to the French Revolution. Robespierre saw Marat as "a fine citizen, a zealous defender of the people's cause"; Marat considered Robespierre "the patriotic orator," "the Aristides of the century," "loyal to liberty." Contemporaries draped them with obloquy.

They hated Marat, in particular. If they portrayed Robespierre as treacherous and gory, they placed Marat among the demented, the diseased, and the criminal.[1] And historians, accepting their estimates, have poked fun at his gestures, his features and his small stature. Perhaps a clue to their aversion was his defense of the have-nots, his never-ending warnings, like siren-blasts, against conspiracies of reaction, and his call to the lowly to be the sentinels of the nation as well as its governors. His ascendancy over them mounted steadily during the first four years of the Revolution until he fairly symbolized their objectives. By the time of his assassination, in 1793, they looked upon him as "The Friend of the People."

9

1

When the Estates General assembled on May 5, 1789, Jean Paul Marat was nearing his forty-sixth birthday. He had left his family and birthplace in Neuchâtel, Switzerland, almost thirty years earlier, and during this long span had been a tutor, a physician, a scientist, a novelist, a writer on politics, criminology and metaphysics, and finally a journalist. He had seen something of western Europe, for he had lived in Bordeaux, Paris, London and Newcastle, and visited Ireland, Scotland and Holland. Several years before the Revolution he seems to have given up a fashionable medical practice in Paris in order to devote himself to research in the physical sciences. Of his eight monographs on scientific research two were awarded prizes by the Academy of Rouen. Also Franklin, Goethe and other contemporaries regarded him favorably as a scientist.[2]

Marat's concern for political and social problems antedated the French Revolution by many years. "I came to the Revolution with ideas already formed," he wrote autobiographically in March, 1793.[3] It is not an overstatement that two of his early books, *The Chains of Slavery*[4] and *Plan de législation criminelle*,[5] contained in substance the convictions that later singled him out for attack and persecution. His own experience from 1789 to 1793 and the events of the Revolution on the whole undoubtedly provided an adequate base for the convictions. But they had had their beginnings in England and Scotland, where he had associated with patriotic societies and observed the agitation over John Wilkes, the great English liberal journalist-politician. Apart from that the two works show considerable scholarship. They validate Marat's subsequent claim that "liberty has always been my favorite goddess."[6]

Marat's early political writings start with the premise that the unequal distribution of wealth is at the bottom of all societal maladies. The acquisition of vast properties is done at the expense of the small man. He loses his independence, in fact is reduced to servitude. "The state then consists only of masters and subjects." In the large towns there are two contraposed classes: one consists of capitalists, financiers, and rentiers; the other is made up of the poor. The first class, regardless of competence or merit, has exclusive possession of the large enterprises in commerce and industry, controls the administration of the public revenue, prescribes the laws of the state and utilizes it for further enrichment. The second class lives by precarious and odious labor. Gold produces gold, but poverty brings demoralization. The man of business "has a price on everything. Gold is no less the value of good posts, heroic deeds, talents and virtues, than it is of wages, products of the soil and works of art." The mercantile spirit makes men predatory and hostile to noble action. They succeed in cornering the basic necessities of life, "thus rendering precarious the people's existence." And they cause false rumors to spread until they net their victims, stocks and all. The rich are without a country. That country is theirs "which offers them the most resources . . . and where they do the most business." Their hearts and minds are as closed to patriotism as to freedom.[7]

Rulers use every device to deceive the people, Marat continued to charge. They are enemies of education and enlightenment; they enlist the aid of the clergy, distract the people with parades and amusements, give out false information, censor publications, prevent their subjects from travelling and employ scribblers to discredit the people's leaders. If this is insufficient, they have recourse to prison and poison.[8] That is why a people's leader must have exceptional qualities, said Marat. He must be courageous, selfless, zealous, and be prepared to face a tempest of abuse. He must be able to rally wavering people and awaken the nation from apathy. Over and above that he has to know how to time events in order to attain the triumph of the people's rising against the despotic ruler.[9] Elsewhere in *The Chains of Slavery* he pointed out that governors, to continue governing, maintain professional armies and embark on foreign adventures. These are the best distractions from domestic issues and the calculated occasions for destroying the people's party. If defeat is to the rulers' advantage, they betray the nation; but "to conceal their treason, they lay the defeat to the soldiers' want of discipline."[10]

The above ideas were Marat's before 1789. The French Revolution but confirmed them for him and anchored them permanently. Oddly enough, he prefigured in these early political works his part in the great revolutionary drama.

2

Marat had been in Paris thirteen years before the start of the Revolution. It is safe to assume that none of the signs of the decaying old régime escaped him. The conflict between those who desired to retain feudal relics and those who championed reforms produced a vast literary crop, most of it ephemeral. This was the golden age of pamphleteers, each proudly bequeathing to the nation his special remedy.[11] Though occupied with scientific research, Marat could not be silent while society was in convulsion. The reform movement probably brought to mind the John Wilkes affair in England, of which he had been an eye-witness.[12] The movement at any rate carried him along, and in February 1789, appeared anonymously his *Offrande à la patrie,* addressed to the Third Estate of France.[13] It marked Marat's début as a participant in the Revolution.

The language of the pamphlet was fairly restrained, but underneath it was the suggestion that the people should take over the government. Marat praised the king, for in February, 1789, the French monarch was held in deep respect. But he called on the king to abandon the feudal class and join the people, for the people, he said, were "the strength and wealth of the state." The people should be firm in demanding reforms. If the government refused to sanction them then the people should boycott it, even refuse to pay taxes. Even now, in this early pamphlet, Marat foresaw that the resistance of the privileged orders would bring civil war and invite foreign intervention.

The pamphlet, appearing among so many others, probably did not have many readers, but did not go unnoticed. It was published at the expense of a patriotic society, implying that Marat already had connections with a political organization. And it caused a small polemic. Marat replied with a second pamphlet that was bolder than the first. He charged his critics with apathy and timidity. In the last analysis such critics amounted to very little in times of crisis. Reform was unavoidable, he held, but the king could not be trusted to introduce it, for he had no interest in the people's happiness. Only a national assembly could free the nation. The people should not expect anything from the privileged and monopolists, warned Marat, but trust instead to their own courage "to break their chains."[14]

The feudal order refused to make its exit from history, just as Marat had foreseen. The flood of enthusiasm engulfing the nation at the opening of the Estates General frightened the court and the privileged classes. It is beyond the present scope to recount the early events that culminated in the storming of the Bastille on July 14, 1789. Suffice it to say that this popular rising against royal authority was a reply to the counter-revolutionary attempts at Versailles to stamp out whatever challenged their ascendancy.

Marat's rôle on July 14, 1789, was not decisive. But he tells us he persuaded a detachment of troops to halt their march against the insurgents.[15] As a member of a revolutionary committee in the capital, he also stayed at his post for three consecutive days.[16] About this time he saw the need of a paper. Other political figures were launching theirs. Why shouldn't he? He laid the plan before his revolutionary committee. But it rejected his offer.

In the absence of a paper Marat addressed letters to deputies on the left. The National Assembly had before it several drafts for a constitution, but all of them, in his opinion, neglected the people's rights. He went on to examine their worth in *Le moniteur patriote*, founded by him in August 1789. Only one number appeared. One constitutional draft, he said, was but "a fabrication of apothegms in morality and jurisprudence"; another was a product of phantasmal speculation; a third, though "interlarded with maxims on rights and duties," left the king with as much power as before the Revolution. All of the drafts had failed to protect "the rights . . . of that large class of unfortunates who have been scorned, spurned, ill-treated and oppressed everywhere and who have never been taken account of by governments." Actually, Marat found himself defending the same cause he had championed in *The Chains of Slavery.* The explanation for it was that the facts of 1789 were sanctioning the premises of 1774.

Once the Parisians had shown the capacity to safeguard the National Assembly against reaction, a large and influential portion of its deputies started back. Their new, ill-clad, defender dismayed them. Besides, reports from the countryside told of peasants' risings against their feudal lords. The insurgents were erasing feudal barriers, razing *châteaux,* and burning records. This threat to property rights persuaded the legislators to abolish personal services, but they left standing the onerous feudal dues that the peasants could redeem. Under the circumstances the Assembly proceeded to stabilize conditions by erecting a new political framework.

Marat published his own constitutional plan toward the end of August 1789. He proposed a constitutional monarchy. The monarchical form, however, was but a wrapper for a design to secure the people's happiness. People would be taxed according to their ability to pay. Above all, society had to guarantee to each of its members what Jefferson had broadly described as "life, liberty and the pursuit of happiness." Marat was rising to the defense of 15,000,000 Frenchmen whom hunger and poverty, he said, were wearing out. "I know," he wrote, "that I am exposing myself to danger by pleading fervently the cause of these unfortunates, but fear will not halt my pen." Marat's program was as distant from socialism as were Rousseau's and Jefferson's and Robespierre's. For in common with them he aimed at a society of small owners, in which property was "the fruit of labor, industry and talent." Where wealth was unequally divided, Marat argued, society owed the working people food and shelter, care during illness and old age and education for their children.[17] Marat's project evoked no response from the constitution framers.

Events were pressing. The Assembly showed signs of bogging down under the influence of conservative deputies, enamoured of the conservative English government. The *jacquerie* was continuing in the rural areas. Were it not for public charity and the opening of workhouses for the unemployed, the cities, too, might have been turbulent. Marat felt the time was propitious for the launching of a paper. Through an arrangement with a book-dealer he was able to begin publication of *The Friend of the People.*[18]

3

Marat considered himself "the people's sentinel." Perhaps no other phrase so accurately epitomized the history and content of his newspapers. *The Friend of the People* and its successors were designed to keep the people on the alert, to focus attention on ineptness and treachery in the governing group, to disclose the internal enemy and its foreign ties, to prevent the new rich class from appropriating the gains of the Revolution that the plebeians had secured by their fighting, and finally to strip the new masters of all make-believe and expose them as no better than the old. Naturally, the paper had many enemies. Its influence even among the lowly, penetrated with difficulty during the first two years of the Revolution. There were times when Marat regarded himself as a voice in the wilderness, and he would then prophesy that the people's political backwardness would permit reaction to triumph. But when the effervescent Parisians showed signs of stirring, his optimism returned.

He mastered the art of adapting the style to the purpose of the paper. Form and content seem to have melted into each other. The liberal Camille Desmoulins indulged in witticisms that sometimes lapsed into the sophomoric. Robespierre was as meticulous about his paragraphs as he was about his breeches. Marat, however, neither aimed to amuse nor stopped to correct the rhythm of his phrases. Forced to produce a daily issue under extremely trying conditions, he wrote rapidly. If the sentences were not eloquent, they were at least energetic, swift-moving, vibrating, and crowded with facts. In contrast to contemporaries who sought precedents and exemplars in classical antiquity Marat kept his footing firmly in the present, and attempted to settle vital issues within the limits prescribed by conditions.

Always Marat put his trust in the people. Despite their lethargy and their faith in the ruling upper middle class, especially in the first two years of the Revolution, he prodded them almost daily, reminding them to be vigilant, predicting their favorite leaders would betray them, and persistently charging that counter-revolutionists were plotting the restoration of the old régime. Marat was aware of the force of tradition; he knew the effect of poverty in making men support decadent practices. But his stay in England and events in France had also taught him that the people could be irresistible for furthering the advance of mankind. Consequently even in his greatest despondency and bitterness he never lost faith in them.

The early numbers of the paper examined critically the National Assembly. It had no plan of work; it was occupied more with royal prerogatives than with the people's needs. Its deputies were either silent or verbose, but concluded nothing. Its composition, moreover, made it incapable of reforming the nation. Marat cited the case of the feudal dues. The purpose behind the concessions of the feudal classes was to pacify the rural areas. The reforms adopted were therefore deceptive, for the peasants had to pay for the seignorial rights. None of the proclaimed sacrifices of the landlords could either bring prompt relief to the starving population or reform the state. The truth was, Marat said, the changes were superficial. Their aim was to paralyze the reforming spirit of the nation. He concluded by demanding the election of a new assembly from which the feudal classes and their allies would be excluded.[19]

The paper was equally critical of the Parisian municipal government. It contained too many highly paid officials of the old school; it functioned secretly; it had erected a wall between itself and the people; it protected speculators and monopolists; it had surrounded itself with "a throng of venal intriguers;" and it was selling adulterated bread to the poor. But the small folk, who were nine-tenths of the capital's inhabitants, he said, were shorn of their rights, excluded from the National Guard and perpetually occupied with the struggle against starvation.[20]

Dauntless criticism earned Marat persecution. Apart from posters denouncing him, his printer was intimidated and the distribution of his paper hampered. A municipal councilor, moreover, sued him for libel.[21] He fled to Versailles, went into hiding, secretly attended sessions of the National Assembly and escaped arrest only because the police agents happened to be his readers and admirers. Returning to the capital he discovered that a spurious *Friend of the People* was circulating. Still in clandestine existence, he resumed the publication of his paper after an interruption of almost a month. The police discovered his whereabouts, invaded the printing shop and confiscated an issue.[22] Thus began his hunted life.

He continued along the course he had charted. His aim was to "unmask traitors, remove from public office the covetous . . . the cowardly, the inept and incompetent," instruct "the poor who have always been subjected and oppressed, and inspire them with a consciousness of their rights." Then, "no human power can stand in the way of the infallible march of the Revolution." The people "will smash the rule of the wealthy just as they have shattered that of the nobility."[23]

Before the meeting of the Estates General in May 1789, Marat had called for the unity of the entire Third Estate to defeat the feudal aristocracy. Once victory over the old order was attained, he began to suspect that the upper middle class was preparing to halt the advance of the Revolution, even achieve the sort of compromise with the feudal class the English had reached in 1688. Suspicion turned to conviction as he studied the doings of the National Assembly and the municipal governments. Only the people, he concluded, could be relied on to complete the Revolution. Their risings had led to the triumph of its first stage. If kept on the qui vive, he reasoned, they would push the Revolution to other stages. Marat was impatient with those who grew "compassionate over the merited punishment of a few profligates. But I see only the misfortunes, the calamities and the disasters of a great nation that . . . has been enchained, pillaged . . . oppressed and massacred for centuries. Who has more sense, humanity and patriotism, they or I? They endeavor to lull the people to sleep, while I strive to awaken them. They feed them opium, but I pour *aqua fortis* into their wounds. I shall continue to pour it until the people have completely regained their rights and become free and happy."[24]

Marat pursued this course until his death in 1793. Compromise would be equivalent to betrayal; or to use his own manner of expression: "A fool can pretend to please everyone in normal times; but only a traitor can claim to do so during a revolution."[25] There were periods when he was a victim of discouragement and despair, particularly in the first two years of his revolutionary life. These spells derived in the main from a want of response to his agitation. For Marat, at this time, was a prophet without disciples.

Economic conditions could best explain Marat's isolation. The plebeians generally followed the leadership of the upper bourgeoisie in the first stage of the Revolution. The peasants had their struggles against feudalism; urban workers had not yet formulated proletarian demands. The industrial crisis and the bread shortage in 1789 and early 1790 caused unrest, but the new authorities reacted quickly first by a show of force, and second by economic measures and relief. National Guards, open to men of property, were instituted; markets were supplied with sufficient flour; the price of bread was kept low; public works were set up in the manner of the old régime; and charity was distributed. Then, too, an improvement in economic conditions aided the bourgeoisie in appeasing the plebeians. The harvest of 1790 was good. Industry was reviving. The export business flourished, for the falling value of the *assignats*, the revolutionary paper money, stimulated foreign purchases in France. People seemed confident. The feeling was current in 1790 and 1791 that the Revolution would bring prosperity, that the best of all possible worlds was about to be inaugurated. Naturally, men like Mirabeau, Lafayette and Barnave enjoyed intense popularity, while Marat appeared as but a Cassandra. There were causes at work, however, to unsettle popular faith in these leaders. Peasants increased their pressure for the total abolition of feudal dues; prices rose as the value of the paper money fell; the new constitution had disfranchised the propertyless; French émigrés on the border, in league with the court, conspired with foreign rulers. And, as if to lend credence to the conspiracies, the royal family made a bold rush to the eastern frontier, but to be intercepted and returned to Paris. Toward the end of 1791 a small democratic party was already looking for converts.

4

Marat was the watch-dog of the Revolution. He followed with unfailing devotion the activities of men in power and held them up to public view. He depicted Necker, the finance minister, as an octopus with an arm in every conspiracy against the nation. Marat accused him of protecting speculators, of sacrificing the nation to the bankers.[26] Jean Sylvain Bailly, the mayor of Paris, was presented as a tool of the court and an enemy of the people because he opposed the freedom of the press, had tried to dissolve the district assemblies and favored imprisonment for debt.[27] Mirabeau, the idol of the nation, was, according to Marat, a prime culprit. He had secured the king's power in the new constitution, permitted enemies of the nation to escape and championed the disfranchisement of the poor. And Marat charged him with being in the king's pay long before the documents disclosed it.[28] For Lafayette, the head of the National Guard in Paris, Marat had but hatred and scorn. The general was a ringleader of counter-revolution, all the more dangerous because of his reputation as a fighter for freedom. With prophetic genius Marat foresaw two years before the event that Lafayette would turn against the Revolution with armed force.[29]

Marat was just as vigilant over the acts of the National Assembly. Its financial policy especially, he contended, was calculated to further the interests of the rich. It had accepted the illegitimate claims of the state's creditors; it permitted financiers and enemies of the Revolution to send their gold and jewels out of the country. By doing nothing to arrest the decline of the *assignats,* it encouraged the hoarding of specie. Marat rejected entirely the purpose of the *assignats.* This interest-bearing paper money with which holders could purchase confiscated church lands, he argued, was but a device of the rich to siphon off the earnings of the poor and to take over the national domain. The confiscated lands, he insisted, should have been allotted to the propertyless. The deputies, furthermore, had made no effort to conceal their partiality in determining the incidence of taxation. Instead of taxing luxuries and incomes, they placed levies on the poor. All these fiscal measures, he concluded, were intended "to reduce the people to servitude through poverty and to force them in despair to call for the return of despotism."[30]

Marat charged that the foes of freedom were enslaving the people under the guise of freedom. The foes, he said, were the great majority of the civil service and of the National Assembly. They treated patriots and friends of liberty as rebels; they protected traitors and conspirators. The National Guard under Lafayette was an organization of the middle class, for workers could not afford the expense of the military equipment.[31] The Constitution of 1791 was a caricature of democracy. It left the king enough power which, Marat predicted, he would use to overthrow it.[32] And it established the reign of the rich by decreeing that only they could vote who paid a direct tax of three days' labor.

Protest against the disfranchisement of the poor assumed broad dimensions after 1792. But in 1789 and 1790, Robespierre in the National Assembly and Marat in his journal were the most forthright advocates of their cause.[33] Marat repeatedly told the disfranchised that their elimination from the political life of the nation was unconstitutional, unjust and impolitic: unconstitutional, because it contradicted the Declaration of the Rights of Man; unjust, because the poor paid taxes on articles of consumption from their slender wages; and impolitic, because it stirred civil strife. The fact that the people "have been despoiled of almost all their earnings," Marat argued, "is no reason for depriving them of their right of citizenship." The decree, dividing Frenchmen into active and passive citizens, into voters and non-voters,[34] was, according to his verdict, "the basest stroke of ingratitude recorded in the history of any people; it mars the annals of the Revolution of the French people; it dishonors the first year of the era of freedom." And finally, it menaced the security of the nation by turning it over "to a handful of ambitious knaves." The decree, he concluded, was signal proof that the National Assembly would avoid doing anything for the people's happiness.[35]

He never gave up fighting against the decree. He enlisted the aid of other journalists, even tried to build a democratic movement around the issue. On June 30, 1790, he published a petition to the Assembly in the name of "eighteen million unfortunates, deprived of their rights of active citizens." At no time had Marat written with greater warmth and conviction than in this number of his paper. He contrasted the deputies' panegyrics on liberty and justice with the new privileges of the rich. The men of toil, he said, carried the burdens of the state, labored, and sacrificed their blood to liberate it from feudalism. Yet to be a citizen of this state they had to give up three days' labor when their wages barely sufficed to purchase enough bread. Then he addressed the deputies as follows:

"You admit that the poor man is a citizen like the rich man; but you say that the poor man sells himself more readily. Do you think so? Look at all the monarchies of the world. Isn't it the rich who form the groveling multitude of courtiers, who constitute the countless legions of self-seekers, searching for favor by every means and selling their honor for it? Save for the small number of poor whom you have corrupted during centuries of servitude, isn't it the rich who are the tools of despotism in the legislature, in the cabinet, in the law-courts, in the army itself? And haven't the poor been the first everywhere to protest against tyranny and to rise up against their oppressors? If they were willing to sell themselves, if they sought but gold they would take it whenever they had the opportunity. Who prevented them from plundering your houses in the first days of the Revolution? Who stopped them from pillaging those they had set on fire? Was a single one of them found fleeing with booty?"

Marat turned on the legislators for their lack of patriotic foresight. Their decree would alienate the stoutest defenders of the nation at a time when its enemies were girding themselves for an assault. "In every revolution," he told the deputies, "he who is not for the country is against it." He appealed to the new aristocracy of wealth to make concessions. While the poor did not demand the sharing of property, "which heaven gave to all men in common," they might be driven to regain it "by taking away your surplus." For the poor were the producers of wealth, Marat maintained. To prove to the rich their complete dependence on them, they had but to declare a general strike, that is "to remain with their arms folded."[36]

Marat's petition appeared while the national government and the municipality of Paris were making costly preparations to commemorate the first anniversary of the capture of the Bastille. Deputies, municipal councillors and journalists, of all political shades, eulogized this event. If they invoked the French revolutionary trinity, like some incantation, they were inclined to dwell longer on *liberté* and *fraternité* than on *égalité*. For to have stressed the last term, after the disfranchisement of millions of Frenchmen, might have called forth the mockery of the multitude. Besides, the word *égalité* was likely to suggest a conception of property that was altogether inconsistent with the conventional opinion, although both derived from natural rights.

Marat, almost alone among the journalists, warned the plebeians that they were being lulled to sleep. "The greatest impediment of an unenlightened people," he lamented three days before the celebration, "is not to know how to choose wisely those they invest with power."[37] While Parisians cried *Vive le Roi! Vive Lafayette!* Marat asked: "Why this unrestrained joy? Why this mad applause, this stupid show of festivity?" Its purpose, he went on to explain, was "to keep the citizens in a state of frenzy, to divert them from public affairs, and to prevent the sections from preparing for the coming elections."[38] Marat, too, desired fraternity, he said, but he wanted it among "sincere patriots, honest citizens, soldiers and non-commissioned officers." All of them "should take an oath to exterminate the enemies of freedom . . . not to put down their arms until the reign of justice and liberty has been established."[39]

5

He had discovered fairly early that the welfare of the common people was inseparable from national security. The more freedom and equality the country had, the more it guaranteed the people a livelihood, the more firmly would they defend it against domestic and foreign enemies. Marat's love of country caused him to lead the fight for the realization of the revolutionary trinity. It was his program; it was inherent in the Revolution; and it held a great human potential. In common with Robespierre and other democrats he demanded full civil and political rights for free Negroes and the gradual abolition of slavery in French colonies. He even saw some justice in the claim of Negroes to self-determination.[40] He protested against the extradition of revolutionary refugees, vigorously defended the unjustly imprisoned Babeuf;[41] and his wrath was as sharp as vinegar after learning that soldiers had been killed or punished for resisting counter-revolutionary officers. Thus the Nancy Affair of August 1790, that had ended in the slaughter of about three thousand soldiers and civilians and had shown the armed strength of reaction, filled him with bitterness. The king, the National Assembly and the Paris municipality thanked the arch-royalist Bouillé, instigator of the massacre. But Marat renewed his appeals to the people and the soldiers to fraternize.[42]

In keeping with his faith in the essential unity of the nation's safety and the people's welfare, Marat singled himself out as an early advocate of the workers' interests. The workers, in his judgment, were "the most useful portion of the people without which society could not exist a single day." They were "those valuable citizens, weighed down by all the burdens of the state without enjoying any of its advantages."[43] He counted on them to complete the Revolution. He aimed at freeing them from organized charity that kept them mute and inactive. His alternatives were national workshops in the already confiscated church buildings and a system of public works, organized like producers' cooperatives. Such reforms, he believed, would raise the physical and moral level of the people.

Consistent with his labor policy, he publicized the inhuman treatment of maritime workers and fishermen, supported the agitation of the Parisian workers for higher wages and opened his paper to their petitions and letters. Among the democratic leaders of the day, he alone disapproved of the law prohibiting workers from organizing.[44]

The revival of industry in 1790 and 1791 made the old guilds totally anomalous. The National Assembly abolished them in March 1791, removing the greatest impediment to a free labor market. An increased demand for skilled labor and higher prices prompted Parisian workers to organize for higher wages. By the spring of 1791 the labor movement in the capital was large enough to alarm the authorities. On an appeal by employers the municipality of Paris warned the workers that their continued organization and agitation would compel the local government to use force.[45] Several days later a decree declared illegal all regulations of labor unions, condemned collective bargaining and ordered the suppression of strikes.[46] It was obvious that the government of the capital, a convert of the tenets of economic liberalism, was determined to enforce them.

Workers continued to organize. They accused their employers of refusing to discuss terms and of scheming to restore guilds for the sake of depressing wages. The workers went on to claim that they had more right to liberty than their employers, since they had won it in the storming of the Bastille. And their labor was the source of the employers' wealth, ran their argument.[47]

The employers had the backing of the government. They intimidated both the municipality of Paris and the National Assembly by reporting the existence of eighty thousand organized workers in the capital, who were planning to form a labor federation. In fact they were already infecting the provinces with their ideas, the report had it. The National Assembly hastened to grant the employers protection against labor. On June 14, 1790, it adopted the Le Chapelier Law, making workers' combinations illegal. Interference with the freedom of labor was punishable by fines and imprisonment.[48] The law remained on the statute books until 1884. Pressure from the labor movement finally forced its abolition.

The law did not provoke the opposition of workers. Perhaps they were insensitive to its implications. Certainly they had not yet arrived at definite ideas about the relation of capital and labor. Marat, however, regarded the law as a menace to the workers' political life. He had protested in March against the outright abolition of guilds. With their abuses corrected, they could have been serviceable, he maintained.[49] Now, in June, when not even Robespierre had made the slightest objection to the Le Chapelier Law, Marat regarded it as a device to harness the workers' political activity. It was evident to him that, behind the argument that workers' meetings might revive the guilds, the deputies had really revealed their fear of the political power of labor. In short, Marat rejected the law as anti-democratic. He cherished the thought that other like attacks on democracy would ultimately force the workers to act.[50] For "they alone," he once wrote, "have the sense and courage . . . to ensure the success of a popular movement."[51]

6

The persuasion gradually took hold of Marat that the Revolution could not go forward like Andreyev's Sabine husbands with two steps forward and one step backward. The deposed feudal class and the court party refused to admit their retirement from history. Their horizons were melancholy, to be sure. And they clung to them both for the sentimental reveries they evoked and the fury they called forth against the revolutionists. But they did not consider their cause totally lost. In fact, in the middle of 1791, as Marat observed, things were in a topsy turvy condition. "Good citizens," he remarked, "need a new dictionary to recognize themselves." Enemies of the country "hold themselves as patriots and regard true patriots as aristocrats. . . . Servitude is accepted as good order, tyranny as justice and oppression as liberty." "It is therefore true," he added, "that we have gained nothing by the Revolution."[52]

Marat believed that all this confusion could be set right again if the people adopted strong, energetic measures. He called on them to delegate full power to a group of their leaders for the duration of the national crisis. The group would act swiftly and decisively. It would stamp out reaction, confiscate the lands of the émigrés for the benefit of the have-nots, use church property to establish national workshops, remove the tax-burden from the poor, give them full political rights, arm the citizens and disarm the foes of the Revolution, purge the administration of all enemies, dismiss the reactionary officers of the army and hold the royal family as hostages. He agreed with Saint-Just that they who made only half-revolutions dug their own graves. "Citizens," he kept saying, "remember that we are at war with the enemies of the Revolution. You are lost if you forget this profound truth."[53]

Marat projected a people's organization, apart from the existing political clubs. Only "good and honest citizens," to use his own phrase, would be admitted. He did not want a "gossiping," social circle, but "a deliberative, acting body," with branches in the capital and in the provinces. It would be a small body, well chosen, and led by democrats of the stamp of Robespierre. It would bar entrance to civil servants, academics, speculators or financiers. It would be "the sanctuary of justice, the asylum of the oppressed, the citizens' torch and . . . infallible guide." In short, it would be the guardian and advance guard of revolutionary France.[54] For a time, toward the end of 1790, Marat was impressed by the "Conquerors of the Bastille," an association formed after the event in the popular quarters of Paris. But he lost faith in it when some of its members took employment with Lafayette's espionage system. Marat then rested his hopes on the democratic Cordeliers Club.

He also advised the common people to organize into fraternal societies, provided they kept out officials.[55] Such societies had grown up spontaneously in Paris, in 1790 and 1791, grouping the humble, the unlettered and the illiterate, passive and active citizens, workers and small shopkeepers. Even women and children came to meetings. Albert Mathiez called these societies "popular universities."[56] At the time of the king's flight to Varennes there were close to sixty of them in Paris alone, federated, and with a central committee making common policy.

It has already been shown that police took steps to prevent Marat's paper from appearing shortly after its foundation. But that was only the beginning of a long hunt that drove Marat from one refuge to another and from France to England. His attacks on Necker and Lafayette earned him surprise visits from police agents in his hiding place or in the printing shop to confiscate an issue of the paper. Moreover, his mail was intercepted and his journal was prevented from circulating in the provinces. Writers were paid to malign him or to launch a spurious *Friend of the People*. One of the writers, Antoine Estienne, was instigated to bring suit against him. Thanks to the "Conquerors of the Bastille" and to the journalist, Jacques-René Hébert, the trial aroused so much feeling in popular quarters that Estienne considered it prudent to absent himself from the court-room. He was in fact ordered to pay the costs.[57]

Marat's sharp pen also brought upon him the ire of the National Assembly. After the enthusiastic celebration of July 14, 1790, he published a small pamphlet, *C'en est fait de nous.*[58] It again drew the attention of Parisians to evil designs of counter-revolutionists. Apparently he was guilty of stirring up discord while fraternity still glowed in men's hearts. Deputies censured the pamphlet, and the Assembly as a whole empowered the attorney general to prosecute authors, printers and distributors of incendiary publications. There was no doubt that Marat was the target, for two days later an amendment to the law made it retroactive in the case of his pamphlet. He replied with a defense of the freedom of the press.[59] At the same time he discreetly changed his living quarters.[60]

His accusations and zeal frightened friends and allies. Camille Desmoulins, for example, whom Marat had considered his "brother-in-arms," threatened to terminate the democratic coalition. "You are really compromising your friends," he wrote, "and you will force them to break with you."[61] Marat answered that his affrighted critic was but a political tyro whose blithesome nature was an obstacle to hard thinking: "You are vacillating in your views; you reprove to-day what you will commend to-morrow; . . . you don't seem to have either plan or aim; and to cap your levity you curb your friend's progress by stopping his blows . . . at those critical moments when the people seem to be turning but to their own despair."[62] He replied again, in May 1791, when Desmoulins accused him of falsely slandering leading men in politics: "To judge men you always demand precise, clear and positive facts; but their inactivity or silence on great occasions is often sufficient for me. You need legal proof to credit a plot. I, on the other hand, watch the general march of events, the relations of the enemies of freedom and the comings and goings of certain people in power."[63]

Marat had little popular following from 1789 to 1791. Even so, his writings, especially his paper, were read by almost four thousand persons, according to one estimate.[64] Also, the *Orateur du peuple,* edited by one of his disciples, shared his ideas. Individuals and organized groups at this time already looked upon him as a leader. For example, in February 1791, when the Cordeliers Club learned of the possible suspension of Marat's paper for lack of support, it formally declared that the disappearance of "the patriot, Marat," from the political scene "would be a public calamity, that his silence would be a general misfortune and the surest sign of the coming ruin of the state." The Club urged him to continue the defense of the people's cause and pledged its membership "to protect his person as well as to disseminate his doctrines."[65]

Marat seems to have won admirers in the second half of 1791. Readers sought his advice, confided in him, and protested against counter-revolutionary officials and policies. They addressed him in the most laudatory terms: "our prophet," "the great magician of the century," "the most zealous partisan of the Revolution," the "true defender of the needy class." Workers communicated to him their complaints against employers.

The fast moving events changed Marat from a comparatively neglected journalist into a people's hero. The royal family, discredited by its attempted flight, the need to buttress the king's position, the outbreak of war only to be followed by defeats, and the invasion of France, these factors and others deriving from them were calculated to give Marat a vast audience. The comeback staged by reaction in 1793, and the civil war resulting from it, threatened the Revolution with extinction. People recalled Marat's earlier warnings and sought his political wisdom as revolutionary France organized itself to meet the challenge of feudal Europe. When the assassin's knife struck him down, he was at the apogee of his fame.

Evaluations of Marat have seldom been free from partisanship. For he articulated the popular aspirations in one of the greatest revolutions of history. He discovered quickly after its start that it could neither be fought with rose water nor its triumph be assured by preaching homilies. If his enemies hated him intensely he hated them as much. He neither expected quarter nor gave it, for he had dedicated himself to a cause in which the issues were sharply drawn and fought over bitterly. Whether Marat wins or alienates sympathies, he must be appraised as a political man who kept pace with history when it moved at a fast tempo. His writings and doings, if examined calmly in their extraordinary setting, are extremely impressive for their penetrating judgments and prophetic insights.

ROBESPIERRE AND THE PROBLEM OF WAR

THE exaltation of the first stage of the French Revolution beginning in 1789 yielded to discouragement and pessimism after two years of internal strife. Toward the end of 1791 Marat observed that the Revolution was perhaps only a passing crisis.[1] Instead of moving forward, instead of approximating the goal a number of democratic leaders had set for France, the Revolution stopped short. The upper middle class refused to go beyond the reforms that had secured its elevation to power. It had of course broken the back of feudalism and of the Catholic Church, created a national market and increased the supply of free labor by abolishing guilds. Though it owed its triumph to the poor and plebeians generally, it had no intention of sharing power with its lowly allies. Nor did it desire to scrap the Bourbon monarchy. If subdued and bridled, it could be useful, just as the English monarchy had been.

The Constitution of 1791 had these objectives in view. It disfranchised 90 per cent of the French people, and it left wide powers to the king.

The middle class, particularly its upper layers, tried to keep a balance between the defeated feudal and clerical forces on the one hand, and the small shopkeepers, peasants, artisans and laborers on the other. The first, it will be seen, refused to lay down their arms, but plotted with the court to regain privileges and power. The second, having lifted the middle class to a ruling place, remained a threat. The bulk of this multitude consisted of propertyless and small owners who wanted a share of the gains of the Revolution. How far they would go few knew, save by the examples of rural areas where landless peasants had seized properties and proceeded to parcel them out. Conditions in Paris proper were not congenial to continued good relations between the middle class and the mass of the common people. There was some unemployment. Rumor had it that speculators and monopolists were causing scarcities of necessities. The falling value of the *assignats* was further helping to raise prices. And when workers combined, struck and demanded wage-increases, the National Assembly hastened to illegalize all such combinations. On top of that the middle class had organized a National Guard that many regarded as anything but national. Only those enlisted in it who could afford to buy their equipment. So constituted, it was meant to hold the common people in check.

Looking at the balance-sheet of the Revolution at the end of its first two years, one could conclude that great strides had been made. The old régime had been shattered beyond repair. The principal beneficiaries were those of the middle class and the many peasants who had profited by the abolition of personal services. But feudalism had not been entirely erased. It required the unrelenting pressure of the peasantry in order to sweep away the final feudal remnants in 1793. The Revolution in its first two years did not improve the condition of the plebeians in the towns. In fact the situation of many of them had deteriorated. The National Assembly, much against the economic liberal creed of many of its deputies, had to resume such practices of the old régime as organized relief and public works. And though the internal political picture was not dismal, it was not optimistic either. The defeated feudal class was still well entrenched in the civil service and in the army; and it had sufficient ground for anticipating a return to its former position. Its leaders and most articulate spokesmen were myopic about what had happened. Unable to read the meaning of the events, they stood their ground, fixed in the contemplation of their sinking world. And while buoyed up by the hope of triumph, they lingered, as Mark Twain put it, "among the cobwebs of the past."

Counter-revolutionists in France plotted the return of the old régime. They bribed leading statesmen, formed secret societies, and appealed to foreign governments to march against France. Royalists invoked the aid of the Church against the Revolution. Debauched nobles turned religious in order to win allies among the clergy for the instigation of a religious war.[2]

Counter-revolution was a cause among officers of the army. Many fled or deserted, often in fear of their soldiers, and joined the émigrés in the expectation of leading hostile armies against their country. Desertions assumed a collective character, so that regiments lost from two-thirds to three-quarters of their officers. The soldiers, by contrast, stayed to defend the Revolution.

Such desertions, planned to cripple the army, coincided with active royalist propaganda both at home and abroad. Court agents organized royalist clubs, circulated royalist newspapers, staged royalist demonstrations with the slogans: "Vive le roi!" and "To hell with the nation!"[3] speculated in order to lower the value of the revolutionary paper money, and bribed club leaders, among them Danton, who was paid 30,000 livres in March 1791. Royalists also channeled their propaganda abroad through émigrés; and secret messages passed from the French court to foreign monarchs. The émigrés, congregated in England and in towns near the French border, execrated the Revolution that had taken from them privilege and position and cast them on foreign soil, without income and often without friends. The more sanguine among them enlisted the aid of nobles and princes; but they trusted their future to foreign governments, provided they could be persuaded to make war on France in order to suppress the Revolution. In return French royalists promised French territory and French colonies.[4] King Louis, too, had been pressing the rulers of Europe ever since October, 1789, to come to his rescue. But they were torn between two fears: one, the rapid spread of the Revolution beyond French frontiers, if it were left to itself; the other, the infiltration of revolutionary ideas among their troops, if they declared war and invaded France. Beyond that, the powers were suspicious of one another. One might take advantage of another's intervention to seize some coveted territory. Thus Spain suspected England, Austria was on the alert against Prussia, and Sweden mistrusted Russia. Louis' agents met with considerable difficulties to smooth out such dynastic rivalries.

The French royal family had meanwhile been seeking an opportune time to escape abroad. There, as the head of the counter-revolutionary forces, Louis XVI would set up a government in exile. He fled on June 21, 1791, financed in the enterprise by bankers. But he was discovered near the frontier and conducted back to the French capital.

Leaders of the upper middle class at once rushed to his defense. They let it be known that Louis had never intended to betray his people. He had simply been kidnapped by the émigrés. Maximilien Robespierre, then a member of the Constituent Assembly, found it hard to believe the story. He denied the king was as innocent as he was painted. Speaking before the Jacobin Club, Robespierre affirmed that the king knew what he had done. He had not been abducted; nor had he resisted in his patriotic devotion to the people. He had fled, asserted Robespierre. More than that he had well timed the flight, for reaction was making progress. Besides, continued Robespierre, the elections to the Legislative Assembly were approaching, when class bitterness would manifest itself. The great mass of the nation would have no voice. Meanwhile the nonjuring clergy were arousing sections of the population against the Revolution.[5] Marat, who had predicted the king's flight several months earlier,[6] demanded his dethronement and the appointment of a loyal and tested revolutionist with full power to act.[7] The monarchists in the government, however, stole a march on democrats by the Champ de Mars Massacre. On July 17, 1791, when a petition was launched in favor of a republic, leaders of democratic clubs were arrested. Radical journalists had to go into hiding. The story was going the rounds that Robespierre was in the pay of a foreign power and that Marat was in the employ of the Duke of Orleans.

Failure to reach his destination but made King Louis more eager to conspire. He took the oath to uphold the Constitution of 1791. At the same time he secretly informed the European courts that he had no intention to be a constitutional monarch. He pressed them to organize an armed coalition against France.

The powers were in no position to wage war toward the end of 1791. Great Britain had decided on a policy of strict neutrality. Spain was exhausted; Tsarist Russia was reserving her strength for a possible attack in the Near East. Prussia and Austria watched each other in Central Europe; and both were deeply concerned over Catherine II's next move against Poland. Obviously the governments of Europe had their own problems to absorb them, and aid to Louis XVI was secondary, for the present at least. Then, too, advisers of European rulers believed the Revolution would weaken France. Why should they spend their military strength to bolster up a state that had been their rival on the Continent? The fact was the European powers hesitated, waited, certainly were in no rush to attack France. The Revolution, concluded Jaurès after examining a wealth of evidence, did not face an immediate peril in the fall of 1791. It had time to organize, to strengthen itself within, "to frustrate intrigue and treachery and perhaps to impose itself on Europe and its rulers through the prestige of its strength, without rushing into a dangerous war."[8]

Yet that was the period when several parties in France sounded their separate war cries. Each had its own purpose, to be sure, but their cries, from the right and the left, blended in one chorus. The court party wanted war in the expectation of a French defeat that would unavoidably result in the restoration of Bourbon absolutism. The moderates or constitutional monarchists, headed by Lafayette, counted on a war to give them the helm of government. The Girondins, representatives of the commercial interests that had suffered from the business crisis caused by the Revolution, argued that a war would fix the Revolution durably in France. It would reveal the king's treachery; it would spread the Revolution to the rest of Europe and destroy feudalism there; and by dispersing the noisy émigrés on the French frontiers it would remove a threat to business men. There were also reasons the Girondins did not utter publicly. They, like the Fayettists, looked to a war to become the ruling party of France. Besides, a conflict with feudal Europe, especially if victorious, would raise the value of the *assignats,* and, what was perhaps even more desirable in the long run, bring together classes that were growing apart, possibly even join them at the edges.[9] It is hard to say whether the lust for power blinded the Girondins to the great risk of their adventure. They might have known that from the military point of view France was incapable of waging war.[10] Its army was badly equipped and provisioned, and it lacked a proper corps of officers. Two years of the Revolution had mauled its loyalty and discipline.

Jacques-Pierre Brissot was the chief Girondist champion of war. He represented a district in Paris, although his principal Girondist colleagues came from the area of the Gironde. He was a talented writer and shrewd parliamentarian. He had been something of a radical before the Revolution, having taken his place among the subtle, if not penetrating, critics of private property. He had even equated it with theft by indirection, thus anticipating Proudhon's rude formula. Two years before the meeting of the Estates General he had argued that three-fourths of the people could not be loyal to the state, since they had no property. As long as they were without it, their education was difficult, even impossible under existing abuses. The whole structure had to be destroyed if the people's rights were to be restored; otherwise they would continue to be plundered.[11] But he abandoned these thoughts in the course of the Revolution, in fact developed into a militant antagonist of the left, especially its partisans of an adjustment in property relations. Even while presenting the above views on property, he had advised the commercial men of France how to gain the American market from England. The advice was contained in a work,[12] written jointly with Etienne Clavière, a Swiss banker like Necker, and like him, chief of the French Finance Ministry. Brissot's colleague was a shady character who had fled from his native Geneva for unscrupulous dealings. In France he had already won notoriety as a swindler and speculator. It is beyond the limits of this essay to enter into his plans on land speculation in the United States. The story is far too intricate to be told here. Suffice it to say that he was a reckless adventurer, tied with many different personalities and totally lacking in principles. With this type of man Brissot established close relations.

Perhaps because the Girondist leader had resided in England and in the United States he considered himself an authority on foreign affairs. His opinion in these matters carried weight, especially in the Legislative Assembly to which he had been elected. Here, on October 20, 1791, he raised the war question. The Assembly had been elected a month earlier on the basis of a restricted suffrage and indirect elections. Brissot demanded stern measures against the émigrés who, in his opinion, were responsible for all the calamities of France. He called for an aggressive policy against the powers.[13] In subsequent speeches, reinforced by the press, Brissot and his Girondist colleagues continued to agitate for war. They claimed that Austria and Prussia were making vast preparations to invade France. Revolutionary France should not wait, but surprise them by assuming the offensive. The path to prosperity and public confidence, they held, lay through the destruction of the nests of the émigrés. The war would not be one of conquest, but of liberation, they promised. Freedom could be carried to other peoples at the point of a bayonet.[14]

There was sufficient and legitimate ground to question the wisdom of the Girondist bellicose policy. The security of the Revolution required peace. Internal problems that had come to the surface obviously could not be postponed. And a war would necessarily cast them aside and leave the Revolution unfinished. Possibly the Girondins had that objective in view.

It called for great courage to defend peace against the protagonists of war. Robespierre had that courage. Almost alone, he fought the battle throughout the debate on the question. Marat's paper had ceased to appear for lack of funds. Robespierre's struggle against war represents one of the most heroic pages of his career in the Revolution. He remained unmoved despite vilification by enemies. They called him a dangerous agitator, an obstructionist working for a foreign power, an enemy of the Revolution, and a paid agent of the court with instructions to divide the nation. When obloquy failed to arrest Robespierre's opposition, the Girondins tried to prevent him from speaking, even planned to prosecute him. Never before, not even during his most ardent defense of the interests of the poor plebeians before the National Assembly had he swallowed so much calumny or been treated with as much angry disdain as when he fought against war. So violent was the campaign against him, so concerted the attack that his popularity, which had been fairly widespread in September 1791, was eclipsed.

Robespierre's reputation had derived from his steady defense of the poor, that dated from his early days in his native Arras. Elected to the Third Estate in 1789, he had brought to Versailles, and afterwards to Paris, the warmth with which he had attacked privilege and advanced the principles he had found in Rousseau, his master.

The Estates General had yielded to the Constitutional Assembly that proceeded to reform the country. As has been shown, the leaders of the upper middle class in the Assembly were so fearful of the plebeian elements, whose strength had prevented the enemies of the Revolution from destroying it, that they halted after a number of fundamental changes. They enacted reforms that released the emergent economy from the feudal strait-jacket. But at the same time they set up safeguards against possible threats from below.

Robespierre stormed these new defenses during his two years in the Assembly. He took a firm stand particularly against the decree that had divided Frenchmen into active and passive citizens, that is, into voters and non-voters. The difference was one of property. On this question he complemented Marat. The provision, said Robespierre, had substituted an aristocracy of wealth for an aristocracy of birth; it had made a mockery of the egalitarian principles of the Declaration of the Rights of Man. Practice had contradicted theory; and this contradiction, he said to the deputies, "casts doubt on your loyalty and good faith."[15] If wealth was the criterion for determining a person's political rights, then the origin of wealth should be looked at. Its unequal distribution, continued Robespierre in the spirit of Rousseau, had its roots in "the vicious laws and governments and in the decadent societies."[16] To correct them Robespierre did not retreat to Sparta, as Mably had done, or with Morelly to an imaginary egalitarian order. Robespierre at best counted on governmental control of wealth, perhaps to the point where it would be equal. That was further than most contemporary reformers were willing to go. Few were prepared to put curbs on property, for economic liberalism was becoming fashionable. The creed owed its acceptance to the proselytism of the Physiocrats. Looked at as a weapon against feudalism, it was fairly advanced. This, however, detracts nothing from Robespierre's democratic convictions. He saw no conflict between universal suffrage and the broad division of property on the one hand and freedom from economic restraint on the other. When experience showed that the second tended to remove the underpinnings of the first, he turned to government intervention as the alternative.

As the Revolution made headway, he and a small minority realized that such intervention had to be comprehensive enough to include the expropriation of the properties of suspects and their distribution among the propertyless. That, he believed, would give an economic base to the democratic order he contemplated.

In line with his assault on the disfranchisement of the poor was his censure of the middle class character of the National Guard. Again he called for state interference by enrolling the poor and providing them with equipment and pay during service. Otherwise the National Guard would be a Pretorian guard, the armed force of the rich against the poor.[17]

The legislation of the Constituent Assembly showed it had not made concessions to Robespierre's arguments. In fact, a proposal was made, giving municipalities extensive power to use their local militias, even resort to martial law. Robespierre denounced it as a class measure.

It severed the nation into two distinct parties: "The people on the one hand and aristocracy and despotism on the other." The second was doing everything possible to subject the first, so that "it might prefer peaceful slavery to freedom bought at the cost of agitation and sacrifice." Disturbance should be forestalled by deeds that were consistent with freedom. "If peace is really the objective," he proclaimed before his colleagues, "it is not martial law that should be given to the people." If the Assembly first inquired into the causes of outbreaks, it would discover a vast conspiracy against the nation. The armed masses were but defending it against enemies.[18]

Consistent with his democratic premises was his defense of the rights of Negroes in French colonies against the exclusive claims of the white slave masters. That was a corollary of his plea in behalf of the gradual abolition of slavery in the colonies.[19]

Robespierre's entire program as a parliamentarian and his siding with causes that were thoroughly unpopular with the men in power isolated him in the National Assembly. Political enemies, and politicos ambitious of repute, regarded him as a fault finding intruder. Some called him hypocritical. Others reserved for him more offensive epithets. Among plebeians generally he was known as "the incorruptible." His experience as deputy had taught him much about politics. He learned first hand how his colleagues had maneuvered and bargained for posts. Above all he had seen the champions of the new class alert to their interests and ready with enactments to anchor it in power. They had proclaimed a new trinity, but few suspected it would inspire the common people to interpret it in accordance with their own understanding. During his two years in the Assembly he had seen the breach develop between the representatives of the rich and the common people. The first feared the second and hated them.[20]

The actuality of the gap was known to men in politics and disturbed them. The problem was unavoidable. Girondins tried to close the breach with promises and democratic speeches, for they were not without forensic talent. Enthusiasm for war, they believed, would absorb discontent like a blotter. Fraternity would then stand triumphantly astride the classes. Other political leaders in the Legislative Assembly, constitutional monarchists for the most part, had faith in the new constitution.[21] They were convinced that once the constitutional monarchy began to function it would be easier to check the plebeians, if need be by force. The same leaders, among them Joseph Barnave, secret adviser of the king and perhaps one of the best political theorists of the Revolution,[22] desired peace. Keen observers, they moved cautiously, perhaps because they had less faith in fraternity than did their Girondist colleagues. A war might well heal the breach if the campaign went well.

But if defeat lay ahead it might raise plebeian anger and place extremists at the helm of government. These leaders at first looked upon war as a gamble and rejected it. But the development of events carried them along with others, in the belief that a war could be advantageous to the monarchy.

Robespierre's reasons for opposing war were quite different from Barnave's. War would pervert the aims of the Revolution, Robespierre argued, divert the people from immediate objectives, fulfill the purpose of ambitious men and invite the return of reaction. His fight for peace was part and parcel of the policy he had pursued in the Constituent Assembly. No longer a deputy when the war issue arose, he brought the question before the Jacobin Club where the Girondins still held sway. Here a series of speeches delivered during a period of several months made him the uncontested leader of the small anti-war party. Peace, he argued, was indispensable to establish freedom and to vanquish the enemy within, an enemy more to be dreaded than the enemy without. A war would inflate the influence of intriguers around the court, permit traitors to conspire, give the executive greater power, and jeopardize the gains of the first two years of the Revolution. "To whom will you entrust the conduct of this war?" he asked the Girondins. If to the agents of the executive power, then the safety of the state would be abandoned to the men who plotted to destroy it. War was "the greatest scourge that could threaten liberty."[23] War, he went on, had always been the first desire of a powerful government that aimed to be still more powerful. "It is during a war that the executive power displays its greatest force and exercises a sort of dictatorship, destroying freedom. During a war the people neglect decisions affecting their civil and political rights in order to occupy themselves with foreign affairs. They turn their attention from legislators and judges and confine their interests and hopes to generals and ministers, or rather to the generals and ministers of the executive power."[24] War was profitable "to military officers, to men seeking power, and to brokers who speculate on events of this character." It was good for ministers, for it cast a veil over their mode of action; it was good for the court, giving it popularity and authority; and it was good for "that alliance of nobles, conspirators, and moderates who govern France."[25]

Robespierre was not a pacifist. He was, he said on January 2, 1792, as much in favor of a war undertaken to spread freedom as Brissot. "But, considering the state of affairs in my country," he continued, "I become uneasy when I view the situation, and I wonder whether the war that will be waged will be the one promised us enthusiastically. I ask myself: Who proposes it? How? Why? Under what circumstances?" He went on to prove that the plan to draw the country into war had been concocted by the internal foes of freedom, by ministers and leaders of the faction that was in close relation with reaction.[26] The war for freedom Brissot was proclaiming was sheer deceit. If he seriously wanted to make the Revolution a force among other peoples, he would first consolidate it in France. "To wish to give them freedom before having conquered it for ourselves," he told the Jacobins, "is to fasten at once our own servitude and that of the entire world."

He asked his audience to examine with him the internal condition of France and the problems demanding solution. It had to establish order in its finances, stop monopolists from plundering the nation, arm the people and the National Guard, and win their support by good and liberal legislation. That alone, he said, "can make us invincible against our enemies." Why send armies against Coblenz (the headquarters of the émigrés), he asked, since Coblenz was in Paris? "Why turn our attention away from our most dreaded enemies and focus it elsewhere?" The Girondist war program, he charged, would benefit reaction, for reaction was counting on a war to create a large army, to separate it from the people, stir up civil war, destroy popular organizations, imprison their leaders, and suppress the party that defended the cause of the people.[27]

Robespierre accused the partisans of war of attempting to stifle debate on the issue. It was the patriotic duty of citizens, he contended, "to search for motives, to foresee consequences, to reflect, to take proper measures both to prevent the enemies of freedom from executing their plans and to secure the safety of the state," rather than "to applaud, idolize, preach confidence, and vote millions." The executive power, he said, was behaving as if war had already begun, for already it was violating the principles of freedom. He announced that he would not surrender the right to expose traitors, despite all the slander cast at him. To the Girondins who tried to prevent him from speaking on the ground that he was disheartening the country, he replied:

"On the contrary I am enlightening it. To instruct free men is to awaken their courage. . . . Had I done nothing more than uncover chicaneries, show the falsity of many ideas and principles, and check rash and dangerous enthusiasm, I would have instructed public opinion and been useful to the nation. I cannot flatter the people in order to ruin them. The proper way to respect the people is not to lull them to sleep by magnifying their strength and authority, but to caution them against their own shortcomings. The people understand more quickly and see better what appertains to the fundamental principles of justice and humanity than those who are removed from them. . . . [But] their natural goodness causes them to be dupes of political charlatans."[28]

Robespierre never yielded to the war party even though it threatened him and confronted him with its combined strength. He remained steady under the fire of the enemy, denouncing treachery and predicting that the war might terminate in a military dictatorship. The best measures, in the interest of national security, were reforms in behalf of the people's welfare. To the reforms mentioned above he added others, such as the return of the common lands to the peasants, the enforcement of the decrees abolishing feudal dues, the extinction of the internal enemy, and the revision of the military code along democratic lines. These changes, by enlisting the peasants on the side of the Revolution, would be the best protection against intervention. Thus, in answer to those who shouted for war Robespierre proclaimed the need of more reform and more democracy as the promising way to defend the nation.

The cause Robespierre fought for had the backing of but a small minority. Less than a handful of journalists plus a tiny group in the Jacobin Club fell in behind him. Danton, at first a partisan of peace, wavered and in time took his place with Brissot. Was Danton promised a post in a Girondist ministry, as Mathiez has suggested?[29] And Desmoulins, whom Marat described as a journalist "without views,"[30] also forsook the cause of peace. By the end of December 1791 he was employing the arguments of the Girondins.[31]

Marat was in England during the controversy. But in the beginning of March he returned and with the help of the Cordeliers Club revived the *Friend of the People*. In its pages he attacked the war party and painted the Girondins as venal and treacherous.[32] For Robespierre he had but admiration. Robespierre, he said, had covered himself with glory "by his steadfastness in upholding the cause of the people." The Girondins couldn't forgive him his popularity among the partisans of freedom, his incorruptibility, and his genuine patriotism. Robespierre's virtues, Marat went on, made the crimes of the Girondins all the more apparent. That was why they were bent on vilifying him and on tarnishing his good name among the people.[33]

The drive toward war rolled over the opposition of Robespierre and Marat. Girondist propaganda, aided and abetted by the followers of Lafayette and by royalists in general, built up an emotional excitement bordering on hysteria. It was sufficient to sweep along the doubtful and hesitant. The power the Girondins had been seeking was offered them in March 1792. They formed a ministry. Two weeks later an ultimatum was sent to the Austrian emperor, threatening him with war unless he renounced all treaties hostile to France and withdrew his troops. The same evening Robespierre again addressed the Jacobin Club in the hope of halting the avalanche. His words evoked hostility from the great majority of the audience. On April 20, 1792, France declared war amidst a general frenzy, and to the deep satisfaction of the Girondist and royalist press. Now that the war was a fact, Robespierre, at the Jacobin Club, called for a people's war. The internal enemy had to be fought as much as the foreign one. The internal enemy had secretly prepared the war and looked upon the Revolution as the great occasion for acquiring riches and power.[34]

Just as Robespierre had foreseen, the internal enemy turned out to be as formidable as the foreign one. The armies were ill clad and badly armed. The queen, moreover, secretly forwarded the military plans to the enemy. The results were French military defeats, the invasion of France and a threat to its capital. The enthusiasm that had greeted the declaration of war changed to rancor and finally to malice against those they suspected of treason. The events that culminated in the insurrections of June 20 and August 10, 1792, and in the overthrow of the monarchy fall beyond the boundaries of the present essay. All that need be said here is that as the war continued the Girondins proved themselves unequal to the problems it raised. In 1793 they had to surrender power to the Jacobins among whom Robespierre had risen to leadership. The war he had so strenuously opposed was henceforth his main burden. He bore it with fortitude and statesmanship.

BRITISH JACOBINISM

THE French Revolution compelled Europeans and Americans to take sides. The titled, the privileged and the propertied in the main likened it to satanry, to be exorcized by prayer, the hangman and the sword. Its defenders were to be found in different social strata, but their greatest numbers were among the common people. These regarded its success as the defeat of their own oppressors at home.

Willy-nilly, the Revolution assumed international dimensions. But its impact on peoples varied with their local conditions. Where history had been given a push, as in Great Britain and the United States, the Revolution inspired an organized agitation to achieve democratic gains. Where feudalism and serfdom were still ascendant, for example in Germany and in Italy, enthusiasm for it was scattered and weak, save in the Rhineland and especially in northern Italian towns, where Jacobinism made converts. The Risorgimento there dated from 1792, according to a lengthy report of Philippe Buonarroti in 1795, found in his posthumous papers.[1] Even so, neither in Germany nor in Italy was the movement strong enough at once to erase the feudal order and to establish national unity. For both countries lacked strong middle classes, with clear objectives, that could take the lead in a war against feudalism, much as the English and French middle classes had done.

1

Party lines were conspicuously drawn in England during the French Revolution. The English seventeenth century revolution had ended in a compromise between the landed aristocracy and the bourgeoisie, that left standing feudal survivals. Parliament remained in the hands of the well-to-do. Still people were not disturbed by the political monopoly so long as the standard of living was not impaired. In the second half

of the eighteenth century, however, real wages tended to decline.[2] The
political scene grew agitated during the decade before the American
Revolution. As in pre-revolutionary France, so in England, liberals
turned their sympathies to the new American Republic. Prominent
among them were Dr. Richard Price,[3] a member of the Revolution
Society that nourished on the traditions of the Glorious Revolution;
J. Horne Tooke,[4] a founder of the Constitutional Society with the object
of obtaining full and equal representation; and Major Cartwright,[5] an
advocate of a more liberalized English government.

The American Revolution had ruffled English politics. But the
French Revolution made them turbulent. English well-to-do saw in the
French attack on privilege an alarming example for the underprivileged
and workers in their own country. Reformers inquiring into the roots
of power had already found in John Locke such theories as the consent
of the governed, the primary common ownership of the land, labor
as the origin of the claim to property and the right of revolution. These
theories, derived from the doctrine of natural rights, also constituted
an essential part of French revolutionary creeds.

Now the same doctrine was serving the business community. The
economic creed, laid down by the Physiocrats and Adam Smith, with
self interest as the motive and competition as the way to the common
good, stemmed from natural rights. That they should be converted
into a weapon against the established order was both perplexing and
unpremeditated. For the propertyless to demand the same rights as the
propertied was to revive the great debates and perhaps even the class
conflicts of the English Revolution. The events in France were in fact
doing that and lending force to the arguments in favor of reform. Where
would it stop once the bars were let down?

Edmund Burke took up the cudgels against the threat to the existing order in England. Stirred by Dr. Price's sermon, "A Discourse on
the Love of Country," that had won the applause of the Revolution
Society and prompted it to send an address to the French Constituent
Assembly, Burke settled down to pen a refutation of the French revolutionary principles. The result was his famous and ill-tempered *Reflections on the Revolution in France*, published in 1790.[6] It presented an
alternative to the theory of natural rights. If we discard Burke's senti-
mentalism for the French royal pair and his distortion of the revolutionary picture, his contention was that a constitution was something
organic. Developed through the centuries, it could not be overthrown
by a popular revolution. The rights of man were metaphysical, created
by men of letters, Burke argued; but the conservative tradition had a
claim on men's minds. It commanded veneration. A government of long
duration represented the accumulated experience of generations, that

a revolution could not erase. The persistence of institutions was an assumption in their favor, was his contention.

The *Reflections* gave a program to conservatism in England and to counter-revolution on the Continent. Its main charges were: The people were "the swinish multitude," incapable of knowing their own good and of making their own laws; the French Revolution was but an abominable usurpation of beggarly tyrants; its guiding principles were atheism and anarchy, and its methods murder and plunder. From this it followed that a war to stamp out the Revolution would be equal to a crusade for a noble cause. Burke actually called on the rulers of Europe to form a coalition before the revolutionary hydra extended beyond France. No wonder Joel Barlow, the American poet, charged him in 1793 with having been an instigator of the European war against France.[7]

Burke's book started a pamphlet war, so great was the controversy over the issues he had raised. The debate produced important contributions to political and philosophical literature, of which the best known were Paine's *Rights of Man*, Barlow's *Advice to the Privileged Orders* and Godwin's *Enquiry Concerning Political Justice*. Paine's book was the most eloquent and the most popular, and Godwin's the most philosophical. Barlow's *Advice* had three editions in little more than a year, despite attempts to impede its sale.

Burke and Paine found confirmation for their principles in different areas. The first, going back into history for the props of his political thought, returned with a deep reverence for things as they were, even though they had gathered cobwebs. The second, impelled by a sense of justice, took his stand on the doctrine of natural rights, attacking from this ground hereditary monarchy and institutions and practices related to it. He traced its beginnings to conquest, violence and plunder. That was in character with what a number of French eighteenth century political theorists had been saying. If the position of these theorists, Paine's included, lacked historical analysis, it was at least more in keeping with the trend of history than Burke's. The French Revolution demonstrated it.

Just as Burke's attack on the Revolution provided arguments in defense of conservatism, so Paine's answer[8] crystallized opinion among reformers and democrats. It rejected completely Burke's theatrical exaggerations, described the sufferings of the people, lauded their humanity in contrast to the brutality of the court and reactionaries, considered civil rights inseparable from an improved, democratic society, and invested the people with the right to establish a democratic government, if they chose. Burke's stress on the solidarity of the past, present and future generations, got the reply that that was an attempt to impose the authority of the dead over the freedom of the living.

The *Rights of Man* was regarded as a call to revolution. For a man to be free it is sufficient that he wills it, Paine said. This appeal to the people to take affairs into their own hands, as they were doing in France, was interpreted by defenders of the established order as the signal for continuous disturbance. Paine's prophecy that the French Revolution promised "a new era to the human race," and that monarchy would not last longer than seven years "in any of the enlightened countries of Europe," appalled advocates of the *status quo,* particularly since the second part of his book presented an immediate program, apparently designed for that "new era."

The program did not promise an invasion of the rights of property, but simply evinced Paine's faith in progress. Far more disturbing than the program, was his disparaging derivation of the political institutions, buttressing the social and economic order.

Paine was conscious of the social problem. The question as it appeared to him was "whether man shall inherit his rights, and universal civilization take place? Whether the fruits of his labours shall be enjoyed by himself or consumed by the profligacy of governments?"

The rights of man seemed to him to contain more than protection from arbitrary government and the exercise of the franchise. They encompassed the right to life, he argued, thus anticipating Fourier. The function of government, Paine contended, did not "exist in executions; but in making such provision for the instruction of youth and the support of age, as to exclude, as much as possible, profligacy from the one and despair from the other."

Paine's renovating proposals aimed at rendering "governments more conducive to the general happiness of mankind." Among the reforms he advocated were: general disarmament through international treaties; replacement of indirect taxes by a graduated income tax; the reduction in the number of offices; abolition of the Poor Law; pensions to all over fifty; grants for children under fourteen; maternity benefits; and national workshops. Taxes on wealth would bear the cost of these benefits. The society Paine preferred was that of small owners. His *Agrarian Justice,*[9] published in 1797, was an addition to his program. He proposed to compensate the propertyless for the loss of their natural rights to the land by paying £15 to each one who arrived at the age of twenty-one and an annual pension of £10 to the aged. But he was not prepared to go to the length of nationalization.

Paine's answer to Burke was a best seller. In an unpublished letter to Paine, written many years later, Thomas Hardy, secretary of the London Corresponding Society, recalled the enlightening effect his book had had on his "fellow-men, removing from their eyes the political bandage which has enveloped them in darkness for ages by the craft of kings and priests."[10] When it was rumored that the government would prosecute Paine, collections were made by popular societies to pay the cost of the defense. Having fled to France to escape arrest, he was indicted and burned in effigy in his absence. Bookdealers who sold his polemic were arrested. But popular societies throughout Great Britain promoted and studied it. A government spy reported in 1792 that Ipswich had "above a dozen clubs and more, to which the common, ignorant people are invited, and a reader is elected in each, and explains Paine's pamphlet to those ignorant people." In November of the same year, another spy told of a well-attended club meeting in Norwich, where "Mr. Paine's *Rights of Man* was read." A report from Scotland in April 1793 had it: "Paine's book, it is now known, has been industriously circulated among the lower classes of our people, and its damnable doctrines eagerly embraced by them. Of liberty and equality they are constantly talking, and of making laws and fixing prices on every necessity of life."[11]

Reports listed Joel Barlow's *Advice to the Privileged Orders*[12] among the publications the societies were promoting. It was the first part of a book by an American poet who had seen service as a chaplain in the American Revolution. Arriving in Europe on the eve of the French Revolution to represent an American land speculating company, he quickly fell in with artists and intellectuals both in England and in France. His English friends and acquaintances were William Godwin and Mary Wollstonecraft, Richard Price, Joseph Priestley and William Hayley, the poet. Among the Americans he met were three painters: John Trumbull, John Copley and Benjamin West. Jefferson introduced him in France to economists and literati in general. All in all Barlow, who had crossed the Atlantic for reasons of business, found himself engrossed in the intellectual currents of Europe. The French Revolution made him its partisan from the beginning. So deep was his interest in it that he planned to write its history, as the notes and long outline in his unpublished papers show.[13] The Revolution confirmed his faith in democracy, of the American form in particular, whose story Jefferson and Madison urged him to tell. And as a consequence of the French Revolution, in which he had a small part, his understanding of liberty and equality ripened. Instead of the nebulous natural rights as its source, it drew strength from science and industry that facilitated "the means of living" and the multiplication of wants. A reading of the French and English materialists awakened his interest in science, and dispelled his metaphysical outlook, as his manuscript notes indicate. Religion, he held, was an instrument to terrorize the multitude. He even

meditated upon the historical and philosophical question whether mono-
theism was to be preferred to polytheism. Polytheists, he said, at least
"never made wars about religion."

Barlow entered the controversy Burke had stirred by his *Reflections*.
In common with Paine, Barlow, during his stay in England, shared
the life of the reform societies. He joined the Society for Constitutional
Information in March 1792, that Paine frequented before fleeing Great
Britain. Barlow's reputation in the society was apparently high, for toward the end of 1792, it included him in a delegation to carry its fraternal greetings to the French National Convention. There is a good
likelihood that he even helped draft the message, just as he had drafted
the address of American residents in Paris, in 1790, requesting the honor
to participate in the first celebration of Bastille Day.[14]

His reply to Burke won immediate recognition. The first part of
the *Advice to the Privileged Orders*, published in London on February
4, 1792, circulated so widely among reformers that the government for-
bade the publication of its second part. Written in the contentious atmosphere of the public debate between conservatives and democrats, the
book naturally had the character of a polemic.

The aim of the *Advice* was two-fold. It set out to answer Burke's
charge that the French Revolution was an anarchic smashup of organic
society; and it undertook to show how the oppressive forms of aristocratic government were no longer able to resist the corrosive power of
reason and progress. While Burke utilized the organic nature of society
with its hereditary orders to close the door to reform and to prevent
any tampering with the class structure, Barlow examined Burke's society and found it had "ceased by degrees to require its continuance."
An aristocracy, he said, always armed itself with theories, laws and
institutions in order to continue ruling. One portion occupied itself
"with the weapons of bodily destruction, and another with the mysterious artillery of the vengeance of heaven." Doctrines, favored by Burke,
were adapted to vindicate the royal prerogative. Even agriculture and
industry were discouraged, lest an improvement in man's condition
threaten the shackles of despotism. The fact was, Barlow continued, the
privileged order, with its feudal practices, prevented economic progress,
put a premium on idleness, nourished rivalries, tempered men's minds
"to an aristocratical subordination." Feudal privileges had lost their
original object of preserving society. But family interest demanded their
survival, even though they were detrimental to the general interest.
Men were inoculated with the idea that what existed was sacred and
unalterable. Barlow's reply was that that was but a habit of thinking,
replaceable by another, nurtured in freedom. And he pointed to the
example of the United States where men were given to think in demo-

cratic terms. The claim that inequality was rooted in human nature was simply groundless "mysticism," he maintained.

Barlow found four main institutions sustaining the power of the privileged classes. First, the established church stimulated religious wars, dulled "the inquisitive faculties of the mind," set up class distinctions in man's "intercourse with God," governed men by incantation, "acquired wealth, and covered arbitrary power with a sacred mantle." Then, the military caste had its standing army that fed "upon human gore." It needed war for plunder and for the exaltation of the ruler. Third, the administration of justice, resting on the "abominable doctrine that private vices are public benefits," permitted lawyers to consider justice a "commodity." Finally, inequality in property divided men and made them artificial beings.

His program was in keeping with the ideas he had absorbed abroad. Its object was to remove the impediments of progress and release "the spirit of investigation which the French Revolution has awakened in many parts of Europe." He would replace indirect by direct taxes, equalize property as far as possible, not ruling out the contingency that "perhaps in a more improved state of society, the time will come, when . . . it shall be found more congenial to the social nature of man to exclude the idea of separate property, and with that the numerous evils which seem to be entailed upon it." He also called for simplified laws, reform of the courts and peoples' in place of professional armies. If the people had "nothing to revenge in the government," there would be "many advantages in their being accustomed to the use of arms," particularly when a nation struggled "for the recovery of liberty." Unlike Burke, who regarded the French Revolution as an ogre, born of the "swinish multitude," threatening to devour the established order, Barlow saw its rejuvenating potential. Among its positive accomplishments, he said, was its challenge to conservatives of Burke's variety to come out openly and say that the people had nothing to do with government.

The same political theme was to be found in Barlow's subsequent writings on the Revolution. They were *A Letter to the National Convention of France, The Conspiracy of Kings* and *A Letter to the People of Piedmont.*[15] But the *Advice,* more than these publications, earned the thanks of democratic clubs and the calumny of conservatives. Government spies reported Barlow's book among those widely circulating. The Manchester Constitutional Society congratulated "the public on the appearance of such works as the *Advice to the Privileged Orders* and the *Letter to the National Convention of France* by Joel Barlow; and they are of the opinion that the cause of liberty will be essentially promoted by extending the knowledge of publications so masterly on subjects so important."[16] On the other hand, *The Morning Chronicle* was abusive, coupling his name with Paine's. That was the worst possible reproach.

Among the many answers to Burke at least seven were by women, among them Mary Wollstonecraft, Catherine Macaulay, Mary Hays and Helen Maria Williams. Of the seven, only the name of Mary Wollstonecraft has survived the test of time. Her *Vindication of the Rights of Men* antedated her *Vindication of the Rights of Woman*. The first was buried in the mountain of rhetoric the controversy had piled up; and the second was resurrected from obscurity by the much later women's movement.[17] The poets Wordsworth, Coleridge and Southey, at first elevated by the French Revolution, turned away from it, and finally found a haven in conservatism.[18] But before passing the peak of their enthusiasm they had awaited expectantly the better time promised by Godwin's *Political Justice*.

William Godwin's book was the most philosophical treatment of the question of government Burke had thrown into the public arena. Published in 1793 in two quarto volumes at three guineas, it escaped prosecution because its price, it was supposed, would limit the number of readers. The authorities, however, had miscalculated. The book appeared shortly before the outbreak of war between France and England that brought with it a period of repression seldom equaled in English history. A number of Godwin's friends stood trial for treason on flimsy evidence. Even so, neither the price nor the cruel curbing of thought and opinion succeeded in casting the book into oblivion. At least 4000 copies of it were sold, and among its purchasers were many workers who had pooled their small sums.[19]

The philosophy of *Political Justice* was as deterministic materialist as La Mettrie's and Holbach's and as optimistic as Helvetius's and Condorcet's. Man's actions, Godwin held, were the result of impressions received by the mind from the external world and transformed through reason into thought. Therefore man's perfectibility was dependent on changes in the external world. But the existence of government perpetuated evils and interfered with the exercise of reason. Godwin belonged to that group of eighteenth century thinkers who drew politically individualist deductions from the new economic doctrine of *laissez-faire*. The best government was the one that governed least. That was a guiding principle for such political theorists as Jefferson, Paine, and Barlow, and it might also have been Robespierre's and Saint-Just's, had they not been burdened with the defense of the Revolution.

Godwin took an extreme individualist position and from a society with the least government arrived at one without government. He distinguished between government and society. The first was an inevitable sequence of corrupting institutions. He referred to it as "that brute engine which has been the only perennial cause of the vices of mankind." The second, society, arose out of the need of living together. The end of progress was anarchism. Although Godwin did not use the word, he already defined it as "a simple form of society without government." Men would then be guided by reason in their mutual relations, and in the relations of peoples; for "mankind are brethren," Godwin asserted. Wars, he held, "do not originate in the unbiased propensities of nations, but in the cabals of government and the propensities that governments inspire into the people at large." He was opposed to the use of violence, save for "the defense of our own liberty and the liberty of others." Reason alone should be used in the service of truth, and that was "indestructible" and "omnipotent."

A political transformation would be pointless, Godwin argued, without changing the system of property. On this question he went to communist conclusions that neither Holbach nor Helvetius had derived from their philosophies. He laid all social vices to private property. It bred "a sense of dependence," brought home "a servile and truckling spirit," and encouraged men to sell "their conscience for the vile rewards that oppression has to bestow;" it directed the mind "into the channel of the acquisition of wealth" instead of into virtue and general welfare; it caused frightful inequality, placed a premium on idleness, extinguished "the sparks of genius," and reduced "the great mass of mankind to be immersed in sordid cares;" it produced crime and violence, gave rise to "an open contention of the strength and cunning of one party against the strength and cunning of the other," and caused despotism and war. Finally, by keeping population "down to the level of the means of subsistence," it strangled "a considerable portion of our children in their cradle."[20]

These were very serious charges leveled at private property. His alternative was a society based on justice, of which Godwin drew but a brief outline. Compared with the carefully worked out Utopian blueprints of Morelly and François Boissel in France, for example, Godwin's logically deduced order was only faintly drawn in its general forms. It was at once communist and anarchist. Decentralized into small associations, it was the type of society that, with modifications, anarchists later had in mind.

Godwin's test of the good society was the amount of leisure people had for intellectual and scientific pursuits. To have this leisure he would be content with a life of necessities. This was a residue of eighteenth century Rousseauism. But Godwin had left behind its crudities. He had faith in the role of ideas to shape man's conduct. Even though modern techniques had begun to change life in the England of

his time, he had neither anticipated their limitless potential nor contemplated, as did Babeuf in France, a society without the alternatives
of leisure and abundance. Even so, peering into the future, he was
buoyant and optimistic. His social vision was as radiant as Fourier's and
equally freed from idleness and unproductive labor. Godwin projected
his society in bare outline:

"If superfluity were banished, the necessity for the greater part of
the manual industry of mankind would be superseded; and the rest,
being amicably shared among all the active and vigorous members of
the community, would be burthensome to none. Every man would have
a frugal yet wholesome diet; every man would go forth to that moderate
exercise of his corporal functions that would give hilarity to the spirits;
none would be made torpid with fatigue, but all would have leisure to
cultivate the kindly and philanthropical affections of the soul and to
let loose his faculties in search of intellectual improvement. . . . How
rapid and sublime would be the advance of intellect if all men were
admitted into the fields of knowledge! . . . It is to be presumed that
the inequality of mind would in a certain degree be permanent; but it
is reasonable to believe that the geniuses of such an age would far
surpass the grandest exertions of intellect that are at present known . . . .
There will be no persons employed in the manufacture of trinkets and
luxuries; and none in directing the wheels of the complicated machine
of government . . . . There will be neither fleets nor armies, neither
courtiers nor footmen. It is the unnecessary employments that at present
occupy the great mass of the inhabitants of every civilized nation, while
the peasant labours incessantly to maintain them in a state more per-
nicious than idleness."[21]

Political Justice had its devotees and enemies. Radicals and reformers found in it a vindication of their demands. Wordsworth, Coleridge
and Southey derived satisfaction from its optimistic rationalism before
they disengaged themselves from its spell and retired behind the spirit
of the age. Others, among them publicists and preachers, denounced
its levelling principles and its criticism of the marriage institution. Godwin was charged with rejecting marriage, inculcating sex promiscuity,
and frowning upon religious worship. The most serious antagonist he
provoked was Robert Malthus, who wrote the *Essay on the Principle
of Population* to counter the happy picture arising from justice with
the pessimistic spectre of overpopulation. Godwin's most lasting influence was subsequently exerted on Shelley, who took over from his
father-in-law such teachings as the supremacy of reason and the perfectibility of man.

Godwin's book scandalized official circles. For he had carried
French doctrines all the way to communism. He rejected the principles

of the English democratic societies, but he defended their leaders whom the government prosecuted. This apparent inconsistency was in conformity with his dislike of coercion from whatever quarter it came.[22] Perhaps because his reasoning on government reached conclusions that had no answer to immediate issues, not his but Paine's book served as the main arsenal of the contemporary British democratic movement.

2

The polemic rent British public opinion into Burkeites and Paineites. The first defended the English Constitution with its highly restricted suffrage and its hereditary privileges. They were conservatives or Tories, and their parliamentary leader was William Pitt. The second advocated parliamentary reform. Its adherents represented separate social strata, from upper class liberals, led by Charles James Fox, to working class democrats, with Thomas Hardy, the shoemaker at their head. This does not mean that Paine's ideas were the common denominator among all of them. On the contrary, upper class liberals either openly dissociated themselves from Paineism or maintained a diplomatic neutrality to conceal their sympathy. Many liberals genuinely wanted reform as an antidote to revolution, and in seeking the remedy they dwelt on "the peculiar necessity of circumspection and moderation."[23] The example of the American Revolution had warned them to avoid disturbances in England, now that the shocks of the French Revolution were being felt. Liberals petitioned the government to make concessions, to abolish rotten boroughs and loosen the landlords' hold on the House of Commons. They did not countenance a broad suffrage to include the entire male population, but they gave their weight to measures designed to rectify political abuses.

The liberals themselves had two main wings: the moderates, organized as the Friends of the People; and the liberal democrats, brought together in the Revolution Society. In either case, a radical title belied a mild program.[24] Neither organization wanted complete democracy, and neither had the backing of the common people. The first, coming to life in 1791 when the reform agitation was beginning to show strength, turned out to be more a deterrent than a stimulant of the democratic movement. The second, the Revolution Society for Commemorating the Revolution of 1688, to use its full name, had been founded in 1780, even before the close of the American Revolution. The Society had among its members such internationally known men as Dr. Price and Lord Stanhope. During more than three years it faced censure and denunciation for defending the French Revolution. As early as November 1789, the Revolution Society sent a congratulatory Address to the French National Assembly on the "tendency of the glorious example given in France to encourage other Nations to assert the unalienable rights of Mankind, and thereby to introduce a general reformation in the governments of Europe, and to make the world free and happy."[25]

The above societies never aroused as much ill will and antagonism as did the unpretentiously named Society for Constitutional Information and the London Corresponding Society. The first attracted small middle class persons; and the second, mechanics and laborers. Both promoted Paine's, Barlow's and Godwin's answers to Burke, defended the French Revolution and cooperated on petitions and agitation. Organized back in 1780, the Society for Constitutional Information fell not long afterwards into a lethargy from which the French Revolution revived it. Its agitation for political reform won it the gratitude of friends and the hatred and scorn of opponents, especially since its program was shared by similar societies in Norwich, Sheffield, Birmingham, Manchester, Bristol and Leeds. Its democratic credo contained the following articles of faith: "that the great end of civil society is general happiness; that no form of government is good any further than it secures that object; that all civil and military authority is derived from the people; that equal active citizenship is the unalienable right of all men—minors, criminals and insane persons excepted; that the exercise of that right in appointing an adequate representative government is the wisest device of human policy and the only security of national freedom."[26] The tenets were obviously a challenge to the existing political order.

The London Corresponding Society was regarded by the high-born and the rich as a grave threat. Two of its warmest propagandists, Thomas Holcroft and John Thelwall, were friends and disciples of Godwin; and Thomas Spence was one of its organizers. Spence was the author of radical pamphlets, advocating imitation of the French and the communal ownership of landed property. His weekly, penny periodical, *Pig's Meat,* a variation on Burke's "swinish multitude," was entirely given over to the cause of liberty and equality in the anticipation of their emergence from the revolutionized system of ownership.

The establishment of the Society on January 25, 1792, on the initiative of Thomas Hardy, who became its active secretary, betokened the interest of British labor in political action. Beginning with eight workers, it grew into a large body with a membership of approximately 5,000, and circulated its resolutions in tens of thousands.[27] The dues of one penny a week were low enough to admit poor laborers and its simple program was nicely adapted to the unlettered. Starting from the theory of natural rights and the doctrine of consent, much as other contemporaries did, the Society claimed the right for everyone "to share in the government," except minors, criminals and insane. From that it went on to say that it was the duty of citizens "to keep a watchful eye on the government" in order to prevent oppression; that a fair and equal representation was the remedy for "oppressive taxes, unjust laws, restrictions of liberty, and wasting of the public money;" and the abolition of "all partial privileges," preliminary to "equal representation." Over and above this program, the Society declared "its abhorrence of tumult and violence." It neither called for a republic nor aimed at levelling property, as enemies charged. The primary of all reforms was an annually elected parliament, fairly chosen by all.[28]

These professions of faith did not secure it from attack. For it had become a center of a people's movement for parliamentary reform. The Society's strength was in London; but its alliance with societies of similar aims throughout Great Britain, the industrialized areas not excepted, set it off as the organization most likely to give the impulse to violent dissent from authority.

The mounting agitation, though peaceful, was taken as an unmistakable threat to the status quo. Conservatives set in motion nation-wide propaganda, and with official aid expected to overwhelm the democrats.

Now opposition to democratic ideas in England had been fairly vigorous during the Wilkite movement in the sixties and seventies. The opposition seems to have slackened after the loss of the American colonies. But it revived after 1789, and with fresh arguments and renewed force met the doctrines of liberty and equality, propagated by publicists and popular societies. Individuals and organizations, disseminating these doctrines, were ridiculed, denounced and indicted. Godwin's expensive *Political Justice* escaped criminal charges, it has been shown. But Paine's *Rights of Man* published in popular editions, and read and listened to earnestly in humble circles, was seized in bookshops. Its vendors were presumed to be equally guilty with the author. Organized mobs wrecked establishments of reformers, among them Joseph Priestley's well equipped laboratory in Birmingham; landlords refused meeting rooms to clubs; writers were employed to flood the market with anti-democratic pamphlets; and "legal associations" were set up to combat the agitation of the democratic societies.

What did conservative pamphleteers and organizations tell Englishmen? A common allegation was that domestic Jacobins were serving France. They were paid to sow dissension among happy, honest, British workers, to turn them aside from job and family with liberty clubs and with promises of some phantasmal equality. But for Paine all this mischief and sedition would not have been abroad. Liberty was natural to England. Here, the theme continued, "people in general may choose whether they will be rich or poor." French ideas, however, made people robbers, destroyed business, caused hunger and immorality. One pamphleteer, claiming he had risen to a competency by "honesty, sobriety, and industry . . . and going to no idle meetings," proposed that businessmen blacklist those belonging to "seditious and mischievous associations" that were "endeavoring to sap the foundations of everything that is valuable to society." Another defined a democrat as "one who likes to be governed by a thousand tyrants, and yet can't bear a king," and equality as the attempt "to pull down everyone that is above him, till they're all as low as the lowest." A third, saying he was a manufacturer and *The Poor Man's Friend*, argued that as long as private property was the rule "you have the foundation of a large estate," and "as long as there is any kind of inequality in the conditions of human life . . . , it is impossible that the representation can be equal, when every individual has an equal right to vote."[29]

A feature of the anti-democratic literature was its abundant and disdainful epithets to malign and vilify radical leaders both in England and in France. According to the ornamented terms, Paine was "ignorant and presumptuous." Hardy, though taciturn and unassuming, was lacking in modesty. Robespierre was represented as corrupt and gory; Marat, as a "scavenger," a "worm," and a hideous monster; and Babeuf, as "scum" boiled up by the Revolution.

The best known of the "loyal" associations was the "Association for Preserving Liberty and Property against Republicans and Levellers," under the leadership of John Reeves. Founded in November 1792 with official blessing and aid, it waged a campaign in defense of English institutions as they had been handed down, and published a series of penny tracts.[30] In keeping with the title of the organization, their object was to refute the current democratic, levelling ideas. They declared flatly that the will of the majority trespassed on private property. If the Rights of Man were really observed, the net result would be the insecurity of men's persons. The tracts went on to ascribe the increase in the number of poor to the disturbances caused by the democrats, whose claim to equality was evidence that their optimism outdistanced the facts of history. For "all history and all experience prove," ran the reply, "that wherever Society exists, there must exist a class of poor." Such was the fixed, natural order. The tracts praised "the excellence of the English Constitution, deduced from the harmony subsisting between the several ranks of citizens;" and they contrasted the English "firmness of soul" with the French "frivolous levity of character." Convinced of English racial "superiority," they expressed amazement at English attempts to imitate the French. So "be quiet," was the refrain of a poem in one of the Association's tracts. Another admonished: "Then stand by the Church, and the King, and the Laws."[31]

Conservative publications apparently failed to convince democrats. The more the issues were debated the more articulate were the critics of the established order. A correspondent of Lord Auckland, wrote in October 1792: "I am very much afraid that Paine's rascally book has done much mischief."[32] Its themes were the burden of a substantial literature. Prose as well as verse, pocket pamphlets and penny periodicals, books serious and witty, interpreted liberty and equality in a popular way. Citizen Lee's pamphlets used the dictionary form to define democratically such words as *alarmist, outcast, labour, rabble, France* and *equality*.[33] Brochures had such suggestive titles as *The Tocsin* and *The Friend of the People*. The "swinish multitude" became a popular slogan, and variations of it were the names of such publications as *The Rights of Swine*,[34] *Husks for Swine*,[35] *Pig's Meat*[36] and *Hog's Wash*.[37] The first, believing that the poor were without protection "against the oppressions and extortions of the rich" and "were robbed wholesale and relieved by retail," held that every "useful person has a right, yea, a *Divine Right* to be satisfied with the good of the Land!" *Husks for Swine, Dedicated to the Swine of England, the Rabble of Scotland and the Wretches of Ireland,* to use the full title, was a collection of lyrics, set to popular tunes, which grunted out in rhythm the complaints of commoners and sang of the "Rights of Mankind." *Pig's Meat, or Lessons for the Swinish Multitude,* Spence's publication, was a penny weekly, made up of extracts from writings on the rights of the poor, democracy and equality. His *Rights of Man,* with its levelling principles, went through many editions.[38] *Hog's Wash or a Salmagundy for Swine,* changed to *Politics for the People,* was a weekly, issued by Isaac Eaton, a bookseller, who was tried for sedition in 1794. It published selections from English, Scotch and French democratic writings.

A keynote of English democratic thought at this time was the brotherhood of man. This dated from the English Revolution, according to a recent study.[39] During the French Revolution the keynote was audible throughout the western world. A study of democratic internationalism in the decade from 1789 to 1799 would undoubtedly show that its principles were already awakening feelings of devotion in Poland and in Ireland, in Italy, Germany and Spain, in France and in America. But this alluring project falls beyond the limits of this essay. All that can be said here, of any relevance at this stage, is that democrats on the two sides of the Atlantic assessed the French Revolution as the harbinger of a new era. Its cause, they said, was that of all peoples seeking freedom from oppression; its principles, their binding force that made them allies against monarchs and feudal princes who waged war against the French Republic in order to root it out. Consequently, France, having lifted mankind to heights from which it could catch a glimpse of new horizons, commanded its entire support.

English reformers shared this view, even communicated it to the French. In their congratulatory addresses to the National Convention they expressed their indebtedness to France for its leadership in liberty and their solidarity with it in its fight for the human race. The addresses were sent before war broke out between England and France.[40] But from what is known of the subsequent activities and thoughts of the reform societies, they continued to hold fast to the brotherhood of man as a guiding motif. It was not uncommon for reformers to contemplate a new social order emerging from international friendship. Society then "will forget all distinctions but those of wisdom and virtue."[41]

British conservatives could ill afford to allow such ideas to circulate. Their efforts to stem the advance of radical thinking, it has been shown, only enlivened the debate. Events, however, favored their cause. On February 1, 1793, war broke out between France and England. For various motives, William Pitt, the Prime Minister, wanted the war. If France were defeated, as he believed, England would annex the remaining French colonies. The war, he calculated, would also strengthen the position of his own party by splitting the Whigs. And conservatism, too, would derive benefit from the wave of patriotism that would inevitably sweep over Great Britain.

There was a flaw in Pitt's calculations, however. He had failed to reckon with the French sans-culottes. In October 1793, England's continental allies were defeated, and revolting cities like Lyons and Bordeaux were subdued. The French recaptured Toulon from the English in December. Besides, the war helped bring on a serious financial crisis, with such results as a run on banks, commercial stagnation, unemployment and general distress.

Still the war fulfilled some of Pitt's anticipations. Liberals, both in and out of the Society for Constitutional Information and the Friends of the People, disowned the French cause, even became hostile. Also, the hardships of the war and the economic crisis weakened many societies. Organizations in Norwich, Birmingham and Sheffield, for example, lost members through unemployment or emigration.

Others, however, gained members and friends. According to the society in the borough of Tewkesbury, the war "has done more good to the cause than the most substantial arguments; 'tis amazing the increase of friends to liberty and the spirit of enquiry that is gone abroad."[42] The London Corresponding Society also increased its membership and influence. Speeding up its agitation, in the spring of 1793, it lent aid to a wide campaign for reform through petitions. And it bade other societies in the country to unite into a large movement. "Our society has met with much persecution," it wrote to a sister body, "nevertheless, we go on increasing in number and political knowledge." In another communication it said:

"Continuing in a slow but steady pace the career which we have begun, we are nearly certain that although the number of our members do not increase so rapidly as from the population of the metropolis we might have expected, yet our principles make their way among the public; and many thousands who, from connection, interest, etc., may be afraid or cautious of joining us overtly, notwithstanding are our staunch friends in private. You very likely do not labour under the same difficulties that we do, who are situated in the very center of corruption; and we have no doubt but that the increase of your society keeps pace with the increase of those national calamities which ever must result from an unjust war."[43]

On the whole, despite the war and the crisis, the democratic movement gave signs of strength in 1793. Maurice Margarot, a delegate of the London Corresponding Society to the Edinburgh Convention of November 1793, ventured to predict that were a conference of Scotch and English societies summoned, "we might represent six or seven hundred-thousand males, which is a majority of all the adults in the kingdom."[44] Margarot of course overstated. By any reckoning the cause of reform was far from having a majority in 1793. But the exaggeration itself reflected an optimism in democratic ranks.

The crisis at home and the military defeats on the continent were not calculated to keep high the prestige of the ministry. It needed buttressing, and Pitt found a way to present his government as the nation's savior from revolution. He launched an attack on the reform societies on the ground that they conspired the overturn of the government. The opportunity was found toward the end of 1793, when Scotch reformers called a convention of democratic societies in Edinburgh. Approximately 160 delegates were present, two of them from the London Corresponding Society. Others represented societies in Norwich, Sheffield, Leeds, parts of Scotland, and even of the United Irishmen. The purpose of the Convention was in its name, "The British Convention of Delegates of the People, associated to obtain Universal Suffrage and Annual Parliaments." The speeches had a French flavor, and the word "Convention" was too Gallic for the average Briton. Moreover, Joseph Gerrald, a delegate of the Corresponding Society, had published *A Convention the only Means of Saving Us from Ruin* that at once brought to mind the French model and implied a dual power. But the sessions were peaceful, being conducted, as Hardy said, "with a regularity, decorum, and dignity, by no means unworthy of the imitation of assemblies of a much longer standing. . . . Their proceedings were open to the public at large, and their resolutions debated and adopted in the presence of all who chose to attend."[45] The aim of the Convention was to win by peaceful reform the "full and fair representation of the people of Great Britain."[46] On December 5, 1793, the government arrested its secretary and several delegates and dispersed the rest. Five, among them the two representatives of the London Society, were tried for sedition and transported to Australia. Only one of the five survived to return to England.

With the breakup of the Convention, the initiative for organizing the remaining democratic bodies passed to the London Corresponding Society. It seems to have been the only surviving, solid organization. Many of the others had either disintegrated or had shrunken in size. The remaining democratic societies in the provinces turned to London for guidance. The united societies of Norwich called on the Corresponding Society to summon another Convention. A group in Bristol wrote for a "sketch of your plan respecting the General Convention." Simultaneously a request came from Newcastle-on-Tyne for advice on establishing a society. A letter from Halifax informed the Londoners that a meeting of delegates, relative to a convention, had withheld decision "until further information from you on that subject."[47]

The Corresponding Society acted in response to the requests. It issued an Address to the People of Great Britain and Ireland, demanding the redress of grievances and the restoration of English rights. With remnants of other organizations, it went ahead with plans for a new convention.[48] But the government arrested its leaders and the top men of the reform movement in May 1794. Then the Habeas Corpus Act was suspended. All the efforts of the government to discover proof of a plot for insurrection failed. Hardy's trial lasted nine days and his acquittal was received triumphantly by the vast crowd outside the court. Also acquitted were Horne Tooke the philologist and one-time follower of John Wilkes, and John Thelwall, of the London Corresponding Society.

The Society seems to have shown signs of a revival in 1795, as economic conditions grew worse. There were bread riots that year and demands for peace. In rural England enclosures went on at a disturbing rate. Alarmed by the rising discontent from which the Society apparently derived recruits, the government introduced two bills, giving it added power to deal with writers and public speakers and illegalizing unlicensed public meetings and reading rooms. A broad protest could not prevent the enactment of the bills. Thereafter the London Corresponding Society declined. What remained of it ceased to meet altogether after April 1798.[49]

The defeat of the democratic movement in England could not be laid solely to rigorous government policy. The inspiration of the agitation was American and especially French, to be sure, but the basis of its origin and growth was unmistakably English. Although the triumph of the Thermidorian reaction in France undoubtedly contributed to the decline of the English movement, the causes of its failure to fulfill its objectives must be sought primarily in English conditions. If workers, shopkeepers and small traders had sufficient ground for complaint in the economic difficulties beginning in the sixties, and anticipated betterments through parliamentary reform, they were, on the other hand, in no position to impose their demands with united ranks. An industrial working class was just emerging; and it was scattered, like the petty bourgeoisie. The French Revolution, moreover, had pushed liberals to the side of conservatism. They, who might have added strength and leadership to the reform movement, rallied around the ramparts of the existing order to defend them against the explosive French revolutionary triad.

Reaction triumphed in England as in France. But the movement, led by the London Corresponding Society, had impressed itself indelibly on the British common people. Looking back at this period after many years and at the Society he had founded and led, Thomas Hardy assessed its place in history as judiciously as when he had outlined its path to the future. The Society, he said, "did more in the eight or nine years of its existence to diffuse political knowledge among the people of Great Britain and Ireland than all that had ever been done before."[50] Neither Pitt's repression nor the unleashed hysteria could erase the deep furrows, made by the agitation for reform. Renewed, even during the Napoleonic War, it reached fresh levels and unexampled dimensions after 1815, finally culminating in the blazing summit of Chartism.

JEFFERSON ON THE FRENCH REVOLUTION

THE French nobleman, the Marquis de Chastellux, travelling through Virginia in 1782, visited Thomas Jefferson in Monticello and drew the following portrait of him:

"A tall, kind man, not yet forty, with a pleasant figure, but whose mind and great attainments can take the place of light, material pleasures; an American who, without ever having travelled outside of his own country, is at once a musician, a draftsman, an astronomer, a geometer, a physicist, a jurist and a statesman."[1]

The Marquis went on to point out briefly the political career Jefferson had already had both in Virginia and in the Continental Congress. For the versatile Jefferson, in addition to his many accomplishments, had turned his talents to American politics. Beginning in 1768 and continuing through six successive years, he had served in the Virginia House of Burgesses, had been a member of the Non-Importation Association organizing a boycott of English goods, and had set on foot a correspondence committee in Virginia to communicate with similar committees in an intercolonial organization.

These activities were but the beginning. A local Committee of Safety, started at the outbreak of the American Revolution, admitted him to membership. He was successively a delegate to the Virginia Convention that framed the state's constitution, a representative in the Continental Congress, and Governor of his state from 1779 to 1781. As a member of the Continental Congress, at the age of thirty-three, he drafted the Declaration of Independence.

Thus at the time of the Marquis's visit, Jefferson was already a prominent political figure in America. The Marquis, himself a man of letters with some claim to original philosophical views,[2] was impressed by his host's hospitality, by his magnificent library, vast knowledge and

57

advanced ideas. Even more than the Marquis, Jefferson was a humanitarian, with a deep concern for "life, liberty and the pursuit of happiness." Born in a wealthy planter's slave-owning family on the western frontier, he had become saturated in his whole being with the egalitarian atmosphere of the region. Here among the settlers, caste and privilege were as tolerable as pork among Moslems. At an early age Jefferson saw democracy in action and warmed to it. It became his standard political system, the only one congenial to his background and tastes. Some time before he became minister to France he had distressed the Virginia feudalistic aristocracy by forcing through the abolition of entail and primogeniture, two of its essential supports.

1

Jefferson's social philosophy belongs to the stream of western thought in the eighteenth century that had the people's welfare as its end. In England Thomas Spence, William Ogilvie and Thomas Paine shared it. And it had a kinship with what the London Corresponding Society tried to achieve after the inspiration of the French Revolution had given it momentum. The English anarchist, William Godwin, Rousseauan and rationalist, equally derived from that general stream of thought.[3] In France it had had champions in Rousseau, Mably, Helvetius and Diderot, to name but four of the better known literati; and during the Revolution it blossomed into programs. Similar trends were present in Italy, Holland and parts of Switzerland.

For in the entire western world, separated by the Atlantic, the ground quaked under the old order, finally giving way in America and in France. The English bourgeoisie sat securely. It had achieved victory over feudal absolutism the previous century and had then made partners of the defeated landed aristocrats. The French Revolution, therefore, did not unhinge the established institutions in England. The tempests, starting in France, blew over it, without leaving behind any wreckage. The revolutions in Holland, parts of Switzerland and Italy were abortive. The bourgeoisie was either too weak to lead the movement or surrendered before it swelled into something uncontrollable. But once the French Revolution triumphed it passed over into the areas of the aborted revolutions and fertilized them with its principles.

Out of the social philosophy shared by Jefferson and many contemporaries stemmed social patterns calculated to close the gap between wealth and poverty. Some banished private property from their realm and extolled crude equality. Godwin, who regarded abundance and leisure as alternatives in a just order, preferred the second. But that was the choice of an intellectual who had not yet discovered the potential of modern science and technique, when the two were at their birth.

And even they, who already caught a glimpse of labor saving machines, retained a nostalgia for primitive egalitarianism and asceticism. Plenty and austerity were to be found side by side, for example in the criticism of J. Louis Graslin and later of Babeuf. Even Diderot, the most brilliant among French eighteenth century writers, whose materialist philosophy drew strength from the science and technology of his day, wandered for a brief interval in the simple, egalitarian land of the Tahitians.[4]

Comparatively few eighteenth century thinkers believed seriously in the possibility of establishing a social order without thine and mine. The great majority of those who visualized a society free from want and poverty were partisans of an equality among small owners. Such was the ideal that inspired Jacobin leaders in France to vote for the distribution of the large estates among the landless and to plan the construction of model rural homes. Small ownership was fundamental to their conception of democracy "where," as Robespierre said in his speech of February 5, 1794, "the country secures the welfare of each individual, and each individual proudly enjoys the prosperity and glory of his country; where all minds are enlarged by the constant interchange of republican sentiments and by the need of earning the respect of a great people; where industry is an adornment to the liberty that ennobles it, and commerce the source of public wealth, not simply of monstrous riches for a few families."[5]

Jefferson, too, aimed at this ideal. Rooted in the unhistorical, yet influential, doctrine of natural rights, it had two important tenets: the individual's right to enjoy property unmolested; and the absence of the exploitation of man by man. Experience was to show the incompatibility of the two. But in Jefferson's social vision they dovetailed. The environment he had been raised in had little of the hierarchical gradations reformers desired to level. And want was practically non-existent, or so it had seemed to the young Jefferson. The good society, in his estimate, was made up of small independent farmers and was devoid of large urban areas. That was his way of preventing conflicts between social extremes and the answer to the large concentrations in cities, where, as he once wrote to Madison, "people get piled upon one another . . . and go to eating one another."[6] Capitalism with its ugly manifestations shocked him, just as it shocked others. He turned from it to rest his eyes on green pastures, on an agrarian order of comparatively equal owners, bound together amicably and sharing the sorrows and joys of neighborly living. There lay the promise of "life, liberty and the pursuit of happiness." Such a community did not seem to be beyond the reach of man in eighteenth century America, where the vast frontier was only beginning to recede. The closer such a society was approximated, the more democratic it would be. The nation, too, would be stronger. In common with Spence and Robespierre he believed that the "cultivators of the earth are the most valuable citizens. They are the most vigorous, the most independent, the most virtuous, and they are tied to their country, and wedded to its liberty and interests, by the most lasting bonds."[7]

Jefferson's pessimism over the emerging capitalist economy did not cause him to seek a haven in a phantasmal land of primitive innocence where, for example, the acute Dom Deschamps had navigated. He was a realist at heart. Commerce and industry could not be turned back from their course, nor their advance arrested, unless they invaded the relatively stable agrarian order. Jefferson yielded to the facts of history. Thus, in 1785 he contended that agriculture "would add most to the national wealth." Twenty years later he conceded that "we must now place the manufacturer by the side of the agriculturist."[8] The western unoccupied lands, he was confident, would absorb the main source of discontent and dull the edges of the social conflicts industrialism was engendering. Here he agreed with Hegel's estimate of the influence of the frontier on American society. But whether he shared Hegel's belief in the transitory nature of the frontier,[9] is less certain. A rural, egalitarian society remained Jefferson's standard. "Those who labor in the earth," he wrote, "are the chosen people of God . . . whose breasts He has made His peculiar deposit for substantial and genuine virtues."[10] His demarcation between lawyers, priests, merchants, capitalists, wealthy landowners and financiers on the one hand and the people on the other anticipated Saint-Simon's parable. The first regarded the second as conquered and servile. To practitioners in law he remarked: "Our ancestors . . . who migrated hither, were laborers, not lawyers."[11] The priest, he charged, had always been "in alliance with the despot, abetting his abuses in return for protection to his own."[12] He held the merchants in low esteem, for they "have no country." Just as Marat declared that to the rich traders the fatherland was where they had "the most resources. . . . and do the most business,"[13] so Jefferson: "The mere spot they stand on does not constitute so strong an attachment as that from which they draw their gains."[14] His antagonism to landowners and capitalists had its rationale in the subsistence theory of wages held by Turgot among other economists. Jefferson accused landowners and capitalists of exploiting the workers, "whether employed in agriculture or the arts, to the maximum of labor which the construction of the human body can endure, and to the minimum of food, and of the meanest kind, which will preserve it in life, and in strength sufficient to perform its functions." This aristocracy of rank and wealth, he went on, "which have the laws and government in their hands," made use of the wage earners and the poor "as tools to maintain their own wretchedness, and to keep down the laboring portion by shooting them whenever the desperation produced by the cravings of their stomachs drives them into riots."[15] He included in the aristocracy of wealth the financiers who wielded authority through the Bank of the United States. They could not be trusted to defend democracy when it was threatened. They might "unhinge the confidence of the people in the public functionaries," he wrote, and by means of their institutions, "penetrating by its branches every part of the Union, acting by command and in phalanx, may, in a critical moment, upset the government."[16]

Jefferson's confidence in the common man was as firmly fixed as Marat's and Robespierre's. Fortunes on the one hand and poverty on the other, his observations led him to conclude, sent tremors through the social edifice ultimately causing it to totter. Only that society could endure in which "the earth belongs always to the living generation."[17] The people, "and not the rich," in his opinion, "are our dependence for continued freedom."[18] Their good sense seemed to him "the best army." They might be led astray for a time, "but will soon correct themselves." [19] Every government declined, he argued, "when trusted to the rulers of the people alone. The people themselves therefore are its only safe depositories."[20] The people alone should rule, and not their masters. "These rogues set out with stealing the people's good opinion, and then steal from them the right of withdrawing it, by contriving laws and associations against the power of the people themselves."[21]

Such complete faith in the people was rooted in him. Behind it was his early experience with the democratic frontiersmen and his knowledge of the people's past in the war for American independence. Jefferson did not become a tired radical with the years. His democratic convictions remained deep and secure. On the fiftieth anniversary of American independence, less than two weeks before his death, he wrote:

"May it be to the world, what I believe it will be . . . the signal of arousing men to burst the chains under which monkish ignorance and superstition had persuaded them to bind themselves, and to assume the blessings and security of self-government. . . . All eyes are opened, or opening, to the rights of man. The general spread of the light of science has already laid open to every view the palpable truth, that the mass of mankind has not been born with saddles on their backs, nor a favored few booted and spurred, ready to ride them legitimately, by the grace of God. These are grounds of hope for others."[22]

Jefferson took pride in America's revolutionary tradition. His country had been an example to other peoples, a beacon of democracy for more than a decade before the French Revolution. He considered it his mission to keep the light shining in the dark periods of history, such as the era of Napoleon's military despotism, followed by years of reaction under Metternich.

To protect democracy and give it enduring force Jefferson advocated public education, for only an enlightened people could be vigilant. Humanity, Jefferson believed, was "susceptible of much improvement," and that would be achieved "by the diffusion of knowledge among the people."[23] Education was most to be relied on "for ameliorating the condition . . . and advancing the happiness of man."[24] The curriculum should lay stress on science in order to extend the frontiers of man's knowledge of the universe, to reveal the secrets of nature, and to promote discoveries that increased his subsistence and freedom. Such discoveries, he said, "must be a matter of joy to every friend to humanity."[25] Democracy to be strong, according to Jefferson, had to keep drawing sustenance from the advances of science, since the main object of all science was "the utility and safety of the human race," "the freedom and happiness of man."[26]

One of Jefferson's tenets was that a democratic society, to function, needed a free press. The people had to be enlightened on public affairs. Therefore newspapers should confine themselves "to true facts and sound principles only," he argued. Jefferson detested a venal press, controlled by the enemies of democracy. As Secretary of State under Washington and later as President of the United States, he learned how the press could mislead public opinion, how it maligned friends of the people and distorted popular movements in America and in France.

"Nothing can now be believed which is seen in a newspaper," he wrote in 1807. "Truth itself becomes suspicious by being put into that polluted vehicle. The real extent of this state of mis-information is known only to those who are in situations to confront facts within their knowledge with the lies of the day. I really look with commiseration over the great body of my fellow citizens, who, reading newspapers, live and die in the belief, that they have known something of what has been passing in the world in their time; whereas the accounts they have read in newspapers are just as true a history of any other period of the world as of the present, except that the real names of the day are affixed to their fables."[27]

Jefferson desired to remove restrictions from minorities and end all forms of servitude. Here again, as in his social and economic principles, he expressed the advanced thought of his age. With Mirabeau, orator and leader of the French National Assembly of 1789, he regretted the persecution of Jews and demanded their equality with other peoples. Just as Condorcet, Brissot, Marat and Robespierre in France and Dr. Price in England, he was severely critical of slavery. Though a slaveowner himself, he had begun a campaign against the slave system when he was still a member of the House of Burgesses. But he encountered stubborn opposition. His draft of the Declaration of Independence had included among the many arbitrary powers of the king his prevention of colonial legislatures from prohibiting the slave trade.[28] The article had to be deleted from the final draft to satisfy the slave trade interests. Even so, this odious traffic was illegalized while Jefferson was President.

He passed sentence on slavery. It encouraged despotism in the master; it had a demoralizing effect on the youth; it destroyed industry and stigmatized labor; it rendered insecure the liberties of the nation; and it made the slave an enemy of the country.[29] The combined strength of southern planters and northern merchants against the abolition of slavery sometimes darkened his horizon, but his faith in the younger generation was a cause for anticipating a better future. "It is to them I look," he wrote, "and not to the one now in power, for these great reformations."[30]

2

In 1784, Congress appointed Jefferson minister to France. Within a short time after his arrival intellectuals, reformers and scientists sought his company or solicited his advice. Writers on philosophy and politics consulted him. The society for the abolition of the slave trade invited him to join it. He had long talks with Georges-Leclerc de Buffon and had friends send samples of skeletons, skins and horns of American fauna to the famous naturalist.[31] He was on friendly terms with Physiocrats, particularly with the abbé André Morellet, whose translation of Jefferson's still readable and useful *Notes on Virginia* appeared in 1786. Men concerned about the political future of France asked for information about the Constitutional Convention in Philadelphia. In feudal France Jefferson was the living symbol of the country that was demonstrating to the world the possibility of democratic government.

Jefferson observed that the American Revolution had had a marked effect on Frenchmen. Noblemen and soldiers returning after the War of Independence spoke admiringly of the American people and of their free institutions. Fact and fiction about the new nation spread through publications. Some of them were translations of works in English; others were original. Also by 1783, there were circulating two translations of the American state constitutions with their bills of rights. According to a reliable student, they served as models for the French Declaration of the Rights of Man in 1789.[32]

If the French pamphlet literature of the few years before 1789 was any indication, the American Revolution had fired the imaginations of Frenchmen. Pamphleteers regarded the United States, if not as an exemplar, at least as a pioneer that had opened a new path. Denis

Diderot looked upon the American nation as the place where the un-equal distribution of wealth might be avoided so that its freedom and government might endure.[33] An essay of Antoine-Nicholas de Condorcet called the attention of his countrymen to America's religious toleration, its freedom of the press and the absence of feudal privilege.[34] The abbé Gabriel de Mably observed that the American state constitutions had established it as an axiom "that all political authority derives its origin from the people."[35] And Saint-Simon, later a Utopian socialist, recalled in 1817 how profoundly the Revolution had impressed him in 1783: "I foresaw that the American Revolution would necessarily set in motion the entire civilized world, and that it would shortly cause great changes in the social order then prevailing in Europe."[36]

The cordial French reception of the American Revolution was a cause of Jefferson's patriotic pride. He advocated continuing the ties between the United States and France because, as he wrote James Madison, "it is the only one on which we can rely for support, under every event. Its inhabitants love us more, I think, than they do any other nation on earth."[37]

The thirteen States had to unite, argued Jefferson, if they were to have the respect of Europeans. This he pressed upon his friends in the Constitutional Convention meeting in Philadelphia. Far from the scene, he followed the progress of the constitution-makers as best he could. He was not alarmed, as many Americans were, by the movement of poor indebted farmers in 1786, led by Daniel Shays, a veteran of Bunker Hill. Jefferson saw it as further proof of the need for greater democracy. But he feared lest the conservatives seize upon the disturb-ance, on the eve of the convention, as an argument for a strong central government, removed from popular influence. He approved of the constitutional plan as it had emerged from the convention. But he re-gretted the omission of a bill of rights, "providing clearly and without the aid of sophism, for freedom of religion, freedom of the press, pro-tection against standing armies, restriction of monopolies, the eternal and unremitting force of the habeas corpus laws, and trials by jury in all matters of fact triable by the laws of the land, and not by the laws of nations."[38] The thought that America was "acting for all mankind" never left him. That was why in his many letters to friends, some of them long political essays, he advanced the importance of a bill of rights. Whether or not his urging had any direct effect in promoting its later adoption is a point of inquiry. In any event the first session of Congress, on Madison's proposal, voted amendments granting civil liberty and submitted them to the states for ratification.

Conditions in France during Jefferson's five years abroad awakened in him almost as much interest as the political scene in his own country.

His communications before the Great French Revolution can still serve as a useful source on the period. He dug deep for the causes of disintegration of feudal society and assessed the privileged classes with discernment. For the poor and exploited masses he had warm sympathy. Clearly he was not an envoy sent by his country to reenforce a tottering régime. The absolute divine right monarchy and feudalism were entirely out of character with his upbringing and principles. If he subsequently seconded the overthrow of absolutism and privilege in France, it was thoroughly consistent with his earlier assault on the entrenched aristocracy of Virginia.

The contrast between the beauty of the French countryside and the poverty of people caused him to search for an explanation. Everywhere he talked with workers and peasants, noted that though the land was rich, the people were overworked. He laid their poverty to "that unequal division of property." Its concentration in France drew the following reflection: "The earth is given as a common stock for men to labor and live on. If for the encouragement of industry we allow it to be appropriated, we must take care that other employment be provided to those excluded from the appropriation. If we do not, the fundamental right to labor the earth returns to the unemployed."[39]

Jefferson learned to like the French people. "The roughness of the human mind is so thoroughly rubbed off with them," he wrote to a friend, "that it seems as if one might glide through a whole life among them without a jostle."[40] That was why their oppression was all the more deplorable. Travelling through the country, he was shocked by the prevalence of ignorance and superstition and "the general prey of the rich on the poor."[41]

Absolutism and feudalism, Jefferson found out, had led France to ruin. Their panoplied grandeur might have blinded them and their entourage to the sores and sorrows of the body politic. But the great mass of the people had grown weary and irritable under the stress. Crop failures had become cyclical; and the bread question, always a challenge, had seldom been more serious than in 1789. Besides, the commercial treaty with England in 1786, favoring the landed interests, had precipitated an industrial crisis. There were bread riots; and the number of beggars and poor generally increased. Paris alone, in 1789, had no less than 120,000 paupers out of a population of 600,000.

Jefferson's letters record the political events from the Assembly of the Notables in 1787 to the meeting of the Estates-General in 1789. Additional revenue had to be found in order to meet the increasing deficit of the treasury. The Notables had refused to make concessions, and the Parlement declined to register new taxes, insisting instead on the summoning of the Estates-General. The old régime was disintegrating and with it the authority of the government. Jefferson, writing to John Adams, had this to report on the state of public opinion:

"All tongues in Paris (and in France as it is said) have been let loose, and never was a license of speaking against the government exercised in London more freely or more universally. Caricatures, placards, bons mots, have been indulged in by all ranks of people, and I know of no well-attested instance of a single punishment. For some time mobs, of ten, twenty and thirty thousand people collected daily, surrounded the parliament [parlement] house, huzzaed the members, even entered the doors and examined into their conduct, took the horses out of the carriages of those who did well, and drew them home."[42]

Jefferson saw the French Revolution unfold. He regretted the lack of leadership, of a cohesive force "in the nation to promise a successful opposition to two hundred thousand regular troops."[43] He hoped that the king might achieve a bloodless revolution by surrendering his power to the nation. But the more he learned of the royal pair, the more he thought it improbable. The short sketches of the two top royal personalities must have amused his friends. "The King, long in the habit of drowning his cares in wine, plunges deeper and deeper. The Queen cries but sins on."[44] Jefferson was persuaded that a change in the French government was inevitable. The prospects of the triumph of freedom seemed bright.

Victory hung in the balance while the three orders of the Estates-General were in a deadlock over the question of procedure. A dispute arose over the verification of the powers of the deputies. The two privileged classes wished to continue sitting separately, as in the past, and vote by orders; the commoners were determined to have a single assembly in which the three orders sat and voted together. This was not a trivial issue. Had the privileged orders had their way reform, especially the abolition of feudalism, would have been impossible. The wrangle went on for nearly two months, keeping political heads in suspense. Jefferson still hoped the king would abandon the privileged orders and ally himself with the progressive forces of the nation.

Jefferson desired to avoid violence. A friend of several influential nobles and commoners, he held secret conferences with them in order to reach a peaceful settlement. He tried to prevail on Lafayette to lead the liberal nobles toward unity with the commoners.[45] Jefferson even went so far as to draft a Charter of Rights, as he called it, that the king would proclaim and all the members of the three orders would sign. The document, according to Jefferson, was designed as a starting point for other gains at the next meeting of the Estates-General. Meanwhile it would break the deadlock. His Charter was in reality a bill of rights, akin to what he had suggested to Madison for the American

Constitution. The ten demands of the document may be summarized as follows:

The Estates-General should be elected triennially, meet annually and determine its own procedure; it alone should control the purse-strings of the nation, and legislate with the consent of the king; arbitrary imprisonment should be ended, the press freed, the military subordinated to the civil authority, and privileged tax exemptions abolished; the nation should assume the king's debts; taxes should continue for another year; and the Estates-General should disband until November 1789.[46]

Jefferson's Charter aimed at ending arbitrary rule in France. If it did not serve immediately as the basis of an agreement among the three orders, it undoubtedly made an impression on the framers of the French constitution that metamorphosed Louis XVI into a constitutional monarch.

Jefferson saw the chances of compromise dwindle. The intrigues of the court party and the weakness of the king left little likelihood of his yielding to the representatives of the nation. He was ready to concede certain fiscal changes, but he was unbending on the structure of the old régime. Jefferson lost faith in Necker, the finance minister and the idol of the bourgeoisie, who had been recalled to his post by the despairing monarch. Necker's proposals of mediation would maintain the separate orders and give but trifling benefits to the commoners. As a wealthy banker, he was closely tied to the old régime.[47]

More than two weeks after Jefferson had submitted his Charter, the Third Estate declared itself a National Assembly. This act of defiance of the court and the feudal classes, a step which had the support of the common people and of a large portion of the troops, ended the uneasy unity of the two privileged orders. When the liberal sections of nobles and clergy joined the commoners, Jefferson believed a new period was beginning in France. To Thomas Paine he wrote that a new French government was being born. Though it preserved monarchy, it would guarantee the rights of the nation.[48]

The absolute monarchy, however, resolved to meet the challenge. The king imported mercenary troops in order to disperse the Assembly and put down any opposition. But the common people of Paris anticipated the plot by storming the Bastille. The insurrection intimidated the court party and sent noblemen scurrying abroad for safety. The event was a new experience for the American minister. It was the first time he had witnessed a large scale mass movement, in which the people had displayed unmatched discipline and honesty, and he could not refrain from writing to his government: "There was a severity of honesty observed, of which no example has been known. Bags of money offered on various occasions through fear or guilt, have been uniformly refused by the mobs."⁴⁹ The bloodshed in no way alienated his sympathy with the French struggle for liberty. Like Charles James Fox he saw in it the dawn of a new era.

Subsequent reports of Jefferson described the progress of the French Revolution up to his return to the United States in September 1789. He painted a dismal picture: unemployment; want of bread; bakers besieged by the people; continued ferment; defection of nobles and commoners to the side of reaction; imminent bankruptcy of the state; waning of Necker's popularity; intrigues of aristocrats against the National Assembly and of the Duke of Orleans against the Bourbon monarchy; talk of the king's flight which promised to precipitate a civil war. On the other hand, the basic changes heartened him. The Assembly had abolished feudal dues, begun the drafting of a constitution, and issued a Declaration of the Rights of Man, modeled to an extent after the American bills of rights. He counted on a coalition of liberal nobles and bourgeoisie to establish a better government for France.

As long as Jefferson was in France he identified himself with the liberal forces whose objectives were the destruction of feudalism and the substitution of constitutional for absolute government. Progress had already been made in that direction by the time of his departure. It can be anticipated, however, that the royal family never reconciled itself to the revolutionary changes. It conspired with foreign powers to overthrow the Revolution, even if that meant extensive bloodshed and the dismemberment of France. The king's oath to uphold the new constitution was pure deception. He bided his time when he could tear it up and set the nation afire.

3

Jefferson planned to return to France after a short stay in his home-land. But upon landing he learned that Washington had appointed him Secretary of State. During his three years in that office the French Revolution moved to the left and Jefferson moved with it, defending it against denigrators. In 1789 he supported Mirabeau and Lafayette; in 1791 he accepted the constitutional monarchy, as the beginning of further advances; in 1793, he aligned himself with the French Republic and the policies of the Jacobins. And if his sympathies were with Brissot, the Girondist, rather than with Robespierre, it was because, as we shall show, he was far from the scene of activity and derived his information from anti-Robespierrist sources. In reality, however, Jefferson's and Robespierre's ideas and policies coincided.

The French Revolution had an international character. It inspired democratic people in Europe and America to enhance the struggle for their rights. The democrats of Mannheim, Germany, congratulated the French Convention, in September 1792, for establishing a republic. The Revolution, they were certain, would "awaken all people to freedom."[50] In Italy Philippe Buonarroti, later a leader of the Babouvist movement, had to flee from Tuscany for disseminating the principles of the French Revolution.[51] Nevertheless by 1792 and 1793, French ideas were taking seed in Italy. In the Italian climate, they soon sprouted into the Risorgimento, or at least its beginnings. In Great Britain, Edmund Burke's *Reflections on the Revolution in France,* apart from furnishing a program to counter-revolution on the Continent, crystallized conservative opinion in England around hereditary monarchy. In a previous essay we showed that he had endeavored to make a monster of the French movement. Burke's pamphlet provoked more than forty replies, the most famous of which was Paine's widely sold *Rights of Man.*[52] Paine, a revolutionist of two continents, it may recapitulated here, exposed Burke's theatrical exaggerations, pointed to the humanity of the people and to the brutality and conspiracies of the reactionaries, defended civil rights as among the basic principles of a democratic society, contended that the people had the right to establish a democratic government, if they chose, and undoubtedly frightened conservatives by prophesying that the French Revolution was the dawn of "a new era to the human race." Denounced and indicted, Paine fled to France while his tormentors burned him in effigy and arrested bookdealers who sold his polemic. Nevertheless, it aided the consolidation of liberal and democratic opinion in England behind the French Revolution.

As in England, so in America, the French Revolution raised partisan controversy. John Adams, even before Burke, had already taken a firm position against the principles that gained popularity in France after 1789. Seeing the movement led by Shays as a warning to men of property, he wrote *A Defence of the Constitutions of Government of the United States of America* to prove the need of a balance of power in order to secure the rich and the well-born against possible dangers and oppressions by the poor. Fundamental to his theoretical system was the tenet "that there must be in every society of men superiors and inferiors, because God has laid in the constitution and course of nature the foundations of the distinction."[53] The French Revolution made Adams an even more militant defender of the rule by an élite. In his *Discourses on Davila,* written with this object in view, he saw no escape from the eternal controversy between the two extremes, no solution of the distinctions that were "as old as the creation, and as extensive as the globe," save through an equilibrium in a bicameral system and "an independent executive authority."[54] His political creed was Harringtonian in inspiration. The main purpose of government was to prevent those without property from having the power to dispose of property. And that purpose should be aimed at in France as well as in the United States. Adams was more temperate than Burke, and certainly more judicious, acknowledging merit in some of the ideas against which he fulminated. Even so Jefferson regarded the entire logic of the *Defence* and *Discourses* as aristocratic. As an antidote he had Paine's *Rights of Man* republished, prefaced, through error, with a brief note by him. An abundance of polemic and epithet followed. Something of the heated controversy was conveyed by Jefferson in a letter to Paine:

"Indeed I am glad you did not come away till you had written your "Rights of Man." That has been much read here with avidity and pleasure. A writer under the signature of Publicola[55] has attacked it. A host of champions entered the arena immediately in your defence. The discussion excited the public attention, recalled it to the "Defence of the American Constitutions", and the "Discourses on Davila," which it had kindly passed over without censure in the moment, and very general expressions of their sense have been now drawn forth; and I thank God that they appear firm in their republicanism, notwithstanding the contrary hopes and assertions of a sect here, high in name but small in numbers. These had flattered themselves that the silence of the people under the "Defence" and "Davila" was a symptom of their conversion to the doctrine of king, lords, and commons. They are checked at least by your pamphlet, and the people confirmed in their good old faith."[56]

Thus the debate on French revolutionary principles was a facet of contraposed classes and parties. Roughly the two sides were: the Anglophile Federalists, led by Hamilton, representing the monied and landed aristocracy; and the Francophile republicans, led by Jefferson, counting on the support of small farmers, artisans, mechanics and western settlers. Jefferson's interest in the French Revolution was constant and enthusiastic. "I remain eternally attached to the principles of your revolution,"[57] he wrote to Brissot in 1793 when France was already a republic. Many intellectuals, in Europe and in America, turned their backs on the Revolution when the Jacobins organized an all-out war. But Jefferson remained firm in his faith, accepting the Jacobin policies as historically necessary.

Jefferson had international perspectives. In his opinion liberty and progress in America were inseparable from their advance elsewhere. Hence he was deeply concerned about the democratic movements abroad. As early as 1787 he was pleased to learn that in Latin America there was combustible material which awaited "the torch only."[58] Twelve years later he observed with satisfaction that the Irish insurrection was "in force and better organized than before."[59]

During the French Revolution he articulated more than ever the indivisibility of democracy. Established in France, it would spread all over Europe "and stay up our own," he wrote to a friend; and conversely, "a check there would retard the revival of liberty in other countries," including the United States.[60] Jefferson noted a monarchist tendency in America, kept alive by the "commercial phalanx". Monarchist sentiment manifested itself in the frontier regions and in New England through the intrigues of ambitious men and of former loyalists who had joined the Federalist party.[61] And Jefferson discerned monarchism in Hamilton's financial policies and in Federalist hostility to the French.[62] In sum, Jefferson had derived from experience the simple fact that nations do not live in a vacuum. The international community was growing closer; what happened in one country inevitably spread to the frontiers and shores of others. Thus, foreign and domestic policies, democracy in France and democracy in America could not be isolated from one another. History had taught him that a new social order came into being with intense suffering, or as he wrote Lafayette "we are not to expect to be translated from despotism to liberty in a featherbed."[63] Come what may, Americans should stand firmly behind the Revolution in France. In protecting it they were fortifying democracy in America. As Jefferson put it: "I feel that the permanence of our own leans in some degree on that; and that a failure there would be a powerful argument to prove there must be a failure here."[64] He feared that if France succumbed to the European despots they might restore monarchy in the United States, "a change which would be grateful to a party here, not numerous, but wealthy and influential."[65] Every victory of the French against the feudal powers sustained his hope that the triumph of the Revolution would "kindle the wrath of the people of Europe against those who have dared to embroil them in such wickedness, and to bring at length, kings, nobles and priests to the scaffolds which they have been so long deluging with human blood."[66]

In common with Paine, Jefferson recognized the rights and independence of other countries. He held that every nation had the right to govern itself by whatever form it pleased, "and to change these forms at its own will." Each people could maintain relations with others "through whatever organ it chooses, whether that be a King, Convention, Assembly, Committee, President, or whatever it be. The only thing essential is the will of the nation."[67] That he called the "polar star" of America's foreign policy. The policy was also consistent with what the French Jacobins wrote into their Constitution of 1793.

The facts of history showed him that nations were confronted with "extraordinary situations which require extraordinary interposition."[68]

That conclusion, already arrived at in 1774, was confirmed by the development of the French Revolution. While Americans in an official and non-official capacity lamented and denounced the Jacobins' execution of the king and their methods of organizing the nation for total war, Jefferson maintained that the continued existence of monarchy "would have brought on the reestablishment of despotism had it been pursued." Besides, the Jacobins had the confidence of the nation. Jefferson was saddened by the loss of life "in the struggle which was necessary." There was no doubt in his mind that innocent people fell with the guilty. "These I deplore as much as anybody, and shall deplore them to the day of my death. But I deplore them as I should have done had they fallen in battle. It was necessary to use the arm of the people, a machine not quite so blind as balls and bombs, but blind to a certain degree. . . . The liberty of the whole earth was depending on the issue of the contest, and was ever such a prize won with so little innocent blood?"[69]

Such was Jefferson's appraisal of the French Revolution. "While we weep over the means, we pray over the end," he said.[70] And the end was the victory of democracy and freedom, its spread to other peoples and its reenforcement in America through Jacobin success. The "glorious news" of the victory of the French republicans over the Prussian army thrilled him. It "has given wry faces to our monocrats here, but sincere joy to the great body of the citizens,"[71] he informed a friend.

Jefferson was not overstating. France had won American popular sympathy after the proclamation of the Republic in September 1792, and the defeat of the reactionary powers was celebrated from North to South. There were civic feasts in Baltimore, New York, Boston, Philadelphia—in fact in every important town in the thirteen states.[72] People erected liberty poles, wore the French cockade, drank toasts to the rights of man and to liberty and equality, sang the Ça ira and addressed one another as citizen. The excitement reached printers and school teachers, merchants who profited from the trade with the French West Indies, and scientists like David Rittenhouse and William Thornton who saw an interrelation between science and freedom.[73]

The main support of France in America was among the common people. They saw the French Revolution as a recapitulation of the War of Independence. By defending the French Republic they were demonstrating their disappointment with the results of their own Revolution. Consequently American celebrations of French victories were a manifestation of the democratic movement. It assumed an organized form in the creation of democratic societies, consisting for the most part of workmen and mechanics, and modeled somewhat after the French Jacobin Clubs and the Sons of Liberty.

Sympathy for France reached Alpine heights with the arrival in 1793 of the French minister, Edmond Genet. He was a young diplomat of aristocratic origin, who had been in the service of the Bourbons in several capitals of Europe. His friendship with Girondins developed after the French declaration of war, in April 1792, which gave them the power they had been seeking.[74] They had declared it their policy to import revolutions into other countries at the point of the bayonet. Robespierre had pointed out the dangers of such a policy during the long debate on the war, but his tiny minority was helpless to prevent it. Defeats brought the king under suspicion. He was overthrown and a republic was established. The trial of Louis XVI was on the agenda of the Convention. From republican clubs and Jacobin leaders arose the demand that Louis Capet should suffer the fate of a traitor. The Girondins, who had warmly professed republicanism, wished to rid themselves of the king without executing him, but, they knew not how, until Genet conceived the ingenious plan of banishing the royal family to the United States. The idea appealed to the Girondins, particularly Brissot, their specialist on the United States and on foreign affairs in general. They had Genet appointed minister to the United States, expecting him to escort the banished Bourbons when he sailed on his mission. Possibly the Girondins had an ulterior plan, if conditions demanded it, of restoring the king to the throne with the aid of the thousands of royalist refugees in the United States. But the plot miscarried. Genet sailed alone.[75]

He was hailed everywhere. In Philadelphia he was awaited by a welcoming committee on which were Dr. Rittenhouse, the scientist, and Charles Biddle of a prominent Philadelphia family.[76] Genet did not wait to be received officially, but proceeded to act like a Roman consul arriving in a subdued territory. On instructions from his Girondist superiors, he fitted out privateers, manned them with American seamen, instructed French consuls to act as courts of admiralty for judging prizes taken to American ports, and started organizing expeditions against Spanish owned Louisiana and British owned Canada.[77] Once these territories were conquered, they would be offered to the United States in return for an alliance in a war against England. The grand design was part of the Girondist plan to embroil neutrals.

The outbreak of war between France and England raised the problem of neutrality in America. If the government permitted France to purchase provisions, recruit seamen and fit out privateers, England might interpret that as a hostile act. And the young republic's position in North America was not too firm. Spain controlled the Mississippi; the Indians were instigated to attack the western settlers; and the British garrisoned strategic points on the borders of the United States.

But the existing treaty with France, dating from 1778, had opened American ports to French privateers and prizes. The questions now arose: what should be the policy of the United States in the war that had broken out between England and France in 1793? And was the French treaty valid now that France was a republic? In reply to the first question, the entire cabinet was at one on a proclamation of neutrality, calling on Americans to desist from aiding any of the belligerents, under pain of prosecution.[78] They answered the second question affirmatively but not without debate. Alexander Hamilton gave two main reasons for renouncing the treaty: it had been made with a government that had been overthrown; the French Republic being unstable, an alliance with it might be dangerous to the United States. On the other side, Jefferson argued that the treaty was binding, regardless of the government in France. Returning to his doctrine that the people in the nation were the source of all authority, he contended that the treaty had been concluded between the peoples of both countries. Then he asked, "who is the American who can say with truth that he would not have allied himself to France if she had been a republic? Or that a republic of any form would be as *disagreeable* as her ancient despotism?"[79]

Jefferson was for neutrality, "a manly neutrality" as he called it, that would not lean to the side of reaction. He defended the right of France to purchase supplies in the United States, a right he upheld despite protests by the British minister whose object it was to drive matters to extremes and involve us in the war. But that was precisely what Jefferson wished to avoid. The United States' entry into the war could not seriously affect the military situation on the Continent; but it would be detrimental both to American interests and to the French Republic. England could then prey on American commerce and France would suffer for want of American shipments.

Genet's lack of prudence embarrassed French friends in the United States and rendered the execution of Jefferson's policy extremely difficult. Drunk with the plaudits of the multitude, he disregarded the President's neutrality proclamation, believing he could appeal to the people against the executive. He even went so far as to express before Jefferson his dislike of the American Constitution.[80]

It was finally agreed to disassociate Genet from the French Republic and to ask for his recall. Jefferson's long letter, accepted by the cabinet and forwarded to Gouverneur Morris, minister to France, related the country's grievances.[81] The case of the United States did not need much pleading before the French foreign office, for long before Jefferson's letter arrived, a revolution had taken place in French foreign policy. The Girondist visionary plan of exporting revolutions was scrapped after their overthrow early in June 1793. The new Committee of Public Safety, to which Robespierre was admitted toward the end of July, followed the Jacobin principle of respecting the rights of neutrals. This was also Jefferson's principle, as it was Robespierre's. In his report to the Convention on November 17, 1793, he denounced Genet's "most extraordinary methods of irritating the American government" against France, declared that the treaty between France and the United States would be faithfully executed and announced that every effort would be made to strengthen the friendly bonds between the two countries.[82] Genet was replaced.

Only within recent years has Robespierre's name begun to be cleared of the slander heaped on it for generations. While he was leader of the Jacobins and a member of the much advertised Committee of Public Safety, he was denounced abroad as an anarchist, a beast and gory dictator. Even Jefferson, seeker for the truth that he was and supporter of Jacobin policies, accepted the stories. Jefferson conceded many years later that after his departure from France he had had no other means to observe the progress of the Revolution "but the public papers, and their information came through channels too hostile to claim confidence."[83]

A sober inquiry into the principles and policies of Jefferson and Robespierre yields the conclusion that there was more in common between them than between Jefferson and the Girondins to whom he leaned during their struggle with the Jacobins. The backgrounds and pasts of the two men were different. But they were intellectually the products of advanced eighteenth century teachings, and they were equally committed to the abolition of slavery. Each fought against the exploitation of the people by monopolists and against the mercantile class whose champions were the Girondins. The same type of egalitarian society, based on small owners, motivated both. These patterns of thought and action earned them enduring places among the great democrats of all times. It was no historical accident that the subsequent labor movements in their respective countries drew on their democratic principles. French workers' political clubs and neo-Babouvists during the Louis Philippe Monarchy, for example, incorporated in their programs a number of Robespierre's tenets, and published a collection of his speeches. The contemporary labor movement in the United States, and the National Labor Union after the Civil War, took over Jefferson's essential articles of faith, even his concept of an egalitarian order.

Jefferson continued to watch over democracy after his retirement from office, in 1793. Napoleon's military rule, however frightening, did not weaken his confidence that the last chapter of the French Revolution would some day be written. For his was the conviction that the insurrection of "science, talents, and courage against rank and birth"[84] could not be halted. It would come to a close only with the victory of science over obscurantism, and of "freedom, the first-born of science," over despotism.[85]

His teachings were like a refreshing spring to Abraham Lincoln. In 1859 he paid the following tribute to Jefferson:

"The principles of Jefferson are the definitions and axioms of free society and yet they are denied and evaded, with no small show of success. One dashingly calls them "glittering generalities." Another bluntly calls them "self-evident lies," and others insidiously argue that they apply to "superior races." These expressions, differing in form, are identical in object and effect—the supplanting the principles of free government, and restoring those of classification, caste, and legitimacy. They would delight a convocation of crowned heads plotting against the people. They are the vanguard, the miners and sappers of returning despotism. We must repulse them, or they will subjugate us. This is a world of compensation; and he who would be no slave must consent to have no slave. Those who deny freedom to others deserve it not for themselves, and, under a just God, cannot long retain it. *All honor to Jefferson—to the man, who in the concrete pressure of a struggle for national independence by a single people, had the coolness, forecast, and sagacity to introduce into a merely revolutionary document an abstract truth, applicable to all men and all times, and so embalm it there that today and in all coming days it shall be a rebuke and a stumbling-block to the very harbingers of reappearing tyranny and oppression.*"[86]

History has confirmed the sagacity Lincoln found in Jefferson, for it derived from the conviction that the triumph of freedom over feudalism in Europe would inevitably buttress and secure democracy in America.

BABEUF AND BABOUVISM

ON MAY 10, 1796, the government of the Directory succeeded in arresting Gracchus Babeuf and his lieutenants of an underground organization. They were preparing to seize political power and to wield it in the interest of the downtrodden. The same day, in the evening, there was a fashionable ball, given by a former vendor of lemonade in a hotel near the Champs-Elysées. The guests, arriving in private carriages, were attired with a brilliance, reminiscent of the old régime. On this very day Parisian salons hummed with conversation about the change of coiffure of Madame Tallien and Madame Bonaparte.

Two social segments in Paris eyed each other from opposite ends. One, numerically small and politically strong, dined and danced, cavaliered and caroused. The other, numerous, ragged and disfranchised, stood long hours in line to receive a ration of bread. Death from starvation was frequent. Some resorted to stealing.[1] For lack of a livelihood, women turned to prostitution.

An economic crisis, fully a decade old, had depressed the already low standards of artisans, laborers and of plebeians generally. That derived from several cardinal causes: the loss of foreign markets during the war, beginning in 1792; the revolutionary measures that discouraged investors in industry and encouraged speculators in land; and an inflation that rocketed prices of necessities far beyond the reach of the small man. But for the war that kept thousands of men under arms and employed many others to make war materials, unemployment would have been even more extensive.[2] Even so, idleness was serious in the large cities of France, particularly in Paris.[3]

The rise of monetary wages since 1790 had been more than offset by inflation. Prices soared as the value of the *assignats* fell. One hundred francs in paper were worth six real sous in 1796. From 1790 to 1795,

77

a bushel of flour rose from two francs to 225 francs, of beans and peas from four francs to 120 and 130 francs each. Bread cost twenty francs a pound in September 1795; two months later it sold for forty and sixty francs.[4] How could wages ever be in step with such rapidly rising prices?

Life for the lowly during the Terror, despite its rigors, had been bearable. Many had believed they were climbing the peak of tomorrow when the firmly rooted republic would begin the building of a better order. But the situation changed for the worse after the Thermidorian reaction. Abuses became more numerous, food arrived in Paris with less regularity, and the lines at bakeries and butcher shops grew more turbulent. Women particularly were clamorous, calling down destruction upon merchants, officials and politicians.[5] Suicides and deaths from starvation were common in police reports.[6] Babeuf's daughter, a child of seven, died for lack of nourishment and his two other children were so feeble that he could not recognize them after an absence of several months.[7]

The rentiers suffered along with the workers. Inflation had ruined them. "With an income of a thousand écus [three francs] owed us by the republic," a rentier complained, "we haven't enough to buy a piece of bread."[8] No wonder many of them added their voices to workers' protests. Several even joined the Babouvist movement.

Social and political demoralization had set in. Debtors ran after creditors; and court dockets were crowded with lawsuits over land speculation. People accused the government of continuing the war in order to keep in power those who had made politics a profession. And the accusation struck home, for their speedy rise to opulence was notorious. A frequently heard charge was that men high in the administration protected speculators and profited by the inflation. Already in 1795 deputies avoided appearing in public, for fear of insult or assault.[9]

For common people had come to believe that the republic under the Directory had been diverted from the purpose their speculations had given it. Ever since its emergence from the insurrections in June and August 1792 it had enchanted many of them. They esteemed it as the English Chartists were to esteem manhood suffrage. It would comfort the weary, feed the hungry, endow propertyless with property, in fine, bring security to the suffering and needy. In some minds republicanism was the synonym of a type of socialism or communism, however primitive or simplistic their vision of it.[10]

Governmental policy during the Terror had inspired such blissful phantasies. According to the Constitution of 1793 society was obligated to provide for its less fortunate citizens. Plans were in the making to divide among landless the properties of the enemies of the Revolution. There were price controls and taxes on the rich. Price regulation, to be sure, was consistent with past custom, but its novel feature was the mass pressure that had imposed it. Government's agents in the provinces had workshops of suspects operated by the workers and the profits apportioned according to need, or, as in Lyons, projected the reorganization of industry and commerce "for the benefit of poor patriots."[11] In Paris proper, the public prosecutor, Pierre Chaumette, favored the nationalization of the abandoned workshops; and the priest, Jacques Roux, the establishment of national workshops and the government control of the grain trade.[12] It was as an employee in the city's administration of the food supply that Babeuf learned some of the tenets he later introduced into his social plan.

To common people, therefore, the republic was the social leveller, the symbol of their high aspirations, and republicanism their patriotism.

In 1795 they rued the fall of Robespierre and viewed with alarm the disintegration of republican standards. Girondins and Dantonists had climbed back to places of power. Ex-radicals were vocal champions of the *nouveaux riches*. Even royalists grew bold. This galloping reaction in the midst of prolonged distress was calculated to brew tempests and violent dissent from authority. Two popular insurrections, one in March and the other in May 1795, each with the slogan, "Bread and the Constitution of 1793," came close to success.[13] Once the insurgents were put down, the Thermidorians hastened to erase what had remained of democratic practices. First, they purged the Convention of those Jacobins who were likely to impede their backward march. Then, they prohibited gatherings of more than five persons. Finally, by the Constitution of 1795, they set up a government, headed by a Directory, that was nothing less than a plutocracy. And to continue ruling they voted that two-thirds of their number had to be re-elected to the new legislature.

The provision slammed the door in the faces of royalists. Now that they could not count on legal methods to regain power, they resorted to force. But General Bonaparte, aided by plebeian republicans, dispersed them. The still lingering Convention rewarded republicans by amnestying imprisoned Jacobins.

1

The ambitions of the Thermidorian politicos and the attempted coup of the royalists convinced republicans on the extreme left of the need for an understanding in order to further their objectives. A meeting in December 1795 at the home of André Amar, a former member of the Committee of General Security, exhibited basic differences among them both on alternatives to the system of private ownership and on the form of transition to the new social order. These disagreements, added to mutual distrust, ended the negotiations.[14]

Meanwhile the government of the Directory tried to find a footing somewhere between the left and the right. In its bid for the support of former Robespierrists it offered them posts and countenanced the reopening of political clubs, however to be shepherded by its agents.

The Pantheon was the most famous of the clubs. Its formal aim was nicely adjusted to the tactics then pursued by the government: "To satisfy the mutual need of reconciling and instructing the citizens, to circulate literature, to offer a wholesome antidote to the aristocratic virus, to counterbalance the secret intrigues of royalists and of public extortioners."[15] From its beginning in November 1795, it had among its habitués friends of the government, spies, democrats and extreme radicals allied to Babeuf. Less than a month after its opening, the Club had more than two thousand members whose debates were reported in the press and in police dossiers. Before long dividing lines became visible between partisans of social change and champions of the status quo. The two sides seesawed for control. Vis-à-vis the government party was another, growing in numbers and directing at institutions and policies a blast of criticism, inspired by, and derived from Babeuf's paper *Le Tribun du peuple*. His friends, Augustin Darthé, Charles Germain and Philippe Buonarroti, led the opposition party. When the government arrested his wife for distributing *Le Tribun du peuple*, in reality to question her on her husband's hiding place,[16] the Club voted its sympathy and made a collection for her children. But the government party gathered its forces and won a majority on an address to the Directory, swearing fidelity to the Constitution of 1795.

The Club became fairly popular. Workers came to its meetings, diluting its large middle class membership. From a society designed to fashion opinion for governmental ends, it had evolved into a hotbed of radicals. The government ordered Napoleon to close it.[17] Driven from the public forum, the left went underground under the leadership of Babeuf and his colleagues.

2

François-Noël Babeuf—he later assumed the name Gracchus—was born in Saint-Quentin in 1760. His parents were too poor to give him a formal schooling, but his father taught him some Latin, German and mathematics. His native province of Picardy exemplified the conflict in France between poor, land-hungry peasants and feudal landlords over feudal exactions and common lands. Here he learned as he grew up how feudalism, in its last stage of decadence, was thoroughly unbearable to the humble people around him. Later study of feudal charters but documented what he had seen and heard in his formative years. Destitution at home forced him at the age of fourteen to seek employ-

ment with a "feudist" whose business it was to search lords' archives
for their rights and privileges. A rising cost of living at the end of the
old régime impelled them to employ "feudists" in the hope of reviving
the payment of lapsed feudal dues. Babeuf learned the business, while
acquiring a knowledge of surveying, and after marriage, set up for himself. His business grew without freeing him from material cares.

Babeuf meanwhile seems to have been busy with the writings of
Rousseau, Mably, Brissot, Morelly, Linguet, perhaps of the Physiocrats,
too, and their critic Graslin. These authors and "feudist" work together
might have set him on the path to a radical social philosophy. "I discovered the dreadful secrets of the nobles' illegal extortions in the dust
of manorial archives," he recalled in 1795.[18] His thoughts in 1787 were
already in the realm of collective ownership. If that order were possible,
he said in a private letter, he would be among its first settlers.[19] In his
Cadastre perpétuel, written for publication shortly before the Revolution,
he saw the need of reforming property relations, if society was to be
spared a rising of the poor against the rich.[20]

There were people in France on the eve of the Revolution who
might have agreed with Babeuf's conclusion and the imaginary framework it was set in. For underlying French literature and social thought
in the seventeenth and eighteenth centuries is a nostalgia for the millenium. For the present purpose it is less important that the millenium often
lay among primitives or distant Orientals or that its brightest horizons
were looked for in antiquity. That was its form and sometimes its content. More significant than its form, and its content, too, was its lasting
quality, even into the French Revolution. Two principal reasons may
be suggested to explain this persistent search for Utopia. The first was
the long period of war from Louis XIV to Louis XVI, that more than
anything else had drained France of resources and impoverished it. The
second, related to the first, but having independent causes, was the
economic dislocation of large numbers of Frenchmen. Prices, during
the eighteenth century, had risen far above wages. The margin between
the two had so widened that increased misery beset artisans and small
farmers. Strains and stresses in the economic sector in time aggravated
social frictions. To the student of the few generations before the French
Revolution, when social and economic tensions were tightest, it is quite
revealing that the period was prolific in blueprints for novel social orders,
in new economic theories and in the emergence of an advanced philo-
sophic materialism. For that was the age of Morelly, Jean Jacques
Rousseau, Dom Deschamps and François Boissel, of Helvetius, Holbach,
Boulanger and Diderot, of the Physiocrats and their critics, and of course
of the Encyclopedists. These thought currents were in full motion while
Babeuf was trying to probe the problems of his generation.

Witnessing the seizure of the Bastille he was at first torn between his private interests and the public welfare. "I was at once pleased and displeased," he wrote to his wife. His business depended on the duration of feudalism. But his whole past and his intellectual development rose up against it. Thus, he went on to say: "They [the people] are right a hundred times and I willingly subscribe to all these changes. I am even prepared to help in destroying the source of my livelihood. Selfish people will accuse me of madness, but that doesn't matter."[21]

Babeuf's material condition went from bad to worse. A word from his wife that the family was in distress brought him back home. His business had practically stopped. Thereafter the Revolution held him with octopus-arms.

His first revolutionary experience was in his province. Here, as elsewhere in the country, peasants were up in arms against feudal taxes and urban small shopkeepers against indirect levies. He took up their causes in briefs, pamphlets and proclamations. But nobles and rich middle men succeeded in having him arrested.[22] After two months in prison, he was back in his native district where he founded Le Correspondant Picard. It was Babeuf's first venture in journalism. He called on the poor to be bold in their protests against their disfranchisement. Since the National Assembly had made them second class citizens because they lacked property, they should boycott military service, refuse to pay taxes and, if necessary, declare a general strike.[23] His stout defense of them cost him a second term in prison. But they honored him with a demonstration and a luncheon directly after his release.

At this point it may be asked how far had Babeuf gone in his thinking since the publication of his Cadastre perpétuel? In that work he had still trod cautiously on the question of property. He had yet to make up his mind in matters of government. But events had moved fast and furiously, and he, along with others had tried to keep abreast of them. In terms of what he wrote after two years of the Revolution, his political and social credo had been evolving rapidly. He was among the first to call for a republic after the King's attempted flight. Not a republic in name, but one thoroughly democratic was Babeuf's aim in 1791, when he wrote to a candidate for the legislature. He wanted universal suffrage, free education and security. And he wanted, too, a democratic army to be employed in useful labor. Above all he was after "the socialization of all the resources that can be infinitely multiplied and increased by means of a planned organization and by the wisely directed labor of all." Babeuf stood four square against palliatives. Looking beyond the immediate situation, he concluded that the final objective of the Revolution was "equality without illusions." Meanwhile he would ·proceed

cautiously, perhaps toward an agrarian law, even though it did not fulfill his demands. But it was an advanced program at the time.[24]

The promise of a livelihood looked better in 1792. Babeuf was
elected administrator, first in the department of the Somme, and later
in the district of Montdidier. So zealous was he in performing his duties[25]
that large property owners sought a chance to discredit him. He provided it when, without knowing the legal procedure, he had substituted
the name of one purchaser for another in a sale of national property.
His adversaries had him suspended from office. Escaping to Paris he
found there employment with the food administration. But his enemies
at home charged him with forgery and condemned him by default to
twenty years in chains. He was arrested for the fourth time. Thanks to
friends, his case was appealed to the High Court, which ordered another
trial. He was finally acquitted.

Back in the capital in August 1794, shortly after the overthrow of
Robespierre, Babeuf went into journalism. For the following month he
founded the *Journal de la liberté de la Presse*. It was a burning hymn
to democracy. His political associates at this time were Hébertists, *Enragés* and Thermidorians, in sum, those whom Robespierre had fought
for one reason or another. Perhaps Babeuf had not yet learned the background of the Ninth Thermidor. Certainly some of his associates still
wore the halos of martyred men. Be that as it may, he now regarded
Robespierre as a "tyrant," and "the most consummate scoundrel." But
Babeuf could not avoid seeing him also as "the apostle of freedom,"
whose Declaration of Rights, "though not perfect, was nevertheless
sublime."[26] He also approved of the social levelling efforts of the Jacobin government,[27] for he was firm in the belief that "paradise is on this
earth" where "he wants to enjoy freedom and happiness, and enjoy
it during his own lifetime."[28] He peered through the mists around the
Ninth Thermidor and reached the conviction that it was not a revolution, but a change of rulers.

The motto of his journal, starting with number 19 was "The aim
of society is the common happiness." He also changed the title to
Tribun du peuple, a notice that he had severed connections with compromising elements. The printer refused to continue after the 26th
number. The 27th was published at the expense of the Electoral Club,
that had come under Babeuf's influence after his return to Paris in
1794.

He was in open war with the government. Already in number 23
he had declared: "When the government violates the people's rights
insurrection becomes the most sacred right."[29] And in a subsequent
issue: "I see in the present state of the public administration the complete overturn of the democratic system, political abstractions in place

of principles . . . the government of an oligarchy instead of a republican régime."[30] After the publication of number 27 he was arrested and spent a few days in prison.

If the government had expected to intimidate Babeuf it had miscalculated. Though his paper appeared irregularly, it continued to aim its shafts at Thermidorians, their policies and at society as a whole. He regretted his earlier anti-Robespierrism. More than that he charged that a new reign of *messieurs* was arising. He was also arriving at a conclusion on class dichotomies. There were two contraposed classes, he said. Both wanted the republic, it was true, but each in its own way. The first desired it the republic of "the million" who had always been "the bloodsuckers of the twenty-four other million;" of the million "who for centuries have been enjoying their laziness at the expense of our sweat and toil;" who "want a small number of privileged masters gorged with superfluities and pleasures and the large mass reduced to the low state of Helots and slaves." The second class looked to a democratic republic of "equal rights and comfort, of a sufficiency of all material needs and social benefits as a just reward for the labor that each will contribute to the common task."[31] He hoped this high aim could be reached by a national petition to the government, laying before it the woeful condition of the people and the reforms they had a right to expect.[32] Did Babeuf believe this form of a national appeal on a concrete program might flare into a vast, irresistible movement, levelling obstacles to what he conceived to be a classless order?

The police hounded him. Arresting his wife, they were disappointed when she declined to disclose his refuge. But they finally located him. He had six francs in his pocket. Still the Convention was told that he had tried to bribe the gendarme with thirty thousand francs, which the incorruptible official of course turned down "with scornful silence."[33]

Babeuf's sixth imprisonment turned out to have important consequences for the organization that grew up around him. Transferred to a prison in Arras, he there met Charles Germain, a former cavalry officer who had been reading works by Rousseau, Mably, Diderot and Helvetius.[34] Germain's ideas of equality were vague on many crucial points and Babeuf took the officer in hand and moulded his thinking.[35] The current system of production and exchange, that Babeuf termed "commerce," was vicious, he charged. Ninety-nine percent of the people suffered by it. His outline of its process brings to mind what such economists as Simon-Nicolas Linguet, Jacques Necker and J. Louis Graslin said before the Revolution.[36] Babeuf maintained that though the worker produced everything he lived in utter destitution. Big owners and speculators together said to him: "Toil much and eat little, or you won't have any work and you won't eat at all. Such is the barbarous law of capital." Babeuf proposed to replace this system of production with a planned society where all would be at once producers and consumers. "There will be neither upper nor lower, neither first nor last." The work of all "will constantly converge toward the great social aim, the common prosperity." Babeuf's new order had "neither masters, nor tyrants, nor cannibals; neither exploiters nor exploited." Following Morelly,[37] he would have public warehouses to store the products of labor, to be distributed equally to all workers, i.e., the farm hand, the artisan, the artist and the scientist. In that way he expected to remove frontiers between producers. The economic system would be "intelligently directed and stimulated with an eye to usefulness and to the general well-being." At a time when modern technology was but in its very initial stage in France, Babeuf visualized the advantages of labor-saving machinery under social planning. Workers would hail the application of science to agriculture and to industry, for "it will mean a certain economy of time and consequently a reduction in fatigue." Society would provide for all its members and put an end to their fear of the future.

Babeuf was mindful of the resistance to be met if the attempt were made to establish the new order. He was still averse to the use of force. For the present, he would set up a model, a sort of phalanx, such as Fourier was to advocate, that would be at once a sample and a center of propaganda. Babeuf in time abandoned the plan of erecting an exemplar in miniature for a full scale, national movement.

Babeuf's letter was a lark-song to Germain. He rejoiced in the vision of a roseate tomorrow. "Your plan is the Code the Gracchi themselves would have proclaimed,"[38] he replied. His zeal was infectious. He converted other political prisoners to the cause he now shared with Babeuf. The two reviewed the political situation after the abortive insurrections in 1795, that turned out to be the last popular billows of the Revolution. And they placed in judgment the Constitution of 1795 in letters to democrats.[39]

Transferred to a prison in Paris, they there met radicals who had been rounded up after the crushing of the insurgents in March and May 1795. The prisoners were politically a motley collection of Hébertists, Robespierrists, Enragés, and men without a party label who were ready to cast their lot with those who were preparing to drive out the new rulers of France.

Of the prisoners who were to be prominent in the Babouvist movement, Philippe Buonarroti and Joseph Bodson deserve notice at this point. The first was of noble origin, a collateral descendant of Michelangelo. His enthusiasm for the French Revolution had been the cause of his flight from Tuscany to Corsica. There, too, his agitation against the feudal order had earned him the wrath of defenders of the old régime. He might have perished had not the French National Assembly intervened. The Convention had found him a trusted and ardent servant in Corsica, Sardinia, northern Italy and southern France, and in each of these areas he had established a reputation as a champion of the downtrodden and won the esteem of Italian political refugees on French territory. His convictions at the time of his imprisonment by the Thermidorians had not yet exceeded Robespierre's or Saint-Just's.[40] Among Buonarroti's companions in prison were Debon and Bodson who had probably opened for him other vistas before Babeuf arrived on the scene. Little is known of Debon, save that he was a severe critic of private property. Bodson, however, had won distinction as a Parisian magistrate, as a member of the governing body of the Paris Commune, and as official envoy in several departments. His thinking was more Hébertist than Robespierrist, although he had shared Robespierre's hatred of arrivistes. But Bodson's social outlook had moved to the left of Robespierre's.

Babeuf's arrival among the prisoners was decisive in the careers of a number of them. Several had already read his views in his *Tribun du peuple;* but meeting him in person and exposed to his zeal and power to convince, they succumbed to his arguments. He, in turn, it may be surmised, derived from men like Buonarroti and Bodson, national perspectives and an acquaintance with broad administrative problems of the Revolution they had themselves encountered.

The prisoners were amnestied after the defeat of the royalists in October 1795. Though the government had crushed its enemies on both extremes, its position was none too secure. The economic situation in workers' districts had worsened, and the routed political elements were regrouping. The left factions looked to Babeuf for leadership. He was tireless; he had a program; he was a talented journalist. Around him developed a movement that before long acquired direction and organization.

While the movement was taking shape, Babeuf's paper became bolder. It chided ex-radicals who had made their peace with the Thermidorians. It called for a return to the Constitution of 1793. And it appealed to all common people to unite for "nothing great" could be done without them. They "must be told everything, shown constantly what remains to be done." For the French Revolution, Babeuf declared, was "an open war between the patricians and the plebeians . . . a war that has been going on continuously, and that begins as soon as the established order permits some to take everything, leaving nothing for others."[41]

Journalists were dismayed. They charged Babeuf was playing into

the hands of royalists. He was likened to Marat and Robespierre. Some
said he was an impostor or madman. But common people who normally
congregated in the Café Chrétien "beamed when the newspaper of
Babeuf was read," the police reported.[42]

Babeuf answered his critics with a frankness that left no doubt
about his convictions. With some of them he was even caustic.[43] But
to sympathizers he patiently explained his understanding of democracy.
It was far more than the Constitution of 1793. If he agitated for it,
that was because "it prepared the way" for the democratic institutions
that would make equality possible. And democracy was not the agrarian
law that would "make France into a chessboard."[44] His meaning of
democracy was social and economic equality in the absence of private
property and the existence of institutions that would prevent some
from becoming masters of others. Each person would work at what he
was best fitted to do. He would turn over the product of his labor to
the common storehouse, and receive in return an equal share of everything. To reach this end Babeuf would no longer rely on peaceful
methods. Henceforth it was a question of "Conquer or die."[45]

The Executive Directory issued a warrant for Babeuf's arrest. He
found a secret refuge from which he went on issuing his paper. The
government tried to discredit him by reviving the old forgery charge.
But in cafés and in the Pantheon Club his support grew. He received
encouraging letters from soldiers and workers. "The patriots who are
very numerous in this army do not read your paper; they devour it."
"The workers . . . who are gathered at a meeting in this commune,
number more than eight hundred. They are enraptured when they hear
your numbers read. They are constantly repeating as their slogan: the
common happiness or death."[46] The influential marquis d'Antonelle
changed from a critic to a partisan of Babeuf's views.[47] Other disciples
were Debon, a believer in the community of goods; the Jacobin Augustin Darthé; Sylvain Maréchal, a prominent journalist; Philippe Buonarroti, who was to be Babeuf's chief associate; the rich Felix Le Pelletier
who helped finance the movement; Didier, a locksmith; and Simon
Duplay, a cabinet-maker and an old friend of Robespierre. Of the
Enragés and Hébertists who fell in line the best known were General
Rossignol, Bertrand, formerly mayor of Lyons, and Joseph Bodson.

A party was thus forming itself under Babeuf's leadership. Germain, a man-about-town, informed him that democrats were looking to
him for directives.[48] And, according to the same source, soldiers were
asking for copies of the Tribun du peuple for distribution among their
comrades.[49] On March 30, 1796, Babeuf, Antonelle, Maréchal and Le
Pelletier formed a directory. Buonarroti, Darthé and Debon were ad-

mitted later. It was a top secret body that planned the overthrow of the existing government and the establishment of an egalitarian order.

3

The Secret Directory of Public Safety, to use its full title, was a central revolutionary committee preparing for a *coup d'état*. It published an extensive literature, drafted directives for the projected insurrection, and sketched legislation and institutions for a new society. Babeuf and Buonarroti wrote most of the correspondence and propaganda that go-betweens carried to subordinate agents. The work kept Babeuf so busy that he had little time to compose articles for his paper.[50]

The Babouvist organization was highly centralized. Underneath the top bracket were twelve civil agents, one for each arrondissement in Paris, and five military agents,[51] all of them appointed by the central committee. According to the initial plan, no agent was to know the identity of any of the others or of the members of the Directory. His communication with the centre was to be through intermediaries who were in the dark regarding the work of those they met. The Secret Directors had tried "to isolate everything, . . . so that each individual employed by it, directly or indirectly, will make betrayal of anyone impossible." But practice compelled a modification of the plan. Several lieutenants were friends or acquaintances of those in the highest rank of the organization.

The twelve principal agents followed specific directives. They had to set up groups, direct discussion, distribute literature, report popular sentiment, designate those who could serve the movement or thwart it, and of course collect funds. Beyond that they were to record the places where food and ammunition were stored, the workshops and their number of workers, and the names of sympathizers who could lodge those arriving from the provinces to assist the enterprise.

The instructions on propaganda were plainly set forth. Agents should plan meetings of groups as quietly as possible. They should be small, numerous and widespread, preferably in the cafés where workers usually gathered, or in homes so as to evade spies. The groups should be anonymous, perhaps referred to as "visits" or "promenades." "Have the real thing, but not the name," read one of the orders. The agents should be part of the audience, yet should be in control of public opinion. They should never let it get out of hand before the troops had joined the masses. Of course, no agent could perform all these duties single-handed. He was therefore urged to train assistants who could organize meetings, post placards and remove those of royalists or of the government.[52]

Other agents were assigned to disorganize the army. These were men with military experience, former commissioned and noncommissioned officers, disbanded soldiers and soldiers still in service. The military agents, too, were briefed on the necessity of prudence and secrecy. They had to submit reports through intermediary agents, stimulate, guide and educate without appearing to do so, and restrain the impetuous until the "majority of the comrades" were disabused. The soldiers were to be told that the French Revolution had been left unfinished, that another and final revolution would terminate to the advantage of the many. Further, the agents should dwell on the soldier's poverty, his small pay, his tattered clothes, the rigid discipline, the insolence of officers, and his dismal future. The agents might then unfold the glorious part the troops could play in establishing their own and the people's happiness.[53]

The Babouvist archives show that the instructions were carried out to a considerable extent. Numerous letters and messages reflect a steady activity of the agents in and around Paris. Those friendly to the movement, according to the reports, were the workers. The shopkeepers were put down as "the enemies of the nation."

Two examples of industrious agents were Moroy, a worker, assigned to the twelfth arrondissement, and Bodson in the eleventh. Posters, Moroy wrote, went up at four or five in the morning so that workers could read them before they were torn down.[54] He had reading circles and discussion groups, where, as he said, he was indoctrinating "uneducated comrades" with the belief that democracy meant "common happiness, real and not Utopian equality." The soldiers, he was convinced, disliked the government. With a little boldness placards might be put up in the camp even in the daytime. "One must be daring in a revolution," he said in passing.[55] Bodson also found channels for reaching people and soldiers. His groups read and disseminated papers and pamphlets. He found small leaflets preferable to posters that were often destroyed before they were read. "More than a hundred soldiers," he reported, "locked themselves in a room in order to read them [*Eclaireur du peuple* and *Tribun du peuple*] in safety;" and a Babouvist song was "known and sung in several battalions."[56]

Other agents were less attentive to their duties than Moroy and Bodson. Morel in the first arrondissement, for example, put his private affairs before his assignment and associated with persons the leaders of the organization had reason to suspect. They sent him a sharp note to remind him of his pledge. Those they had once decided to employ, they warned, either had to serve "or know what to expect."[57] Cazin of the eighth arrondissement was culpable in a different way. An overdose of alcohol had made him indiscreet. For abusing the confidence placed in him they reprimanded him.[58]

Conditions were not congenial for a large organization. Still within its narrow limits leaders and subordinates seem to have learned from one another. There is ample proof that some of the party's best techniques of propaganda had their origin at the bottom. Even the style of certain literature was suggested by rank and file.

The evidence on the occupational make-up of the party is not enough for any statistical evaluation. All that can be said is that within its ranks were many artisans and unskilled laborers. They seem to have been the most numerous, as far as it is possible to judge. Also represented were the professions of law, medicine, pharmacy, journalism and teaching. And if the list of subscribers of the *Tribun du peuple* were any indication, even merchants and manufacturers might have belonged. Among the most active members were military men, discharged soldiers and officers.

How did the Babouvists try to reach people and soldiers? The unfriendly *Courrier républicain* of the 25 Germinal (April 15, 1796) described how a group, drilled by one of the agents, caried out the task of organizing a public meeting: "Four or five Pantheonists [Babouvists] meet and begin to speak about public questions. They lament the poverty of the people. Idlers approach and join the chorus. Working-class women [*tricoteuses*] come over, bewail the tyranny of the merchants, the royalist plots, above all the despotism of the five hundred kings and royalists in the two Councils. . . . They talk of liberty and equality. . . . comment on Châles, Antonelle and Babeuf and point out how everything would run smoothly if the . . . profits of industry belonged to all. Finally, the awful Ninth Thermidor is anathematized pitilessly. The conversation then turns to the blessed days of the incorruptible Robespierre. He brought the rich to reason, gave bread to the people, kept the *assignats* at par, distributed money to the workers and sent aristocrats to the guillotine by the cartload. . . . We need another Robespierre to make things move as in the days before the infamous Ninth Thermidor."[59]

Posters, pamphlets and songs were important media of propaganda. Squads posted placards where they could be noticed and guarded them against destruction by enemies. Letters to the central committee are filled with reports about the enthusiastic reception of the posters. One of the most popular, according to the police, was the *Analyse de la doctrine de Babeuf*. In fifteen articles it declared that the era of the revolution was not over, that the rich had become the new privileged class, that the final end was to assure happiness to all.[60] Crowds in front of posters discussed or disputed, and then the police appeared. Newspapers and pamphlets were better adapted to military camps, police and groups behind closed doors. The approximately 800 subscribers of the *Tribun du peuple* represented the most important re-

gions of France; and the *Eclaireur du peuple* circulated among soldiers
in and around the capital. Both papers were also read in cafés and
homes. Here, too, were to be found the pamphlets of the Secret Directory.
Babeuf wrote most of them, and a few were the work of Bodson.
Buonarroti's *Réponse à une lettre signée M. V.* was perhaps the best of
the series.[61] The themes of the pamphlets were more or less the same
as in the posters. They argued that the privilege of wealth had replaced
the privilege of aristocracy; the undemocratic Constitution of 1795 had
been imposed on the nation by a small minority; it was the people's
duty to restore the democratic Constitution of 1793; the soldiers were
the tools of the rich minority to keep the poor majority in subjection;
both soldiers and people were exploited; they should fraternize to overthrow the usurpers of the people's rights and inaugurate the society
where the planned labor of all would be to the good of everyone. Art
would have a social function. Ceasing to be the diversion of the frivolous few, it would have social responsibility.

The celebrated *Manifeste des Egaux*[62] has been erroneously accepted as the official expression of Babouvism. Written by Sylvain
Maréchal, who was at once a journalist, a dramatist and a poet, an
atheist and a precursor of anarchistic communists,[63] it demanded social
and economic equality, "the community of goods," "one education and
one standard of living for all," and another revolution "to found the
Republic of Equals." The Babouvists rejected the *Manifeste* on two
counts: (1) it set little store by art and science when it proclaimed:
"Perish, if need be, all the arts as long as we have real equality;" (2)
it leaned toward anarchism by saying: "Vanish at last the revolting
distinctions of . . . governors and governed." Babeuf was probably disposed to use it for propaganda if the offensive sentences were deleted.
But Buonarroti, its severest critic, defined it as "the incomprehensible
product of an extravagant mind," and referred to its strictures on government as "pitiful madness."[64] Apparently the conflict between anarchists and socialists was already present in the Babouvist party at least
fifty years before the controversy between Proudhon and Marx.

Almost a dozen poems, written by Babouvists and set to popular
tunes, served a useful purpose. The *Chanson nouvelle,* for example,
written by Maréchal, was quite the vogue for a time. *L'Eclaireur du
peuple* published it, agents posted it and had it sung in cafés. The poems
portrayed the popular distress, decried the tyranny of the men in power
and summoned people and soldiers to unite.[65]

Women were among the best assistants of the agents. They distributed literature, visited camps and police barracks, acted as emissaries
and popularized songs in cafés where Babouvists and soldiers congregated. The two most successful female propagandists were Marie-Adé-

laïde Lambert, a working girl, and Sophie Lapierre, a school teacher.[66]

Madame Babeuf and the thirteen year old son, Emile, must be counted among the party's aids. They tended to the circulation and finances of the *Tribun du peuple* or carried messages to and from agents. In correspondence, the son was the amanuensis of his illiterate mother. They kept the father abreast of subscriptions, the popular temper and the reception of the party's literature.[67]

The Babouvist party had its strength in Paris. But it also had some support in the provinces where its literature penetrated and its friends collected funds. It had followers in Arras, Béthune, Soissons, Lille, Pas-de-Calais, Toulon, Marseilles, Cette, Montpellier, Toulouse, Grenoble, Lyons and Reims. The party drafted an address to the departments and even set up a special bureau to encourage friends to come to Paris and hold themselves in readiness for the anticipated rising.[68]

The party was not allied to an international organization, simply because no such organization existed. But within its own ranks were members of different national origins. Jean Fion, a military man, was of Belgian descent; Buonarroti was Italian; and Bodson might have had a Scandinavian background. The Babouvists had admirers in the London Corresponding Society. At their trial in 1797, Babeuf and Germain said that their cause was that of an international movement to achieve democracy. And research in Buonarroti's posthumous papers and in French archives suggests that, through Buonarroti's influence among Italian refugees and his connections in Italy proper, the party anticipated a movement of national liberation in the peninsula. If the Babouvist and Italian movements synchronized, the one buttressing the other, the position of the Thermidorians would be untenable. The Babouvists were acting on the principle that democracy was indivisible. But Napoleon's victories in Italy and his contempt for popular movements upset the Babouvist party's calculations.[69]

Despite precautions the authorities knew of the underground organization. Spies, police reports and the propaganda in the armed forces gave the governing Executive Directors a basis for alarm. They passed stringent measures against the press and public gatherings and labelled the Babouvists foreign agents. Several members of the highest governmental bracket, regarding them as useful to their personal ambitions, made overtures to their leaders. Director Barras even had secret conferences with Babouvists, offered to place himself at their head and professed devotion to democracy. But they rebuffed him.[70] And Babeuf wrote in his paper: "Those who govern make revolutions only to continue governing. We, on the other hand, want to make one to secure forever the people's happiness through genuine democracy." He warned the people against offerings from on high: "You are mistaken in thinking that you can do nothing by yourselves. Nothing great and worthy of the people will ever be done save by the people themselves."[71]

The government was aroused to the sense of danger by increasing disobedience in the armed forces.[72] Police and soldiers pillaged shops, publicly denounced the worthless paper money and fraternized with workers. The Paris legion of police was a hotbed of discontent, and in it the Babouvists had set up a revolutionary committee. All the attempts of officers to keep the men in line were to no avail.[73] On April 24, the Executive Directors ordered three of the battalions to leave for the front, but two of them refused. Fiquet, the agent of the sixth arrondissement, hurriedly informed the underground committee that things were critical for the government. There were eight thousand rebellious men who could "form the vanguard of the popular and insurgent army." Shall he hasten events or wait? A dispatch from the agent of the second arrondissement told of soldiers' "violent language" against the government's order. Babeuf naturally seized upon the discontent to point out "the villainy of the rulers;" and legionnaires, perhaps aroused by the agitation, swore to use their bayonets on the Executive Directors before departing for the front. Another dispatch reported that the battalion stationed at Vincennes had sent delegates to Paris to learn what course would be followed. They urged the police to resist. Fraternization between people and soldiers was reaching extensive proportions. Germain, one of the men behind the mutiny, wrote that rebels were associating with those sent to replace them, and that their committees were getting friendly welcomes in other camps. The two battalions, he went on, were planning to march from the barracks in order to unite with the troops in Vincennes. If that were done, it would be a triumph for the Babouvists.[74]

The mutiny had surprised the underground committee. It was irresolute and clearly unprepared for the events. Its information on the strength of the rebels was incomplete; the organization of its forces had scarcely begun; and the plan of insurrection was but in raw state. It could not act decisively as its agents had demanded. Almost four days passed before the committee could adequately assess the nature of the mutiny. It finally ordered its lieutenants to keep the two battalions in Paris so as to make them the armed nucleus of the insurrection.[75]

It was too late. The governing Executive Directory stole a march on the insurrectionary Secret Directory. The mutinous battalions were disarmed and conducted under escort to the Military School. Realizing it had missed the opportunity, the underground committee called on its agents to calm the rank and file. It promised meanwhile to intensify its propaganda in the army and complete the plan of insurrection.[76]

4

Twelve days intervened between the police mutiny and the arrest of the Babouvist leaders. During this time they called into conference their five military experts: Germain, Rossignol, Fion, Massard and Grisel. Present, too, were Babeuf, Buonarroti, Maréchal, Darthé, Debon and Didier. Babeuf read the Act of Insurrection, containing numerous "Whereases" and twenty-one articles, that would be distributed by the tens of thousands the day of the rising. It summoned the people to destroy the existing governmental machinery, provided for their feeding and lodging, the return of their articles in the pawnshops, the care of widows and orphans, the liberation of political prisoners and the distribution of the enemy's properties among the poor and the soldiers.[77] The last provision, according to Buonarroti, was designed to placate the small owners. By the distribution of property, he added, was meant the distribution of its fruits.[78]

A discussion followed on the way to put the Act into force. Rossignol, an old Hébertist, would do it through terror. Fion opposed it.[79] Grisel, a spy, criticized the Act for its failure to lay down the form of authority for the period of transition. Rossignol interrupted with the question: "What concern is it of yours? Do you lack confidence in the Committee's forethought? . . . Remember you have been called here as a soldier only to advise on carrying through [the insurrection] and not to interfere in other matters." Realizing he had gone too far, Grisel recommended the burning of the châteaux around Paris in order to divert the government. Fion and Babeuf opposed the scheme. The new order would lose what was useful and beautiful,[80] they said. The five soldiers present were then organized into a military committee and given the task of drafting a plan for the technical execution of the rising. The Secret Directory reserved to itself the supreme command of the movement.[81]

The military committe held ten short meetings within eight days but never finished its work.[82] The material for the plan was still in raw form. A study of it reveals that the Babouvist party had about four hundred firearms and several rounds of cartridges to an arrondissement. But plebeians still had their pikes. Buonarroti estimated that the Babouvists had in Paris 17,000 trained men, not counting the workers, who were expected to rise against the government.[83]

The military committee left but a rough outline of a plan. Briefly it was as follows: after the distribution of the Act of Insurrection, tocsins and trumpets would sound, preferably at dawn, signalling the people to assemble with their leaders and Babouvist slogans. Sentries would be placed at the exits of the city. Insurgents would surround the two Councils, the Executive Directory, the ministers and the general staff. Others would seize the national treasury, mint, post-office, telegraph, stores of food, arsenals and the homes of ministers; arrest officials found in the street; prevent royalists and rich property owners from assembling; construct barricades; and spread the rumor that the military posts at Grenelle and Vincennes had joined the revolutionists.[84]

The central committee had a list of instructions for its civil agents. Among others, the orders were to distribute the manifestoes, rally the people in the districts, spread the word that the government had fled Paris in order to return with an army to restore monarchy, obey the insurgent commanders, fraternize with soldiers, requisition horses and vehicles, provide the bakers with flour and guard key points to intercept communications between enemies.[85] Further orders were to arrest foreigners, protect the provisioning of Paris, confiscate the properties of enemies, move the poor into their homes, purge the army, and call on the provinces to revolt.[86]

What form of authority did the Babouvists have in mind after seizing power? They agreed that a transitional power had to intervene between the victory over the old order and the final social system they had in view. The aim of that power would be "to free the people forever from the natural enemies of equality and to endow it with the unity of will necessary for the adoption of republican institutions."[87] Authority would rest with firm and gallant leaders. Buonarroti pictured them as men "deeply imbued with a love of country and humanity." They had "searched for the fundamental causes of social evils, . . . freed themselves from common vices and prejudices, seen further than their contemporaries and, with a complete scorn for material rewards, sought happiness in the immortality gained by securing the triumph of equality."[88]

Babouvist policy makers had different conceptions of the transitional power. According to Debon and Darthé, it should be a dictatorship of one man. Had that been done in 1793 and 1794, they argued, had Robespierre, for instance, been invested with full authority, the Revolution would have been completed. Babeuf demurred. A one-man government would look too much like monarchy. Besides, a single person might abuse his power or be utterly incompetent. Babeuf was against the use of the word "dictatorship." It "would shock people," he said. But he did not rule it out as a policy, if necessary, provided the man at the head had the wisdom and ability of a Robespierre. "An emancipator", he wrote, "must have broad views. He must level all obstacles, everything encumbering his path and preventing him from reaching speedily the objective he has in mind."[89] Babeuf and a majority of the secret committee preferred a government of a small group to the rule of one man. The committee, continuing as the provisional government, would summon a national assembly, composed of one member from a department. Each would be nominated by the committee and approved by popular vote. The new government would initiate and enforce legislation, set up administrative bodies, enforce decrees, and put down all opposition.[90] After exacting obedience to the measures prescribed in the Act of Insurrection, the government would carry through the following program: disfranchise those not engaged in "useful labor"; arm the people and disarm the enemies of the revolution; censor the press; abolish inheritance; confiscate the property of counter-revolutionists, of those who had made fortunes in public office, and of persons who "neglect to cultivate their lands;" compel all able-bodied citizens to perform useful labor; introduce machines "to reduce men's toil;" establish public stores; usher in economic planning; establish a popular system of education; enable all producers eventually to participate in the making of laws; cancel the national debt; abolish money; and monopolize foreign trade.[91]

5

While the Babouvists were making plans, Jacobins set up their own committee with the object of restoring the Constitution of 1793. The Babouvists, regarding them as rivals, charged that they had compromised the interests of the people. But conditions compelled the two organizations to unite. The Jacobins were too weak to carry on alone. The Babouvists, for their part, had discovered at the time of the police mutiny that they were quite unprepared for their great enterprise. Money was needed and the Jacobins had rich men who might open their purses. And Drouet was on their side, the same Drouet who had earned vast popularity for having intercepted the King's flight in 1791. Darthé was his friend, and Babeuf had tried to bring him around.[92] Also, Fion and Rossignol had good friends among the Jacobins. Political considerations, they urged, made unity necessary. Debon disagreed. He could not forget the part the Jacobins had had on and after the Ninth Thermidor. Besides, he added, they opposed common ownership. The secret committee outvoted him and decided to meet with them. On May 7, 1796, three days before the arrest of Babeuf and others, the two committees reached an understanding.[93]

Their first meeting was the following evening at Drouet's home. The Babouvists outlined anew their motives. Lindet, for the Jacobins, endorsed the immediate program in the Act of Insurrection. Grisel, who by the way had already posted Director Carnot on the details of the underground movement and on the meeting, promised the support of the camp of Grenelle where he was stationed.[94] There was entire agreement that the Babouvist committee should quickly complete its plans. A subsequent meeting would hear a final report and set a date for the rising.

The group had no sooner left than an officer followed by a detachment of soldiers invaded Drouet's apartment. Finding only the host and his friend Darthé, the officer withdrew. There had been a misunderstanding on the time between Grisel and Carnot.

The incident naturally alarmed the Babouvists, but did not stop their preparations for the taking up of arms. The military committee called on the civil agents to submit further data. Its five men decided to meet the morning of May 10, in order to study the information they were expecting.

Grisel's chance arrived. The son of a tailor, and trained for the trade, Grisel had left his father's home, eager for adventure and the fortune it might bring. He had enlisted in the army and risen to the rank of captain. Darthé, after meeting him, had decided that the officer would be an important link with the camp of Grenelle."[95] But the Babouvist movement was too weak and too poor for his ambitions. He resolved to betray it in the hope of promotion or financial reward. He wrote to Carnot for an interview and promised not to remit his vigilance. The attempt to surprise the leaders at Drouet's home had miscarried. On May 10, 1796, however, they were arrested. Drouet, Darthé, Didier, Germain and others were trapped at the meeting called to fix the day of the insurrection. When the police entered Babeuf's hiding place, he was writing number 44 of his *Tribun du peuple,* while Buonarroti was drafting a manifesto to proclaim the success of the uprising. Resistance was futile. Babeuf rose and exclaimed: "It's all over . . . . Tyranny is victorious."[96]

People did not stir to save them. For the people had to contend with high prices and unemployment. Privation and two abortive risings in 1795 had sapped their vitality. Then, too, Napoleon's rapid successes in Italy diverted them. They would sooner follow a Bonaparte than a Babeuf.

The growth of royalism disquieted many republicans in the government. This Babeuf knew and leaned on it for some political maneuvering. He thought that by convincing the Executive Directors of their common interests with democrats he could save his friends. Two days after his arrest, he sent the Directors a bold, and, what turned out to be, a tactless letter. He invited them to treat with him as "one power with another." A public trial would but alienate the democrats from the government. He acknowledged the existence of the clandestine organization, in fact pictured it as powerful. But it did not aim to be bloody, he said; it counted on "other means than Robespierre's." Babeuf urged them to "govern popularly" and rally the people behind the republic.[97]

The letter dismayed the Executive Directors, and they proceeded to plan an important trial. But Drouet was among those arrested. As a member of the lower house, he had to be tried by a special High Court of Justice. Director Barras, however, arranged for his escape. The others were moved from Paris to Vendôme like wild beasts in grated cages, followed on foot by wives, children and relatives. There they waited almost three months for the start of the trial. So elaborate were the precautions to guard them that Vendôme looked like an armed camp. They were charged with plotting the overthrow of the government, the outbreak of civil war and the pillage of private property. Darthé and Sophie Lapierre refused to be interrogated. All the others, except Pillé, the naive and deaf copyist employed by the Babouvists, contended that there had been no plot, that the movement had been organized against the royalists in order to save the republic. They in turn accused the government of contemplating the restoration of monarchy. Babeuf was interrupted several times as he defended the insurrections of 1795, and presented his teachings with long citations from Mably, Morelly and Rousseau. Buonarroti was calm and dignified; but Germain was bitter and caustic in his retorts and fiery in his defense. Many were the wrangles between the accused and the state's prosecutors. The prisoners, after each session, marched out singing one of their songs.

The trial lasted three months. On May 26, 1797, the verdict of the jury was read. Fifty-six of the sixty-five were acquitted. Babeuf and Darthé received the death penalty; Buonarroti, Germain, Moroy, Cazin and three others were condemned to deportation.[98]

Babeuf and Darthé attempted to escape the scaffold by suicide. Hearing their death sentence, they stabbed themselves, but had only inflicted painful wounds. After two days of suffering, they died on the guillotine on May 28, 1797.

The evening before his death, Babeuf wrote a final letter to his wife and children. It was his requiem. Only a portion can be cited here: "I don't know how my memory will be appreciated, although I think I conducted myself most irreproachably. I don't know what will become of all the republicans and their families . . . in the midst of the royal fury the counter-revolution will bring. Friends! How these thoughts are tormenting me in my last moments. To die for one's country, to leave a family, children and beloved wife would be endurable if I did not foresee the loss of freedom and the horrible destruction of everything republican. My dear children, what will become of you? I can't control my sentiments. Don't think I have any regrets for having sacrificed myself for the greatest of all causes. Even if all my efforts for it were useless, I have performed my job. . . . I conceived no other way of making you happy than through the happiness of society. I have failed and sacrificed myself. I am dying for you, too."[99]

6

Babouvism did not die with Babeuf. During the July Monarchy, his companion, Philippe Buonarroti, exerted considerable influence. His book, *Conspiration pour l'égalité dite de Babeuf*, published in 1828, was widely read not only by French people but also by German political refugees in France, and by Chartists in England. Louis Auguste Blanqui, the arch-leader of the underground movement against the July Monarchy and Second Empire, has often been considered by historians the heir of Babouvist strategy and methods. But available evidence does not readily establish such direct descent. Blanqui's early manuscripts, that might have yielded the necessary clues, were burned. All that is known is that Buonarroti and Blanqui were acquainted with one another during the years immediately after the Revolution of 1830. In any event, there is a resemblance between the organizational structures and methods of the Blanquists and Babouvists. But Babouvist influence in the French political clubs of the 1830's is less subject to doubt. Club leaders derived many of their articles of faith from Buonarroti's history, and none were more indebted to him than Charles Teste and Voyer d'Argenson, two of his disciples who were responsible for the programs of a number of clubs.[100]

Babouvism also impressed English Chartists. Thus Bronterre O'Brien, perhaps their best theorist, translated and annotated *Buonarroti's History of Babeuf's Conspiracy*, and Henry Hetherington, another Chartist, published it in 1836.

Although traces of Babouvism might be discovered in the immediate program of *The Communist Manifesto*, Marx appraised the Babouvist doctrine as crude and Utopian. It could not be otherwise before the appearance of the modern industrial economy. After the June Days of 1848, Babouvism ceased to have any effect on radical thought, save on isolated individuals. It went the way of other Utopian creeds. The subsequent labor movement ranked the Babouvists with its other pioneers who had charted new paths.

SAINT-SIMON'S PHILOSOPHY OF HISTORY

HENRI DE SAINT-SIMON has a distinguished place in the history of socialism. Marx placed him among the great Utopians.[1] Engels, apart from considering him a great precursor, likened him to Hegel, "the most encyclopaedic mind of his age."[2] Long before Saint-Simon had been elevated to a top place in the history of ideas, he had been the founder of a school with many disciples. Economic and social changes in France from 1830 to 1848, however, had caused them to drift apart. Many took the route back to their class of origin, and became engineers, financiers and orthodox economists. Others shared the cause of the rising working class. The conclusions they had derived from their master's premises brought into focus the need of resolving the problems of labor as the preliminary to the emancipation of society as a whole.

In view of the undeveloped economic conditions of his time, Saint-Simon's social philosophy could not take into account the modern proletariat. All he could see was abuses. Differences between classes, marked off by capitalist growth, were necessarily peripheral to his thought system. His efforts to erase the abuses led him into fantasy. But his search for an alternative to the unfettered order of the classical economists and to the military order of Napoleon, yielded a theory of historical progress that reached its summit in a peaceful society sustained by science and industry. Not Saint-Simon's peregrinations in the land of phantasmal speculation, but his philosophy of history was the source of inspiration for later socialist writers. It is this historical philosophy that will be the subject of the subsequent pages.

To find the privileged road to salvation in a secular way was the high purpose of Saint-Simon. Eighteenth-century reformers who had had a fairly similar aim had either championed panaceas or called for the imitation of some system in antiquity, or were themselves the archi-

tects of blissful social orders. This optimism, having inspired French
revolutionists, finally had its fulfilment in the Babouvist program. Neither
Enragés nor Hébertists, neither Robespierrists nor Babouvists, however
deep their sense of justice and however well intentioned their solutions,
had the answers to the important problems, brought into focus by the
French Revolution, and aggravated by the Napoleonic system. The problems were quite apparent while Saint-Simon's vistas were attaining well
proportioned dimensions.

Saint-Simon's mature life spanned the old and the new eras. The
political and social alterations that had separated them gained depth
and meaning with the application of science and technology to the pursuits of production. Inquiring minds were already discovering in the new
techniques the possibility of abundance and universal unity through the
free exchange of goods. The social and economic changes, it was also
noted, had the tendency to weaken the supports of absolute, feudal
governments.

The experience of the American and French Revolutions, in particular, had convinced Saint-Simon that economics and politics were
kindred. From 1779 to 1783, that is from his nineteenth to his twenty-
third year, the young nobleman had commanded expeditionary troops
France had sent to aid the American revolutionists. The War of Independence had appeared to him the dawn of a new historical epoch;
first, because the force of its example and principles would help topple
feudalism in Europe; and second, because the American republic was an
illustration of the thesis that peaceful labor was the cause of progress.
His reflections on the United States had led him to conclude that they
had four advantages over Europe: (1) They did not consume their
energies in religious feuds; (2) they had not been impeded by feudalism and its social frontiers; (3) they did not have a single family that
regarded governing as its patrimony or the allotment of posts as its prerogative; and (4) they had grown up with a regard for thrift and industry. The four advantages, Saint-Simon believed, would serve Americans to outdistance Europeans on the road to liberalism and democracy
and prevent the formation of a military caste. Consequently the greatest
statesman in America would be he who had a way "to diminish most of
the people's burdens without damaging the public service."[3] It is beyond
the present scope to apply the historical test to Saint-Simon's appraisal
of the United States. What was significant in it was the marked
importance assigned to the economic factor in a country's history and
politics.

The French Revolution, even more than the American, had impressed itself deeply on Saint-Simon. In Picardy, where Babeuf had first
waged war on privilege, the nobleman was in the company of *sans-*

culottes, wrote a *cahier* for poor peasants, and propagated the republican persuasion. Business connections with land speculators and financiers, however, made him suspect to the revolutionary authorities, and he spent a term in prison in 1793 and 1794. He came ultimately out of his business speculations a poor man with only a small income. What was even more consequential, the Revolution had declassed him psychologically, had filled him with irreverence for old castes. He emerged cognizant of the great advances that had been made.

The changes he had witnessed further revealed kinship between economics and politics. The feudal classes, deprived of their lands and privileges, had lost their political power. Power had passed to the bourgeoisie, enriched by its new acquisitions. Politics and property seemed related. In fact, closer study showed each form of property tending to beget a political structure that best conformed to it. American and French experience, therefore, validated the contention of Adam Smith that economic conditions had a decisive effect on a people's history. Social philosophers leaned to the conclusion that historical movement was consistent with a people's economic status and with the social class that apparently held the destiny of that movement.

Saint-Simon did not discover the class approach to historical science. French pamphleteers on the eve of the Revolution had already associated the growth of freedom with the rise of the bourgeoisie. Its champions, after its first victories over the feudal classes, maintained that its coming into power was inevitable. It had risen to the top in obedience to the law of historical progress. Two men, Rabaut Saint-Etienne and Joseph Barnave, argued with some evidence and persuasive force that progress was inexplicable without the development of the bourgeoisie. The first wrote a history of the Revolution during its first two years to show how the Third Estate unavoidably became the nation.[4] The purpose of the *Introduction to the French Revolution* by the second was to explain the thesis that politics followed the expansion of trade and industry. "A new distribution of wealth causes a new distribution of power," Barnave averred. "Just as landed property placed the aristocracy in power, so industrial property places the people in power."[5] The "people" meant to him the nation as a whole, without the numerically small feudal minority, led by the confident and triumphant bourgeoisie. It alone claimed to be the voice of the nation, its agent appointed by history. Barnave nowhere, in his remarkable *Introduction,* referred to the proletariat, as Jaurès has shrewdly observed.[6]

The cardinal objective of Saint-Simon was to found the science of man. The end of science, as he conceived it, was the improvement of mankind. In common with other great Utopians, he counted on those in power to fulfill this end. At first he looked to Napoleon to build a

social order in which scientists, artists and producers would take the
helm as administrators. Later, he called on the Bourbons to achieve that
aim. Steadily, he tried to persuade the rising industrial class to complete
the unfinished business of the French Revolution by securing the greatest
happiness of the greatest number.

Saint-Simon laid the foundation work of his social philosophy in
the Napoleonic period. His writings from the *Letters of a Genevan* in
1802 to his *Memoir on the Science of Man* in 1813, charted a global
organization, headed by a parliament of scientists, artists and industrialists. Its mission would be to guide humanity in its onward march. There
is, of course, good ground for questioning Saint-Simon's faith in the unity
of interest between scientists and artists on the one hand and industrialists on the other, if by industrialists are meant the captains of industry. Important, however, was the part he had assigned to intellectuals
—scientists and artists. They were the inseparable allies of the advanced
class.

The general outline of his blueprint suggested a hierarchical order
in which scientists took the place religious leaders had once held. Science,
directed by the Council of Newton, would have laboratories and workshops instead of churches and temples, and technical administrators in
lieu of clergy. The scientific élite would plan to erect paradise on earth.
Humanity would then be one, united internationally, and free from
the subjection of one people to another. "All men will work," said Saint-
Simon in his Genevan *Letters*. "All will regard one another as brothers,
attached to a workshop."[7] The goal would be reached when industrialists and intellectuals stood hand in hand. Their separation during the
French Revolution, he contended, had permitted the movement to fall
into the hands of non-owners and caused it to miscarry. Such a catas-
trophe could be avoided in the future provided artists, scientists and
proprietors joined in the common enterprise of improving humanity.
Obviously, Saint-Simon had set aside equality and democracy, proclaimed during the Revolution.

His new society stemmed from his philosophy of history. Taking
up the problem of historical lags, that the French Revolution had forced
on the attention of partisans of historical progress, he sought their causes
in the growth and decay of ideas and institutions. Eighteenth century
rationalists had taken the position that progress was unbroken and
gradual. But Saint-Simon, having had the benefit of two revolutions,
considered it an untenable hypothesis. He held instead that "the march
of civilization does not, strictly speaking, follow a straight line." History
was "a series of continuous, progressive oscillations, more or less slow
and far-reaching," he observed. The oscillations, moreover, could even
be shortened and accelerated.[8] The theory of continuous perfectibility

implied that history was an accumulation or an addition. Historical experience taught, however, that institutions and ideas had their periods of childhood, vigor and decline. In their vigorous stages they had a progressive character, otherwise they could not overcome the hostile forces that resisted their advance. Institutions in decay yielded to higher forms, thus permitting humanity to go forward. The problem, as it presented itself to Saint-Simon, was not one of emphasizing or neglecting, praising or condemning institutions of the past, as Condorcet had done in his *Esquisse d'un tableau historique des progrès de l'esprit humain,* but of assessing their worth and the reasons for their decline in their respective epochs. If history and politics were a science, if their laws of development were known, man's next stage could be foreshadowed.

It was Saint-Simon's ambition to prefigure the succeeding period and to convince rulers and industrialists to anticipate its coming. Just as the eighteenth century Encyclopedia had constituted the ideological arsenal for French revolutionists, so a new encyclopedia could provide the intellectual tools for erecting the new order. "After the French materialists who were predominantly mechanical," to cite Engels, "the need became evident for an *encyclopaedic comprehensive treatment* of the entire natural science of the old Newton-Linnaeus school, and two men of the greatest genius undertook this, Saint-Simon and Hegel."[9] Saint-Simon aimed at classifying the sciences and at establishing their interconnections. His task was far from completed. Still he looked to science to furnish the means and to point the way for achieving the greatest happiness of the greatest number. He insisted that before science could make rapid strides it had to be organized, and freed from academic control and official tutelage. The academic spirit, he claimed, tended to be conservative, even reactionary. "How furiously academies have persecuted men of genius who combated their views," he declared as early as 1802.[10]

Before Saint-Simon had finished his *Memoir on the Science of Man* and worked out his historical philosophy, Napoleon was in full flight from Russia. After 1814, the Bourbons returned to France, followed by the feudal classes who had grown even more moldy in exile. Unable to erase the principal gains of the Revolution, the reinstated classes sat uneasily on the new system of property. They could not restore the old economic base of their power without causing social upheavals. On the other hand, the bourgeoisie could not long continue in their inferior position without attempting to regain political power.

The Restoration, in Saint-Simon's opinion, did not hold out the promise either of a peaceful France or of a peaceful Europe. Neither could the Congress of Vienna successfully redraw the old boundaries. The reorganization of the Continent was possible, he was convinced, if its unity, once provided by the Catholic Church, rested on a secular and scientific base, and had as its purpose the happiness of mankind. That was the thesis he had expounded under Napoleon. It is not without interest, moreover, that his appeal to history and science was a service to the cause of liberalism that was then engaged in a struggle against Catholic romanticism.

Just as he aimed at establishing the unity of the sciences, so he endeavored to lay the groundwork for the unity of nations. In his *Reorganization of European Society* (1814) he called for an international peace organization, broader and more political than the Council of Newton he had proposed in *Letters of a Genevan*. Earlier plans, those of Henry IV and St. Pierre for example, were visionary, according to Saint-Simon, because they had perpetuated the existing order. An international organization to be effective had to be "systematically homogeneous,"[11] that is, it had to be made up of governments having similar forms and aims. He projected a European parliament with the power to legislate over European affairs and to undertake such enterprises as interoceanic canals and international education. Scientists and proprietors, elected to the parliament, would have a major part in rebuilding European society.

Saint-Simon would initiate the society of nations by forming an Anglo-French alliance. To have championed such an alliance in 1815, directly after Waterloo, was in itself an act of courage, as Engels remarked,[12] to say nothing of the statesmanship of the plan. The alliance had a historical basis, he argued, for the two countries had had parallel revolutions. The principal difference was that France had not yet had the last phase, that is, the final expulsion of the restored dynasty. The French Bourbons could secure themselves against this possible occurrence by allying themselves with England. The alliance would strengthen liberalism in England and stimulate it in France. It would also hasten the development of constitutional government in European countries, particularly in Germany. Saint-Simon anticipated the importance of the evolution of Germany from feudalism to parliamentarism, and believed that an Anglo-French combination would do well to make it a partner.

His preference for the parliamentary system in 1815 did not mean that he regarded it as the best of all political forms. He was of the opinion that it was but a transitional stage in the development of a higher social order in which peoples cooperated to attain general well-being. Of course, the establishment of such an order could be begun at once, if rulers and upper classes willed it. Then France and Europe as a whole would be spared other revolutionary disturbances.

Saint-Simon's brand of internationalism was a projection of his

Utopianism. It corresponded to the simultaneous conceptions of Fourier in France and of Owen in England. Saint-Simon, no less than Fourier, never ceased to appeal to men of talent and property, rather than to the people, to inaugurate his society. The two Frenchmen, nevertheless, were historically minded. To Fourier the past seemed dark and his own period, topsy-turvy and torn apart by dissension. His phalanx was Paradise by contrast. Saint-Simon, on the other hand, considered previous epochs necessary in the evolution of mankind. One social structure gave way to another, because the old one had ceased to fit changes within it. A new edifice then arose that was in harmony with man's needs. Seeing history advance through incompatibilities he confined himself to a general outline of the future society. He never indulged in its details, as Fourier did. Saint-Simon's writings are remarkably free of an elaborate blueprint of his Utopia.

The steadily growing friction between feudal aristocracy and bourgeoisie after 1815 yielded further evidence for Saint-Simon's social philosophy. He thereafter put great stress on the economic factor and on class relations. As causes of political and social changes they were influential in contemporary historical writing. Barnave, we have shown, had made them the essence of his important essay. French students of history and politics after Waterloo were inclined to see the French Revolution as the counterpart of the seventeenth century English Revolution. The middle classes in both countries had been victorious over their feudal rivals and each victory had had a liberalizing effect on the nation.

The historical investigations helped to shape Saint-Simon's thinking. From 1814 to 1817, Augustin Thierry acted as secretary to the philosopher. The young liberal historian, inspired by the older man, discovered in the communal revolution of the middle ages the forerunner of the bourgeois revolution of 1789. As a result, Saint-Simon's own understanding of the rise and decline of institutions and classes settled on a more solid base.

In his *Reorganization of European Society* he had already sought the explanation of political relations in economic conditions. Governments and institutions changed with the law of property, he said, and "there is no change in the world order without a change in property."[13] The outcome of such a change, the French Revolution had proved, was civil war between propertied and non-propertied. His anticipation of a revolution with the consent of the upper classes and without popular participation was in character with his Utopianism. The enduring thesis of his teachings, however, reappeared in his subsequent writings: the law that constituted property was the most important; it was "the basis of the social edifice."[14] The law establishing the division of powers and regulating their exercise was but secondary. The implication was clear:

if the law of property, underlying social relations, was changeable, society and its political institutions could be changed.

Continuing to dwell on this cardinal philosophical question, Saint-Simon approximated the materialist outlook on history. He held that man's relation to man became more rational as his contact with production grew closer. Early conquerors learned to spare the fruits of the earth, and instead of killing captives enslaved them in order to exploit them. Then followed the introduction of "machines to feed and supply man." It was industry and science, "peaceful and patient industry," that strengthened the reflective powers of man. "In bringing about a great change in things, man acts upon himself."[15] In other words, he grew rational as he subdued nature.

There was an interaction between industry and the superstructure, according to Saint-Simon's theory. In antiquity, industry was alienated from society, for it was left to slaves who were not part of the state. War was the big industry in the sense that it was the source of wealth. Industry became an active part of the community in the Middle Ages, affecting politics, and generating ideas of freedom and peace. Warlike times, when trade and industry were hampered, set limits to the trader's outlook. The expansion of industry and peace broadened his views, made him the bearer of liberalism. The more the feudal class ceased to inspire confidence, the higher was the regard for the industrialist. The state finally had to call on his services because he was the most respected and the most enlightened of the citizens.

The advance of industry and commerce also changed ethical values. Christianity could not provide moral standards for a changing order, for the fraternity it preached lacked a solid base. "It is by multiplying needs and different works that fraternity among men can be practiced," Saint-Simon insisted. "The true Christian society is that where each one produces what others need, while they produce what he lacks . . . the unifying medium is labor."[16] Christian fraternity, derived from mysticism, and the French revolutionary triad, stemming from the unhistorical natural rights, were meaningless to Saint-Simon unless they had roots in labor. The triad, like the imprisoned chrysalis, would finally emerge in a society of production and abundance. For "the real purpose of the sciences and the arts is to unite in order to adapt nature to man's advantage." By increasing the means of subsistence, by instructing and civilizing men, science and industry "tend more and more to cause the disappearance of the three greatest causes of disorder: poverty, laziness and ignorance."[17]

Industry and freedom need peace. That was their fundamental condition, according to Saint-Simon. Peace is the primary interest of a people aiming at production and abundance. War is the greatest calamity to a people desiring freedom. During war freedom is suspended, abuses increase, even become acceptable.[18]

Labor and industry, Saint-Simon showed, were the sinews of a people and the decisive factor in its history. The German Empire was the most warlike in the twelfth century; yet the Emperor's seven military expeditions against the industrial communes of Lombardy failed completely. In the sixteenth century the Flemish manufacturers defended their independence against the military might of Spain. The thrifty and industrious American colonies triumphed over the British Empire. The French revolutionary armies defeated a feudal-monarchist coalition principally because industry in France was further advanced than in the feudal states. Consequently, industry and labor made "a hero of a citizen who was not even a soldier."[19]

Saint-Simon observed a close relation between the economic factor and social classes. Before the French Revolution Simon-Nicolas Linguet had already pointed out class dichotomies in history, but he had neither regarded them as a cause of historical movement nor expected them to culminate in a classless order. Barnave's understanding of class forces in history had been in keeping with the outlook of the optimistic bourgeoisie. According to him, a particular system of production and the class in power were congruous. The summit of the social pyramid to which the bourgeoisie had climbed during the Revolution had hidden the broad base from his view. The accelerated rate of industrial progress after the Congress of Vienna provided Saint-Simon with data for a new appraisal of social classes. He not only linked them with the movement of history. He even warned that the working class would be a serious challenge to the class in power unless steps were taken to secure the greatest happiness of the greatest number. That end would be reached when politics was the science of production and the administration of things replaced the government of men.

Let us look at Saint-Simon's canvas of the succession of classes through history. In ancient times, slaves were the producing class, while the masters performed civil and religious functions. The break-up of the Roman Empire was accompanied by the gradual change from slavery to serfdom. That was an improvement, Saint-Simon contended, for the serf was better protected against the lord than had been the slave against the master. Meanwhile the industrial class in the communes won political recognition and freedom from feudal lords. The monarch in time acknowleged its usefulness to the state by inviting it to send deputies to the national parliament. But the conflict between the industrial and feudal classes went on. Saint-Simon credited the English Revolution with having begun, and the French Revolution with having completed, the process ending in the triumph of the industrial class.

Since then "it has invaded everything, taken over everything," remarked Saint-Simon.[20]

He called on this class to assume leadership in the march of progress. It stood between two extremes, between the class he described as parasitical,[21] and the lowest class that Saint-Simon had learned to know during the French Revolution. Though he did not disassociate the last class from the industrialists, he already saw it as a threat to the bourgeoisie.

A modern working class was just beginning to emerge. Still its antagonism to capitalism was sufficiently in evidence to make Saint-Simon aware of the labor problem. The tempo of technical innovation was speeded up in France after 1814. Workers at this time did not anticipate socialism as the alternative to capitalism. Many vented their hostility to machines by wrecking them, or combined against employers, despite existing legislation.[22] The new trend in class alignment forced itself on the attention of students of the social and economic scene. Simonde de Sismondi, for example, argued in his *Nouveaux principes d'économie politique* (1819) that the workers bore the cost of capitalist development.

Saint-Simon's writings from 1820 to 1825 show that he, too, took more notice of the workers. His last work, *The New Christianity* (1825), was a call for a social order, free from exploitation and founded on the productive labor of all. In another sense it rebuked those romanticists who desired to return society to the domination of the Church. Saint-Simon regarded such an aim as absurd, in view of the immense strides made by science and industry. He affirmed the need of a new morality, corresponding to the realities of history and consistent with the happiness of the greatest number.

He likened society to a pyramid, with the workers as the base. This young class, he recalled, had shown its capacity to administer affairs during the French Revolution. Agricultural workers had demonstrated their ability by managing the small properties many of them had acquired; industrial workers, by superintending the workshops they had opened. French workers, he contended, had reached a high level of civilization and culture. Did Saint-Simon imply that they would endeavor to act independently of their employers?

The evidence indicates that his aim was to erase frontiers between the two classes. It would be achieved when politics was absorbed in economics. The minority would no longer need force to subordinate the majority. The problem was not one of perfecting government—that was the error Saint-Simon laid to the French revolutionary leaders—but of substituting the administration of things by an élite for the government of men by the inept.

The ruling class, under the government of men, Saint-Simon reasoned, tried to maintain the status quo. Consequently it employed armies of soldiers and civil servants, spent the bulk of the taxes on activities that were useless to the producers of society.[23] The political situation, as he saw it, was "the spectacle of the topsy-turvy world: those who are directing public affairs are greatly in need of direction; the very able are in the class of the governed, while the governors . . . are very mediocre men."[24] Under the administration of things, however, only the most competent would manage affairs "in a way completely satisfactory to reasonable men in all classes. Then there will be no longer be the dread of insurrection, and consequently no need of maintaining large standing armies to resist it." To those who held that armies were necessary to repel invasion he answered that "thirty million men, finding themselves happy, would repulse the attack of any coalition against them."[25]

The administrative élite, though drawn from the most talented in society, was but the instrument of historical progress. Its policies and functions were consistent with the laws of social development; it followed a prescribed path. Government in the sense of commanding was reduced to zero, for "decisions can only be the result of scientific demonstration . . . and open to discussion by all who are sufficiently competent to understand them." The administration of things would bring "the highest degree of freedom compatible with the state of society . . . . The maintenance of order will then easily be, almost entirely, a duty shared by all citizens." The problem would not be burdensome, because where society's improvement was the objective "the mass of the people exercises a passive force that is almost alone sufficient to check an anti-social minority."[26]

Saint-Simon's philosophy of history, therefore, had its culmination in a socialist society. It was hierarchical, anti-democratic, Utopian. The workers' part in creating it was passive. They would enjoy the advantages of a social order built by industrialists, scientists and artists in accordance with the trend history had disclosed.

The Utopianism in his teachings was in vogue among his disciples in the twenties and thirties. If they reduced it to an absurdity, they also hastened the demise of their school. Saint-Simon's faith in an élite inspired sociologists and historians, among them Auguste Comte, Joseph Mazzini and Thomas Carlyle. His theory of history, however, was his legacy to socialism. A class lost its hold when it ceased to lead people in the trek to a more advanced social stage. Saint-Simon showed, for example, how the feudal-theologic class had surrendered command to the bourgeoisie after profound changes had undermined the feudal structure. The scientific discoveries, the Protestant Reformation, the opening of the new world—all these revolutions had caused old institutions to atrophy while they stimulated the rise of new ones. Increasingly outworn standards and ideals had retarded the expansion of industrial society. Under feudalism, a noble's indolence was honorable, and labor degrading. The spiritual power placed the safety of the soul through privation above the security of the individual through work. In other words, the emerging economic order had been encumbered by outlived traditions and ideologies. The French Revolution threw them on the scrap-heap.

Saint-Simon regarded the Revolution as the crowning achievement of a long development that had begun with the rise of medieval communes. To this general process belonged the American Revolution. He never forgot how it had weakened the supports of French institutions. Criticism, intensified by the Encyclopedists, had made a hollow shell of the superstructure. If the task of 1789 was the demolition of old institutions, the object of 1793 was the construction of new ones. Saint-Simon's explanation for its failure was in line with what Marx later said in *The Holy Family* (1845). Both observed that, unversed in the laws of society, the leaders of 1793 had to seek exemplars in classical antiquity.[27]

History, therefore, as Saint-Simon viewed it, had a rhythm. As one social stage decayed another grew up and pushed out what was incompatible with it. "There are times," he wrote, "when through an uncommon vicissitude, what was possible ceases to be so, and what was wise and useful becomes insane and fatal"[28] By 1789 the old social pyramid was quaking from the summit to the base. The feudal classes were cast from their supreme position. To it rose the vigorous bourgeoisie, confident of its ability and firm in the conviction that it held the potential of the best of all possible worlds.

Eighteenth-century rationalists could not explain historical lags. Unable to fit them into the theory of uninterrupted progress, they considered them unfortunate retardations. Saint-Simon, however, undertook to interpret them. What seemed a retardation, he held, was in effect a transition, an adjustment to a higher social level. We have seen that he regarded the march of civilization as a series of progressive oscillations that could be more or less slow and far-reaching, even shortened and speeded up. His medium for hastening the construction of the new order, however, was in keeping with his Utopia and its hierarchical scaffolding. His concept of a historical transition lacked the magnitude and popular quality of the Babouvist system. For a brief period after 1815, he counted on the Holy Alliance to lay the groundwork of real international unity. Similarly he looked upon the parliamentary system as a preliminary stage for his industrial society. Subsequently, he appealed to the king of France to decree such measures as the abolition of the nobility, the substitution of a national guard for the standing army and the organization of a council of scientists, artists and industrialists. Saint-Simon recommended that the king exercise dictatorial power in order to secure the shift from the feudal-theologic system to the scientific-industrial. "The exercise of limitless power in the present circumstance," he pointed out in *Du système industriel* (1821), "will obtain for you great advantages, and it cannot have any great inconveniences. Since the purpose of the dictator is to make society achieve the aim which has been clearly determined, public opinion will not permit him to deviate from the road he must follow." The dictatorship would inevitably transform the monarchical institution. As a result of contact with the interests of science and industry, it will lose its feudal-theologic character. The king would then become "the first of the industrialists."[29]

His scheme of transition, it should be repeated, rested on an élite. Everything, though done for the people, was done without them. Behind his conception of class succession in history there was an inevitability in which the people had no part. His optimistic picture of man's progress held out the promise of a peaceful and bounteous future; but he did not count on the workers to create that future, even though he had witnessed their first stirrings. Like Fourier, he was frightened lest their activity retard the coming of the next society that only geniuses could beget.

Saint-Simon wrote at a time when modern class friction was just beginning to show iself. His term, "industrialist," included all who had a share in the productive system: that is workers, manufacturers and merchants. Nowhere in his writings is to be found the claim, that is frequently met with in Robert Owen's, that the fruits of production belonged to the workers on the ground that they had created them. But when this is said, there still remains his enduring thesis that humanity was moving ahead, however tortuous the road; that, marshaled by an advancing class, it was going toward a society where politics was the science of production and the government of men yielded to the administration of things.

FROM SOCIAL UTOPIA TO SOCIAL SCIENCE*

THERE are many antecedents of *The Communist Manifesto*, but only four of them can be referred to here. Historians have often cited, however erroneously, Maréchal's *Manifesto of the Equals* of 1796 as the expression of Babouvist principles and aims. Emanating from Rousseau-ism and eighteenth century materialism it foreshadowed anarchism rather than socialism. In the first half of the 19th century there were Georg Büchner's *Der hessische Landbote* of 1834, which, in the spirit of sans-culottism, appealed to the oppressed to rise up against their oppressors, and the catechism of Moses Hess in 1844, calling for a society that would free man from the reign of money.[1] The previous year the leading Fourierist, Victor Considérant, published in his paper *The Manifesto of Peaceful Democracy*,[2] restating the principles of the Fourierist School. These manifestoes have long been relegated to obscurity. Only the *Manifesto* of Marx and Engels, published in London in February 1848, still commands attention.

Earlier manifestoes, to be sure, had indicted prevailing conditions. But their programs at best had relied for their realization either on the will of an individual or on the force of reason. The social systems they had projected were without roots in the historical process, for they had left man outside of historical change. In *The Manifesto* of Marx and Engels, on the other hand, men are the makers of history. They are no longer regarded in the abstract, but as members of a social class, growing out of the productive relations. The final fulfillment of the program no longer rests with an individual or with exalted reason. That eminent assignment is given to the working class, raised into prominence by the new industrial system. Here was a totally new outlook on history.

---

* The substance of this essay was read at a meeting of the American Historical Association on December 29, 1948, in Washington, D.C.

The Manifesto was written as the program of the Communist League, an international organization with its headquarters in London and nuclei in France, Belgium, Switzerland and Germany. The League, under the influence of Marx and Engels, had renounced Weitling's chiliastic anarchism and French egalitarianism, substituting for them the principles held by both men. It had commissioned Marx in 1847 to draft a program. The manuscript was sent to the printer a few weeks before the outbreak of the February Revolution in Paris.

The program did not at once win partisans. In fact, it had but a comparatively limited circulation from 1848 to 1871. However, it had already been translated into English, French, Danish, Polish and Russian. The English version first appeared in 1850 in London, in the paper of George Julian Harney, the Chartist.[3] *Woodhull & Claflin's Weekly* in New York republished the same text in 1871.[4]

As the principles of the program were adopted by socialist parties, it became the subject of controversy. Governments tried to stifle its teachings by legislation and police measures. Enemies assailed it as a paraphrase of works by others. At least a half dozen men, notably Georg Brandes, Georges Sorel, Morris R. Cohen and Harold J. Laski, have either said or implied that the authors of the *Manifesto* had plagiarized Victor Considérant's *Manifesto of Peaceful Democracy.*[5] It can be said at the outset that their evidence has not been convincing. A brief inquiry into the charge of plagiarism is in order.

Considérant's indictment of the social and economic system was both eloquent and arresting. In place of the old feudalism, he said, a monied aristocracy had arisen, that imposed a new type of servitude and stood as a threat both to the working and middle classes. The accumulation of capital by a tiny minority tended to divide society into two large classes: a small number owning everything and the large number having nothing. The new feudalism henceforth formed the real government. Considérant predicted that unless there was a solution for this "social hell," as he called it, revolutions would result.

Considérant never went into the economic structure to study its inner workings. If he sought the laws of social change he could not discover the reasons why the society he arraigned broke down periodically. The disturbing picture he drew in his *Manifesto,* as in his earlier works, had an uncommon likeness to the portrayals by socialist contemporaries. For the kind of capitalism they all contended with was the financial, speculative variety of the July Monarchy. Since credit was political economy's standard for valuing men, their panaceas for the pressing problems, their ways of achieving their different versions of justice, depended rather on the organization of credit within the existing order than on the organization of labor, called for by Marx and Engels. All leading Utopians, Considérant among them, were genuinely alarmed at the growing power of concentrated wealth and at its perversion of the egalitarian and libertarian principles of the French Revolution. Turning their backs on the new situation born out of the technological revolution, they looked with confidence either to their special schemes or to the terrestrial paradises they planned to erect.

For they discounted labor's part in bringing about socialism. In fact, their grand designs left labor and socialism separate and distinct. Considérant, as much as other socialists of his day, thought in terms of class differences, even considered them central to the long historical process, though his analysis of them was inferior to that of the contemporary labor press, certainly to that of the economist, Constantin Pecqueur. Whatever quality Considérant's diagnosis had, he owed it in a large measure to the Saint-Simonians, especially to Armand Bazard and Barthélemy-Prosper Enfantin.[6] He believed, as they did, that as humanity went forward the spirit of fraternity intervened to cushion the conflict. Classes, instead of mauling each other, would ultimately join hands and travel together toward the promised land. This conception of a gradual class rapprochement, terminating in collaboration and harmony, derived from the eighteenth century persuasion that human history developed rationally and uninterruptedly; it implied, too, a faith in the willingness of the rich, propertied classes to accept the dictates of history, to step down from their places of power in order to bask in the brilliant rays of fraternity. Thus for Considérant, as for Utopians in general, the future did not emerge out of practical human activity, as it did for Marx and Engels. With a firm trust in the final triumph of reason, Considérant set up ideal conditions, counting on their convincing power to inspire men to establish them.

It may be further observed, in view of the charge of plagiarism, that, unlike Marx and Engels, Considérant regarded the political order as secondary to the immediate social issues. Hence he accepted the July Monarchy, established in 1830. On the political question, as on class antagonisms, it should be recalled, he was representative of many contemporary socialists. The same question was an impenetrable block between himself and such socialists as Pierre Leroux, Louis Blanc, and especially Louis Auguste Blanqui and the editors of the second *Fraternité*. Economic factors and state forms were apart and unconnected, in Considérant's philosophical scheme. Consequently, the existing political régime did not seem to him incompatible with social progress. The democratic principles of equality before the law and the elective system of representation had already been won, he contended. They but needed developing. And who would do it? Not the workers, for class conflicts as propulsive forces in history were not in his design. The principles would develop in accordance with social evolution, impelled by an innate justice and marked out by the progress of "the dogma of fraternity," to use Considérant's phrase. Marx and Engels probably had in mind a socialist like Considérant when they said of the Utopians that they "endeavor, by small experiments, necessarily doomed to failure, and by the force of example, to pave the way for the new social gospel."[7]

All indications point to the conclusion that Considérant's historical outlook was much akin to that of eighteenth century perfectibilists. Implied in his doctrine was a faith in anticipative destiny, in an abstract principle of justice, steadily revealing itself in history and finally blossoming in a cooperative order. His own blueprint was in keeping with the dreams of Utopians in general. His *Manifesto of Peaceful Democracy* discloses that his view of society was a static instead of a dynamic one; that, like Proudhon, his contemporary, he was at bottom a conservative. For both aspired to resolve incompatibilities in a social equilibrium. "Thus," Engels estimated the Fourierist phalanx in 1843, "after all the beautiful theories of association and free labor; after a good deal of indignant declamation against commerce, selfishness, and competition, we have in practice, the old competitive system upon an improved plan, a poor law bastille on more liberal principles."[8] Apparently the evidence behind the charge of plagiarism cannot stand the test of investigation. Yet the accusation persisted, gained validity through repetition and became standard belief among reputed writers on social thought.

There is no intention here to rule out the indebtedness of Marx and Engels to their precursors. In fact they were the first to acknowledge it. No one ever wrote more warmly of the great Utopians than Frederick Engels.[9] And Marx esteemed the penetrating judgments on capitalist production of such economists as Simonde de Sismondi and Thomas Hodgskin, for example, although he rejected their remedies.[10] But unlike their forerunners, Marx and Engels held that the movement of history was independent of phantasies, that no *a priori* social device could bring it to a halt. For in their diagnosis of capitalism they believed to have found out why it grew and declined. They concluded that it begot both the conditions of the future and the social class that would construct it.

Now the existence of a class struggle had been recognized long before Marx and Engels, and they admitted it.[11] We have seen that class friction was a representative theme in the writings of the Utopians. But the theme had already been present in eighteenth century literature. Adam Smith, in the chapter on "The Wages of Labor," described the latent and open antagonism between masters and workmen.[12] His French contemporaries, the Physiocrats, had a class theory of their own, by which they explained the circulation of the net product.[13] Significant was their contention that while the productive class provided the life blood of society a parasitic class alienated a portion of the net product. Opponents of the Physiocrats, for instance Necker and Linguet, acknowledged a continued antagonism between employers and wage earners. But the antagonism, in their conception, was both unavoidable and insoluble. It was intrinsic to the permanent order.[14]

The French Revolution brought class differences into sharper focus. Henceforth writers on politics and economics linked classes with the forms of property. Thus, as early as 1792, Antoine Barnave held that property relations were behind class divisions and the distribution of power.[15] Saint-Simon went beyond Barnave. Instead of considering property in general the basis of the class antagonism, Saint-Simon saw it conditioned by property in the means of production. From this he concluded that politics was the science of production.

Class distinctions were also cardinal in the writings of English socialists and economists in the first half of the nineteenth century. Notable examples were Charles Hall's *The Effects of Civilisation on the People in European States* (London, 1805), Thomas Hodgskin's *Labor Defended against the Claims of Capital* (London, 1825), and the many articles of the Chartist, James Bronterre O'Brien.[16]

Class antagonisms, therefore, had been accepted as an overriding factor in social relations long before Marx and Engels. What they did that was new was to exhibit it as a law of social change, premised on the activity of the workers in order to achieve their political supremacy.

How had the two men come upon this law? Marx discovered it via a criticism of Hegel's theory of the state and of the classical economists; Engels, through the investigation of industrial and labor conditions in England. The first concluded that legal relations and political forms were best explained not by the progress of the human mind, but by seeking their roots in the material conditions of life. Study and observation in England convinced the second that increasing concentration of wealth and sharpening class friction would finally terminate in a system of production, founded on men's collectivity.

The paths travelled by Marx and Engels converged and there began one of the great partnerships in history. Marx supplied his learning and his creative genius; Engels, his knowledge of labor conditions, his business experience and his skill in marking out foundations. The two steeped themselves in classical German philosophy, English and French political economy, and French and English socialism; and both were in the thick of practical activity.

The principles they arrived at by 1848 were put down in their *Manifesto*. Though it was the statement of their Party's credo, it had also the polemic quality of several of their earlier works. In the third chapter they took exception to the various schools of thought that did not represent a realistic position in relation to the general body of the workers. Their own position, to be sure, had assimilated aspects of earlier social movements; but it had avoided their drawbacks. In this respect it was qualitatively distinct from all previous social systems. Earlier socialist writings, said Marx and Engels in the *Manifesto,* "attack every principle of existing society. Hence they are full of the most valuable materials for the enlightenment of the working class." Their practical measures, however, the two men continued, "point solely to the disappearance of class antagonisms which were, at that time, only just cropping up, and which, in these publications, are recognized in their earliest, indistinct and undefined forms only. These proposals, therefore, are of a purely utopian character."[17]

Looking at the *Manifesto* after the lapse of more than a century, we find little in it that is dated. The program at the end of the second chapter was drafted in the anticipation that the expected revolution would make the workers the political arbiter in the most advanced European countries. Then there is chapter four which lays down policy towards the various opposing parties. These sections have a bearing on the general political climate of the time, and may be useful for assessing the period.

The third chapter, already referred to, apart from telescoping the theoretical controversies before 1848, establishes the differences between the new principles and the older ones championed by precursors and contemporaries. Since the tenets of these earlier theorists have reappeared in many versions since 1848, the third chapter can continue to serve as a basis for modern criticism. The authors of the *Manifesto* took their stand against those they characterized as reactionary socialists who today have their successors among those who aspire to reimpose a fixed hierarchical order of the past; they disassociated themselves from the partisans of conspiracy, from "the alchemists of revolution,"[18] as Marx once called them, who were detached from the labor movement and who counted on a small, secret group to seize the reins of power; and they could not find common ground either with a Joseph Proudhon who desired to redress social grievances in a system that stabilized and continued the existing forms of property, or with doctrinaires of the type of Victor Considérant and Etienne Cabet, who appealed to philanthropists to help them set up their paradises in miniature.

By contrast with these system builders Marx and Engels refused to be distracted from immediate issues by an apocalyptic contemplation of the future. They applied themselves instead to examine conditions critically and to evaluate the general results of the social movement. Their appraisal of the historical process yielded them the conclusion that the rise and decline of classes and institutions but demonstrated the law of contradiction. The *Manifesto* lauded the great achievements of the bourgeoisie in more glowing terms than can be found even in the literature of its stoutest apologists. But it already spoke of this class as in a funeral oration. The antagonist, the working class, growing to maturity as a result of the new productive relations, stood ready to become heir and successor. For the working class, in the social philosophy of Marx and Engels, held the promise of a vast human potential. The experience of the French and English workers in the third and fourth decades of the nineteenth century had inclined them to believe that. If on the eve of 1848 they underestimated the reserve, expanding power of capitalism; if they did not foresee the growth of the world market after the decline of the economic crisis, starting in 1847; if, as Engels said later, they failed to include in their calculations both Russia and the United States, they nevertheless looked far into the future. Instead of drawing in outline the society they expected would eventually replace capitalism, they formulated the laws of social development, according to which the alternative society would finally emerge.

Their conviction was the outcome of a new conception of history, that has come to be known as historical materialism. This philosophy starts from the thought that men make their own history, "but in the first place," as Engels wrote, "under very definite presuppositions and conditions. Among these the economic ones are finally decisive. But the political, etc., ones, and indeed even the traditions which haunt human minds, also play a part, although not the decisive one."[19] Engels admitted years later that he and Marx were "partly to blame for the fact that young writers sometimes lay more stress on the economic side than is due to it. We had to emphasize this main principle in opposition to our adversaries, who denied it, and we had not always the time, the place or the opportunity to allow the other elements involved in the interaction to come into their rights."[20] According to their line of thought, the new order was neither the architectural creation of fancy, nor the final product of an even, unretarded progress of humanity. Neither was it the outcome of the power of reason in the eighteenth century understanding. On the contrary, the two men argued, the new society was begotten by a tortuous and painful historical development, forever impelled by the antagonisms of incompatible classes. And if it was rational, that was so because it was the dénouement of the historical process, exhibiting a logic totally different from that it was believed to have. Historical movement did not consist in the march from one idea to another, but in the transition from one system of production to another.

Marx and Engels explained why they placed their faith in the workers alone to achieve the new society. First, they said, "in the conditions of the proletariat, those of old society at large are already virtually swamped. The proletarian is without property." Modern industry transformed the workers' psychology and life pattern, revealed to him the cold, cash nexus between himself and his master, and dispelled the halo around existing conditions and institutions. Social classes that had formerly risen to power had their newly won positions to defend. The workers, however, had nothing of their own to protect. They had but to level the ramparts of private property in order to take over the forces of production. Second, Marx and Engels went on to contend, the workers' movement, unlike all previous ones, was "the self-conscious, independent movement of the immense majority, in the interest of the immense majority." This broad base of the social pyramid could not shift its position without overturning everything above.[21]

Such were the historical perspectives of the *Manifesto*. It closed the gap between labor and socialism, that had been of the essence of Utopian thinking. Its confidence in the workers' capacity to erect the alternative to the capitalist order was indeed a long jump from the realm of fantasy to the realm of primary and unavoidable historical conditions in which men lived. In this environment, that changed men and was changed by them, were to be found the elemental factors and the vital forces to advance, perhaps accelerate, the historical process.

FRENCH DEMOCRACY AND THE
AMERICAN CIVIL WAR

THE Civil War in the United States had international dimensions. Its ruinous effect on European economy caused governments, especially the English and the French, to countenance intervention on the side of the slave-owners. It is common knowledge that in the Fall of 1862 Napoleon III and Lord Palmerston were planning an armistice that they expected would terminate in conciliation. If the North rejected a truce England and France were prepared to recognize the Confederacy. Several reasons, however, persuaded the two powers to hold back. There was the fear in England that a war with the United States would cut off the American wheat supply on which England depended. The suffering this would bring might outweigh the benefits to be derived from a reopening of the avenues of commerce.[1] Then, the two Western powers had failed to win Russia's cooperation. The Tsar's government, acting in its own interests, had promised to support the North against England and France. Finally, English and French public opinion would not tolerate intervention in behalf of the Southern Confederacy.

The assistance of the British workers to the North has been the subject of inquiry since the Civil War.[2] A recent article[3] concentrated on the large public meeting of March 20, 1863, at which John Bright was the principal speaker. The meeting, endorsed by British organized labor, was a measure of their sympathy with the cause of anti-slavery. Students, however, have tended to overlook the part of French workers in promoting the same aim.[4] The purpose of this essay is to bring into focus their opposition to Louis Napoleon's pro-slavery policy, with the hope of suggesting further investigation into this neglected chapter of their history.

121

1

French labor's suffering, owing to the cotton famine, was relatively as severe as that of English labor. The wretched in France were, to be sure, not as numerous as in England because French industrial capitalism, and the cotton industry in particular, had not reached the proportions of its English competitor. The French cotton industry needed approximately 700,000 bales in 1860, the bulk of which came from the United States. But the Northern blockade of Southern ports reduced French imports from America to a mere 1,911 bales in September 1861.[5] The cotton industry employed from 130,000 to 140,000 workers. Including dependents, the estimate of those directly affected by the blockade rose to about 1,500,000 men, women and children. To this figure should be added the tens of thousands of workers who earned their livelihood through the carrying trade. Further, the Civil War had drastically cut into the French silk and ribbon industries, causing unemployment in such cities as Lyons and Saint-Etienne, for the United States had been a large purchaser of luxuries.

Could colonial areas supply enough raw cotton for the textile industry? was the question asked in France after the start of the Civil War. Egypt, India and Algeria were potential sources; so were Mexico, French Guiana, the West Indies, even Tahiti and Senegal. But these projects, if ever undertaken, were remote at best. A number of factors, official irresponsibility and shortages of labor and capital among others, prevented these colonies from challenging the supremacy of the Southern United States.[6]

Big French manufacturers, with large stocks of raw cotton, continued to run their factories at maximum profit. Others, with capital reserves, bought the raw material at higher prices. In either case the cotton crisis was their chance to extend the working day, introduce labor saving machinery and lower wages. Wherever it was possible, women and children took the places of fathers of families. The fall in wages was so general and steady that even a conservative Procureur in a stricken area had to admit it was "regrettable, because it is perhaps not sufficiently justified."[7] Needless to say, smaller manufacturers could not stand the strain of the cotton shortage and had to shut their factories.

Distress spread through French industrial areas. By the end of 1862 the Seine-Inférieure alone had 130,000 unemployed.[8] Another estimate for January 1863 put the number in the same department at 300,000.[9] Even allowing for possible exaggeration the reality was grim indeed. The accounts in the contemporary press, as they have been summarized, told a dismal tale of the workers' miserable state. "Some of them," the summary runs, "tried to sustain themselves with a kind of pasty made of coarse bran, water and herbs. Those who could sometimes get bread were considered fortunate. Half naked children went into the country to beg soup or potatoes from the farmers. Sometimes they had to go so far that they could not return to their homes until the next day."[10] Adult workers either relied on odd jobs to eke out an existence or, if they were semi-proletarians, returned to rural life as agricultural laborers; others found work in the revived woolen industry. The vast majority, however, starved. The police reports of the Seine-Inférieure paint a heartrending picture of the workers' conditions; and one police commissioner, writing to his superior, remarked: "Poverty is great indeed."[11]

Little help came from the rich or from charity, for philanthropy under early capitalism was not regarded either as a virtue or as an insurance. Besides, relief was at first not held to be urgent, for Napoleon's government, part of the press and sympathizers with the Confederacy were predicting that the North could not withstand the military talent of the South. Men in French ruling circles counted on a short war, anticipating at the end of it the return of their markets and prosperity. Nevertheless, the spread of unemployment caused fear in the same upper social strata. Officials, the press, the Catholic Church, all vied with one another in benevolence. Prefects called on civil servants to contribute one-third of their salaries; mayors were instructed to collect funds in their communes; newspapers published lists of contributors and requested workers to pledge part of their wages. Church hierarchs and royal princes were no less mindful of their Christian duty. The Archbishop of Rouen circularized the clergy of his diocese for special appeals, while nobles and princes gave substantial sums to the Committee for the Relief of the Unemployed. On its list of contributors were Bourbon and Orleanist pretenders to the throne of France, for charity also had a dynastic motive.[12] The total contributions fell far short of the needs, and the government had to vote millions of francs.

Labor leaders in Paris set up their own committee for the relief of the unemployed. Its appeal to workers for contributions was signed by men like Henri Tolain, J. J. Blanc and Perrachon.[13] All three, we shall see, had given a kind of independent status to the labor delegation at the London Exhibition of 1862. For the next two years they also led the movement for labor candidates. Tolain and Perrachon were among those who established the First International in 1864. Clearly there was a continuity between labor's organization of relief and its share in the founding of the International Workingmen's Association. This is not to claim that the Civil War in the United States was the immediate issue on which workers' representatives from different countries united. But it can be said that workers' distress, from the same cause, both in England and in France, further convinced them of their common interests. If the Polish Question served as the occasion for bringing together their delegates at public meetings that finally ended in the establishment of the International, the American war against slavery provided the setting and created the conditions for it.

French labor's inclination in the early sixties to act independently was a disappointment to the imperial ruling hierarchy. Napoleon had suppressed the labor organizations upon his rise to power in 1851. In the following six years capitalism rose to heights that François Guizot, the Minister of Louis Philippe, had never contemplated. The mania for getting rich governed political life. The "thirst for lucre," "the infatuation of gambling," Count Montalembert observed, carried away men in small towns and villages.[14] But the economic crisis of 1857 rudely shook people's faith in the permanence of the imperial system. To what extent the faith lost its hold on workers cannot be established for they had no means of publicizing their views. Their votes, however, helped to elect five deputies of the liberal opposition in 1857. Then, too, they waged a number of strikes for higher wages to check the steady decline of their standard of living.[15] After 1857 a new strike movement began for the defense of existing wage scales. Observers saw, however, that the penalties imposed on strikers were milder than they had been, and that the victims were often pardoned.

The Emperor apparently signified an intention to take the course toward liberalism. The amnesty of political prisoners and his aid to Italian unity in 1859 were two signs of his new policy. Indicative, too, was his benevolence to labor. Under the influence of ex-Saint-Simonians, he made a bid for workers' support in exchange for a number of concessions. He subsidized papers that were partial to labor; he gathered around him labor men to advise him on labor policies, and a team of them published a series of pamphlets to show that he was the workers' best friend;[16] and he permitted them to elect delegates to the International Exhibition of 1862, even contributed to the expenses. Two years later he modified the combination laws, permitting workers to organize.

It is difficult to learn the degree to which Napoleon's new policy of tolerating labor persuaded workers to seek guidance at the Imperial Palace. But it is a fact that after 1860 they exhibited an increasing hostility to the Empire, and either took their stand with the liberal opposition or followed their own path. Several events signalized this trend. First, workers continued to strike in an effort to equate wages with rising prices. Second, the labor committee in Paris, headed by Tolain, won the concession of electing the labor delegation to the Exhibition of 1862. Committees in other cities imitated the one in the capital. The election in Paris brought out almost 200,000 workers who chose 200 delegates.[17] Since the total number of French delegates was 750, according to the official estimate, electing them became a workers' movement that the police regarded with suspicion. Third, in the general elections of 1863, the labor ballots helped to raise the number voting for the liberal opposition to almost 2,000,000 that entitled it to thirty-two deputies.[18] Already, in this election, the labor group, led by J. J. Blanc and Henri Tolain, ran two independent candidates in Paris. Though their vote was too small to be of any account, the candidacies were a token of the political reawakening of French labor.

The small vote for labor candidates in 1863 did not discourage the nomination of Tolain for a by-election in Paris in 1864. This was the occasion for sixty workers to issue a manifesto. Known as the Manifesto of the Sixty, it was not a call to arms, not even a summons to form a labor party. All it asked for was labor's right to send deputies to parliament where they could present its demands. The program was mild enough. Apart from the freedom of the press and the separation of church and state, the workers desired free and compulsory education and the freedom of labor. With that they coupled free credit in the hope of saving the artisan and small producer from going under.[19] In sum, the Manifesto was a moderate document many liberals might have endorsed. Proudhonist in inspiration, it in turn inspired Proudhon to write his last work, *De la capacité politique des classes ouvrières*. Still the Manifesto was the starting point of a broad labor agitation. The law on coalitions, authorizing workers to organize, and following the by-election by four days, was not an act of Napoleon's benevolence but a concession to the quickening labor movement. It is not without interest that nine of the signers of the Manifesto joined the First International, founded approximately seven months later.

2

If the object of Louis Napoleon was to bridge the gap between his government and the workers, his policy in North America was not calculated to achieve it. The defense of slavery was the least popular program, especially in a country that had pioneered in slave emancipation. It was obvious towards the end of 1862 that Napoleon's government could not recognize the Confederacy. Instead of remaining neutral he secretly countenanced the pro-slavery propaganda of its envoys in France and inspired the press and pamphleteers to champion intervention or mediation. Further, he embarked on the far-reaching plan of becoming the next-door neighbor and possible protector of the Confederacy by invading Mexico. There he counted on setting up a Catholic Latin Empire.

The expedition at first neither stirred strong opposition nor aroused enthusiasm in France. It had its apologists, of course, just as the Confederacy did. But the expedition and the Confederacy also had articulate adversaries. We cannot, for want of space, explore French public reaction to the Mexican adventure. If the unpublished reports of the Procureurs généraux and of the police in the various departments are any test of opinion, the expedition was clearly unpopular by 1865, and demands for the withdrawal of the French troops were fairly general.[20] Though interference in Mexico was in the general pattern of Napoleon's North American policy, our primary concern here is with its relation to the struggle over slavery. We need not dwell long on the arguments of its French defenders, for their reasoning was identical with that of Southern slave owners in America and their friends in Great Britain. But there was a Gallic twist to pro-slavery propaganda in France. Its partisans here maintained that both economically and ethnically the South was closer to Europe, to France in particular, than to the North; economically, they asserted, because the major portion of their raw cotton went to Europe; and ethnically, because they were more Gallo-Roman than Anglo-Saxon. It was true that Europe consumed more bales of Southern cotton than the North. England alone bought almost 2,700,000 bales in the United States from 1859 to 1860. French imports of American cotton in the same period, however, amounted approximately to 590,000 bales, and its total consumption of raw cotton was sizably below that of the North.[21] The ethnic argument was pure fantasy. Propaganda, however, need not rest on scientific evidence. Its purpose, in this instance, was to justify Napoleon's intervention in Mexico and his future claim to the Louisiana territory his uncle had sold to the United States.[22] Louis Napoleon had dreams of empire that were every bit as great as his predecessor's, but his talents and statesmanship were of the mediocre variety. And his reckoning omitted public opinion at home.

French partisans of the Confederacy were men of high social status and influence. They were makers of policy, cotton manufacturers, merchants in Bordeaux and Le Havre, bankers who had floated Southern loans in England and France, and the Catholic hierarchy. Further down in the social ladder were purchasers of Confederate bonds, rentiers and peasants who had staked some of their savings on the Mexican adventure. It should be said in qualification that a number of Catholic laymen, among them Count Montalembert, an ultramontanist and a prominent political leader, and Augustin Cochin, the sociologist, and the Church dignitary, Bishop Dupanloup, came to the defense of the North. On their side were the Duke de Broglie, who had presided over the Committee of 1843 for the Abolition of Slavery; François Guizot, historian and member of the French Academy; Edouard Laboulaye, a member of the Institute of France and a popular lecturer on American institutions at the Collège de France;[23] Henri Martin, the famous historian; and other esteemed scholars and publicists. These eminent representatives of French culture came together at the end of 1864 and organized the French Committee of Emancipation. Its two main objectives were to refute falsehoods of pro-slavery champions and to promote the cause of liberation in the United States.[24]

The opponents of slavery had the backing of influential newspapers —the *Siècle,* the *Temps,* the *Journal des débats,* the *Opinion nationale* and the *Phare de la Loire.* With them, too, were the liberal opposition in parliament and dozens of writers and scientists. Among them were Agénor Gasparin, a grandson of a member of the Committee of Public Safety in 1793 and the author of a book on the United States that had two American editions;[25] Elisée Reclus, the famous geographer; and Eugène Pelletan, publicist and parliamentarian, a sort of John Bright without his forensic talent. Gasparin's book can be summarized as a noble plea for human rights. Reclus contended that the slave owners were wasting themselves in a hopeless cause. Even if they won a separate existence, they could not maintain themselves economically, he held, for the raising of cotton with slave labor required constant expansion into virgin territories, and that had its limits.[26]

Eugène Pelletan's defense of the North was one of the most ardent and cogent. He portrayed the planters as hypocritical, idle and pleasure seeking men whose conscience about slavery had long been unburdened by their clergy. Then he charged that they had been plotting the Civil War for a long time. Regarding themselves as cotton kings, they calculated that they could dictate terms to the North. The Yankees, they reckoned, would not risk throwing their industries into disorder and their workers on the streets for the sake of national unity. Nor would the European powers allow the Southern ports to be sealed. Any party in a nation that counted on foreign intervention to achieve its end, he said, was afflicted with moral leprosy. The South, he was certain, could never be victorious, for it lacked resources and high principles. Turning to the Emancipation Proclamation, he said that it had given the North the moral initiative and a worthy program that would inspire the slaves to seek their freedom. At this point he paid tribute to the patient genius of Abraham Lincoln whom he likened to Admiral Coligny, the French Huguenot leader, and to William of Orange, the gallant fighter for Dutch independence. Touching on the Mexican adventure, Pelletan warned his countrymen that it would embroil France in exhausting campaigns. He looked to the revolutionary traditions of his country to keep it from being the ally of such an anachronism as a slave state. And he reminded Frenchmen that their great Revolution "was the first to give freedom to the Negroes."[27]

Both sides of the controversy over slavery undoubtedly won converts in France. But the anti-slavery side seems to have had the great mass of opinion with it, according to a Confederate agent in Europe. Writing to his superior, the Southern Secretary of State, on September 26, 1863, he assessed the situation as follows: "With the exception of the Emperor and his nearest personal adherents, all the intelligence, the science, the social respectability is leagued with the ignorance and the radicalism in a deep-rooted antipathy—rather than active hostility against us." The Emperor would never dare provoke this array of opinion, the agent regretfully reported. Comparing the different outlooks on slavery in England and France, he found an almost complete antithesis between them. His explanation was as follows: "It is much easier for the English, accustomed to a hierarchy of classes at home, and to a haughty domination abroad, to understand a hierarchy of races than it is for the French, the apostles of universal equality, and who have sacrificed so much to their creed. Few of our friends understand the full force of this fact in its bearing upon the political action of the Government. The Emperor, from the very magnitude of his power, cannot afford to offend so universal a feeling, and he cannot act as he wishes, unless by conciliating that feeling with some manifest and dazzling material advantage, or by creating such a situation as to give him the excuse of necessity."[28]

The Confederate agent in reality confirmed Eugène Pelletan's point on the pervading power of the French revolutionary principles. Nor was the agent alone in doing so. His Secretary of State, on the basis of independent research, concluded that "Abolition sentiments are quietly assumed as philosophical sentiments too self-evident to require comment or elaboration. . . ."[29]

The French anti-slavery current, in other words, was deep and broad. It was so wide and strong that Napoleon himself, save for his entourage and the subsidized press, felt isolated. Indeed the Procureurs généraux, the Emperor's faithful servants, were reporting that merchants and manufacturers in such cities as Bordeaux, Le Havre and Rouen regarded the secession of the Southern States as a *fait accompli* and counted on the Emperor to recognize them.[30] But the mass of the workers remained cold to pro-Confederate propaganda. Though they were without jobs or food, they did not call for intervention on the side of the South. Like the workers in England, they preferred to suffer rather than to be allies of slave owners. If they did not publicly demonstrate their stand with free labor, as their English brethren did, the reason lay in the political restrictions. Meetings of more than twenty were forbidden. French workers were silent; but theirs was the silence of the penitentiary. The following themes recur in the reports of the Procureurs: the workers are calm; the workers bear their suffering patiently; the workers avoid any demonstration likely to disturb the peace.[31]

At no time, during the American Civil War, when they were reforming their organizations and starting on an independent political course, were there reports of workers' disturbances that might have challenged the authority of Louis Napoleon. To provoke such a challenge, a Procureur wrote on January 9, 1862, "exceptionally important events would be needed."[32] Such events came eight years later. Meanwhile the Mexican expedition incited hostile sentiments that even merchants and industrialists shared. How much resentment it produced among workers is impossible to gauge. But they seem to have joined the ever mounting opinion against intervention in Mexico. That was a less suspect way of opposing intervention on behalf of the slave owners.[33]

Circumspect, even devious, in their sympathy with the North, French workers nevertheless exhibited it in every available way. Silence before official propaganda was one. The use of the ballot Louis Napoleon had left them after his coup d'état was a second. Thus the Procureur of Lyons reported that the increase of the opposition in the election of 1863 derived from many causes, among them "the American war and the Mexican campaign."[34]

3

News of Lincoln's assassination released French popular feeling for the Northern cause. Emotional restraints were thrown off, regardless of possible reprisals. The general sadness the tragedy caused in Northern France, for example, where the cotton famine had had the worst effects, showed how deep the feeling was. Reporting the extent of the sorrow, the Procureur wrote: "After having gone through many confusions and anxieties, at one time produced by personal interest, at another by humanity, current opinion unanimously applauds the stubborn resistance of the North and its triumph. It is, after all, the triumph of the good cause."[35]

The office of John Bigelow, American Minister to France, was flooded with messages of condolence from all over the country. The reaction to Lincoln's death was quite unexpected and unprecedented. To William Cullen Bryant, Bigelow wrote: "Familiar as I supposed I was with the current of public opinion here towards the U.S., I had no idea of the interest with which the progress of our war has been watched by the masses. I am quite sure the death of no other foreign sovereign or subject, by whatever means, would have produced so much emotion."[36] His dispatch to Secretary William Seward, enclosing testimonials, had this to say: "they will suffice to show not only how profoundly the nation was shocked by the dreadful crime which terminated President Lincoln's earthly career, but how deep a hold he has taken upon the respect and affections of the French people. It is difficult to exaggerate the enthusiasm which his name inspires among the masses of Europe at this moment—an enthusiasm before which the ruling classes, however little disposed to waste compliments upon anything tainted with republicanism, are obliged to incline."[37]

Even Napoleon's government had to bow before the national sentiment. The *Corps législatif* had to be called together in special session to satisfy the public demand. The official message to the United States was reserved. But seventy-four deputies of the Left signed their own address, saying: "United from the bottom of our hearts with the American citizens, we desire to express to them our admiration of the great people who have destroyed the last vestiges of slavery, and for Lincoln, the glorious martyr of duty."[38]

A subscription for a medal, "to glorify the hero of American democracy," forced the government to reveal its true position. An appeal for ten centimes (two cents) per person, "to recruit the greatest number of adherents," according to the police, had so much response all over the country that it had to intervene and confiscate a number of lists. Still, forty thousand persons answered the call. The medal sent to Mrs. Lincoln bore the following inscription:

"To Lincoln, twice chosen President of the United States, from the grateful Democracy of France. Lincoln the Honest abolished slavery, reestablished the Union, saved the Republic, without veiling the Statue of Liberty."[39]

Letters and addresses arrived at Bigelow's office from numerous organizations and eminent persons, from students and workers. The French Committee of Emancipation recalled Lincoln's humble origin and several of his great speeches.[40] Masonic lodges conveyed their sorrow over the loss of the famous American. An expression of grief, signed by the editors of four leading liberal newspapers in Paris, was, by implication, a rebuke to Louis Napoleon. "Abraham Lincoln," they said, "will be lamented as he has been admired by French democracy."[41] Elisée Reclus wrote from Sicily to convey his deep concern over the death of the great man.[42] And Professor Edouard Laboulaye's letter was in a sense his students' too. Speaking on Benjamin Franklin, he "embraced the occasion," to use his own words, "to speak of President Lincoln. Never in my life as a professor have my words awakened so much sympathy. Three times in succession the hall applauded with an enthusiasm which was not for the speaker, but for the noble victim of a cowardly assassin. You ought to see how great is the emotion in Paris— far greater than I supposed."[43]

The American Minister already had some knowledge of the student's feelings. For on April 28, 1865, he had received a delegation bearing an address by a students' committee. The address had just been the cause of a demonstration of students of whom at least twelve hundred had set out to escort the delegation. But soldiers and police stopped them and made a number of arrests.[44] The signature of A. Rey, a medical student, at the end of the address showed it had some connection with the socialist groups of the University, where Louis Auguste Blanqui was exerting influence. Towards the end of 1865, Rey went as a delegate to the international student Congress at Liége where his materialistic and anti-Napoleonic statements brought about his expulsion from the University.

The address of the students to Bigelow mirrored some of the radical teachings then taking seed in France. "In President Lincoln, we weep for a fellow citizen" they said; "for no country is shut up now; and our country is that [there] where there are neither masters nor slaves; where every man is free, or is fighting to become free." After this romantic excursion into internationalism, the students identified themselves with John Brown, Abraham Lincoln and William Seward, as exemplars of real democracy. It continued, "We young people to whom the future belongs must have the courage to found a true democracy; and we will have to look beyond the ocean to learn how a people who have made themselves free can preserve their freedom."[45]

The last sentence was in the nature of a threat to the imperial system. The threat seemed all the more actual after the endorsement of the address and of similar ones by workers' groups. Workers in the muslin industry of Tarare, not too distant from Lyons, associated themselves, "heart and soul, with the addresses of the students and the four journals of Paris—addresses so conformable with the true sentiments of liberty, justice, and hope, and stamped with such grievous sympathy."[46]

Though the address of the workers from Tours to the American minister made no reference to the above students' communication, it was as optimistic and had a similar warning to Napoleon's régime. The document merits citation, because it so genuinely expressed the sentiments of French workers and their difficulties under the Empire. Save for the opening sentence it reads:

"It was hard to obtain 208 signatures in a city where there is only one newspaper, where the press only speaks the official language of the prefecture, where liberty is limited by policemen and public functionaries, and where democracy's warmest partisans are among the common people.

"Our document will reach you after passing through the soiled hands of our hardy workmen, who cannot leave the sheet spotless, whereon they have put their hearts with the signature of their hands to express their sympathy for the great republic.

"It is not you, a representative of a country where labor leads to the highest dignities of the nation, that will disdain our address because it carries the visible impress of hands devoted to work.

"These are the hands that will break, in this country, all the bonds and fetters that are put on liberty, under the specious pretext of measuring and regulating its gait; these are the hands that will shake most cordially those of your citizens."[47]

Workers in Paris seem to have been less articulate on the American struggle against slavery than workers in the provinces. A possible explanation was that their leaders in the capital were Proudhonists who tried, as their master had done, to dissuade workers from embarking on political action. But even Proudhonists could not long resist the march of history. Beginning in 1863, it has been shown, they asked the workers to vote for independent labor candidates. The same leaders, impelled by the international events, crossed to England where, together with English trade unionists and political exiles, they organized the International Workingmen's Association. Set up in London in September 1864, it gradually spread in Europe and the United States.

Its corresponding members in Paris, Proudhonists from first to last, could not withstand the flood of sympathy Lincoln's death had released. They did not draft their own address; nor did they affix their names to those of students or workers. They accepted instead the moderate and cautious address of the French Committee of Emancipation, signed by the historian Henri Martin, appealing for conciliation between the conflicting parties of the Civil War.[48] The address was so much milder than, programmatically almost the reverse of, the one of the General Council of the International, calling on President Johnson to avoid "any compromise with stern duties," and to complete the task of emancipation,[49] that it is difficult to believe both could have been endorsed by the French representatives of the International. Yet, that was probably the case. For, however much French labor leaders had countenanced the emancipation of slaves they had no settled policy calculated to secure the rights of the freed Negroes.

There is nothing in the unpublished minutes of the General Council to indicate that the Paris bureau of the International took exception to the Council's address. In all likelihood the Parisian delegates at the Conference of the International in 1865 associated themselves with the rest at once to celebrate the founding of the International and to commemorate the triumph of national unity and free labor in the United States. An address issued by the Conference to the American People, dated September 25, 1865, exhorted them fully to emancipate the Negroes if they wished to secure the nation against violent disturbances. The words of the address on this point were as follows:

"Injustice against a fraction of your people having been followed by such dire consequences, put an end to it. Declare your fellow citizens from this day forth free and equal, without any reserve. If you refuse them citizens' rights while you exact from them citizens' duties, you will sooner or later face a new struggle which will once more drench your country in blood. . . .

We therefore admonish you, as brothers in a common cause, to sunder all the chains of freedom, and your victory will be complete."[50]

The anti-slavery sentiment of French workers thus came into the open. Though they were still subject to severe, imperial, scrutiny, though they could not yet manifestly repudiate government policies, though their trade unions, partly through retarded industrial development and partly through legal restraint, lacked the organizational strength of the British unions, they were already challenging the Napoleonic system. It is safe to say that the American Civil War, during which they endured extreme hardships without falling prey to the propaganda of interventionists, served to crystallize among them a feeling of unity, national and international. Their grim, silent, suffering had a power and an eloquence all its own. It helped stay the hand of the pro-Confederate party in France.

THE FIRST INTERNATIONAL IN FRANCE, 1864-1871

MEN and things were slipping from Louis Napoleon's grip towards the end of the sixties. Intervention in Mexico had turned out a fiasco. Holders of Mexican bonds could scarcely continue confidence in the Emperor of the French who had been behind the sordid and humiliating adventure. Almost timed with it was Prussia's rapid triumph over Austria in 1866. Napoleon had counted on an exhaustive war, with himself as peace-maker in Western Europe, possibly rewarded with territory for his trouble. Instead he found facing him a strong, victorious state, blocking his path to the center of the Continent. It was a diplomatic defeat. Without allies, he could depend only on his military prestige and perhaps on a united France. Neither one had been seriously tested since the Austro-Sardinian War of 1859, when the cause of Italian unity was at stake. Napoleon's aid to the Italians had then earned him popularity, not to mention Nice and Savoy in payment for his assistance. What could he expect after 1866? Prussia was a real challenge. And his power at home had weakened since 1859. The republican opposition was stronger; the labor movement had grown; strikes were more numerous; the press was more articulate and defiant. In short the domestic scene had impending signs of coming tempests.

Each wing of the opposition had its objectives. On the extreme right were conservative republicans whose principal aim was to replace the Emperor with their own men. Their republic was the kind the Girondins had visualized and the Thermidorians had established. Then there were radicals who modeled themselves after the old Jacobins. Theirs was a democratic republic that would at once secure private property and probably enact some social reforms. Radical leaders were fairly popular among urban small owners, shopkeepers and artisans. Left of the neo-Jacobins were socialists of different persuasions, principally Proudhonists and Blanquists.

134

1

Since the law of 1864 that had relaxed restraints on labor coalitions, French labor had grown into the best organized part of the republican opposition. By the end of 1869 trade union councils had arisen in Marseilles, Lyons, Rouen and Paris. In March 1870 they held a congress and set up a provisional committee with the high aim of calling into being a national federation. A summons for a national labor congress to be held in May went out from the labor federation of Rouen, led by Emile Aubry, a printer. Postponed to the end of June, the congress was finally forbidden.[1] The government had meanwhile arrested leading members of the First International in France and had already begun the third trial of its Paris bureau.

Evidence of labor's antagonism to the imperial system was the strike waves that passed over France, beginning in 1865. Most of the strikes seem to have been waged for higher wages. People were quick to lay them to the toleration given to trade unions by the law of 1864. Undoubtedly there was a connection between the law and labor's mounting unrest. With larger organizations workers were better prepared to defend their demands. But the deeper causes of the strikes must be looked for in the economic conditions with which the political situation was bound up. The cost of living had risen during the sixties in France,[2] in fact in all of western Europe. The high cost of government in France, due to foreign adventure and preparations for war, had contributed to a reduced standard of living. But it also had its roots in the rebuilding of Paris in order to forestall street insurrections, in the rapid rise of modern industry, the wide employment of women and children, the beginnings of industrial concentration, and the larger world supply of precious metals after the discovery of gold in California. All these conditions were behind the many strikes in France during the sixties. In another respect, they were symptoms of opposition to the imperial system as a whole.

Labor had revived from the prolonged silence and sluggishness it had been cast into after 1848. Its press after 1864, ephemeral and heavily censored, stubbornly exposed social wrongs and maladies. In addition to the liberal press that reported labor news and fought for elemental freedoms, there were newspapers of comparatively long duration, *Le Courrier français*, *Le Réveil* and *La Marseillaise*, that were outright defenders of labor's interests. Though the chief editors were not strictly labor leaders, their immediate associates on the staff and their important contributors were trade unionists and socialists. Among them should be singled out Emile Aubry in Rouen, Henri Tolain and Eugène Varlin, both from Paris, and Benoît Malon, a self-taught farm hand, who had established himself in the capital. Then there were Albert

Richard of Lyons, son of a foreman in a silk factory, with leanings to journalism, and André Bastelica, a Corsican, working as a clerk in Marseilles. The two, if evaluated in terms of the entire French labor movement at the time, were perhaps lesser figures than the first four. Two of them, Tolain and Varlin, ranked high among men of labor. The first, a metal worker and the organizer of his trade, had led a campaign in Paris for labor's independent political action,[3] and had been one of the founders of the First International. But his general theories did not mix readily with the events. He found himself outdistanced by younger men as the pace of the times increased and the mood of labor became more resolute.

The second, Varlin, was perhaps the most respected and far seeing of the younger men. He was a bookbinder by trade, and a tireless organizer of trade unions and labor cooperatives. From his experience he had derived conclusions that put him far in advance of other labor leaders. He had first been a Proudhonist, but the stubborn political issues under the Empire had forced him into political action. The paths of labor intersected and converged, he held, and none could be neglected. The future belonged to the trade unions, he believed, for his credo was akin to what was later known as revolutionary syndicalism. The first step towards that future was a national federation of trade unions. It alone was the surest link with organized labor in other countries. Varlin, a zealous champion of the First International, was considered in France one of its best brains.[4]

The story of French labor from 1865 to 1871 would be defective and jejune if it omitted the First International. Its history in France has been so overcast with vituperation, so coated in fustian and imbedded in ideological controversy, that a good account of it still awaits the historian.[5] Within the space of a short essay can be given only its very general historical outline in France.

Many currents met to create the Association in London in 1864. The principal ones were: the renewed struggles for national liberation; the cotton famine in Europe, growing out of the American Civil War and painfully revealing labor's common interests, regardless of frontiers; the need of workers' mutual assistance against the menace of militarism; the bloody suppression of the gallant Poles in 1863; and finally the urgency on the part of labor, especially in England, of preventing the importation of scabs.

The first French bureau of the International was set up in Paris in 1865, in extremely modest headquarters and with an empty treasury. Its growth was very slow during the first two years. Inner friction between manual workers and intellectuals, Blanquist hostility to the Proudhonist program of the Paris branch, government suspicion and officially inspired rival organizations, charges of ties with the imperial palace leveled at its leaders, and emphasis in its program on credit and co-operation and on political neutrality, all of these factors together kept it from fanning out in its early period. Still in the first two years the bureau managed to distribute 20,000 copies of the rules and statutes of the International. A possible reason for the bureau's survival in its nascent period was its reliance from the start on the remaining cadres that had been formed around the Manifesto of the Sixty.

The changing political and economic climate steadily brought adherents to the International in France. Already in 1866, the General Council in London received news that sections were in existence in a number of French cities—in Rennes, Rouen, Lyons, Bordeaux, Vienne and in many smaller areas. They asked for more membership cards, announced large meetings organized by Internationalists and reported that employers were threatening to discharge workers if they joined the Association.[6] In September 1866, its first congress in Geneva, attended by seventeen French delegates from four sections, officially adopted its statutes. Four of its resolutions called for the abolition of the wage system, the eight hour day, cooperation, and the united effort of workers in all countries to check the importation of strike-breakers.[7] The congress had enough notice in the French press to bring upon it harassment by Napoleon's government.

From 1867 to the outbreak of the Franco-Prussian War in 1870 French Internationalists felt his heavy official hand. They inevitably became leaders of strikes, however incompatible that was with their Proudhonist convictions. They took part in politics by openly demonstrating against French reoccupation of Rome. And they countenanced the republican League of Peace and Freedom. This was too much for the imperial government. Two trials of the Paris bureau in 1868 ended in orders to dissolve and in penalties for its members.[8]

The orders prevented the branch in the capital from functioning or solidifying its strength. But it apparently spread to the provinces. Of the eighteen French delegates at the third congress of the International in 1868, a number spoke for sections in new towns and cities, among them Caen and Marseilles, where a section had been in existence since October 1867. Twenty-seven French delegates at the congress of 1869 represented eight towns and cities. Sections in Amiens, Nantes and Avignon, for example, either could not afford the expenses of a delegate or were intimidated by the police.

The International in France went on growing, official pressure notwithstanding. Its strength derived principally from its close bonds with trade unions. Wherever important strikes went on, there Internationalists were in leading posts. This is not to suggest that they provoked strikes, for the policy was to avoid them whenever possible. But once workers laid down the tools or were locked out, Internationalists did what they could to achieve victory. They drew on strike funds and collected aid for the families. They appealed for help to local organizations and to the General Council in London; they organized meetings, assisted in the negotiations and dissuaded the strikers from acts of violence. Also, when a call for help came from other countries, French Internationalists asked workers for contributions. Actually that had become the practice in the entire organization.

Persecution naturally disorganized many sections of the International in France. They could not meet save secretly. The collection of dues was difficult, not to mention the recruiting of members. But the energy with which Internationalists built trade unions and defended strikers won workers' gratitude and enlistments. Entire unions allied themselves with the International. Inspired by Internationalists, they tended to unite in central labor councils. The first seems to have arisen in the fall of 1869 in Rouen, and the second in Marseilles, with twenty-two unions.[9] Others followed in Lyons and Paris; and in March 1870, it has been pointed out, they held a special congress to project their federation. Further plans to unite nationally were cut short by an official order.

Seen superficially, the International in France gave the appearance of a powerful body that could marshal its millions of members. Government agents, whose secret reports indicate that they knew better, let it be known that the French branch alone had in its heyday from about 500,000 to 5,000,000 on its lists. But their estimates were fantastic. While an accurate count of French Internationalists has never been made, in view of the absence of reliable evidence, students of the organization in France have set the number of its followers much below that claimed by the authorities. And the students' estimates are at best very approximate. Louis Reybaud, a semi-official publicist, credited the entire organization in Europe with 1,000,000 members in 1867,[10] even though it then had but small nuclei in Western Europe. In 1868, when it had barely begun to spread outside of the French capital, the government said it had 160,000 members in France.[11] The figure for 1869 jumped to more than 357,000, and for 1870 to 433,485.[12] More extravagant reckonings, on a par with Reybaud's, gave it millions of adherents. If we turn to comparatively sober accounts we are told that the organization had at most 250,000;[13] and Benoît Malon, one of its leaders, set the figure at 200,000.[14]

Even if we allow the inflated figures, the International was weak and badly knit. Reports of French sections to the General Council in London disclose a frightful lack of cohesion, a highly fluctuating membership, a perpetual struggle to keep alive, to hold meetings and collect dues. They were almost habitually poor. Sections usually inclined before the tenets of their leaders, and there were many different persuasions. Some shared Proudhon's faith in credit and cooperation, his political abstentionism and rejection of strikes, even his conservative views on women and education. Others, having started as his disciples but having found themselves at odds with the raw facts, scrapped his credo. Still others were drawn to Michael Bakunin's anarchism and talked of revolution as if it were a toy or an exciting escapade. Others still nourished their creed with memories of 1793 or were in sympathy with Louis Auguste Blanqui's teachings without enrolling in his party. Available evidence discloses that not a single leader of the International in France before 1870 subscribed to Marx's teachings. One explanation was that Marx's name was practically unknown there before the Paris Commune, to say nothing of his principles. Léo Frankel, who adopted them after 1871, was a Proudhonist; and Varlin, perhaps the top Internationalist in France, came close to a syndicalist outlook, as we have already shown. A reading of the published and unpublished writings of French Internationalists prior to 1871 reveals a looseness of thought and a thoroughly meaningless, even reckless, use of concepts and terms commonly met with in labor theoretical literature. They were moved by some vague and ideal order that had not yet taken form in their minds. But political difficulties and the problems they encountered as leaders of trade unions saved many of them from violent fits of fancy, even held them knee-deep in reality.

Peripheral to the International were radical elements. The principal ones were the neo-Jacobin republicans and the small party headed by Louis Auguste Blanqui. The first, rejoicing in the expectations of yesterday, had their eyes fixed on the past rather than on new horizons. To them 1793 represented what had once and for all been settled and clarified. In enthusiasm for principles they had few equals. And though it was wedded to a cobwebbed cause, it was highly serviceable to the republican and democratic movements of the sixties. The second, the Blanquists, formed a compact group that took its orders from the small, austere, thin and ascetic looking, white haired Blanqui. He had had long practice in planning insurrections. His name inspired devotion and fear. He had the complete allegiance of disciples and of members of his party. Bonapartists, right republicans, even Proudhonists, however, trembled at the sound of his name. In economic thought he had not advanced beyond the Utopians of the third and fourth decades of the nineteenth century. His social theory was eclectic, an aggregate of many strands drawn from as many schools. But his political creed inspired apprehension. For his was the belief that a group of daring men of unquestioned obedience to the leader, could seize political power by a sudden, surprise attack. Such a group or party was necessarily clandestine, removed from the people, subject to a plan, worked out in advance in the highest echelons. Once the insurgents had taken up arms, the movement, it was expected, would assume a broad character and take in the workers.

The Blanquist party was pyramidal and closely united. Practically all its strength was in Paris, in the first place among students, and to a small degree among workers. In numbers it never exceeded 2,500 men; and its propaganda, at one time noisy and at another mysterious, was at best limited. Its press was ephemeral, designed more for the *déclassés*. Among workers it gained comparatively few recruits. Despite Blanqui's instructions "to pay more attention to the workers," the organization never succeeded in setting roots in labor groups.[15] Actually its framework and tactics were utterly inadequate for agitation among workers, and all its efforts to compete with the Proudhonists for labor's following turned out to be fruitless.

For Proudhonists were trade union leaders whose programs promised either to secure the economic status of the craft worker through cheap credit or to restore his economic independence *via* cooperation. The failure of the cooperative bank in 1868 naturally shook confidence in the remedy and caused workers to rely more on political action. But many others continued to regard cooperation as the way to economic betterment, perhaps to salvation.

Blanquists made war on this persuasion, declaring it to be an illusion that enervated the labor movement. Partly because cooperation persisted as a fundamental tenet among French Internationalists, a breach existed between them and the Blanquists. Watching the proceedings of the Association from his exile in Belgium, Blanqui grew more mistrustful of it. All advances from London to reconcile Proudhonists and Blanquists were in vain.[16] They remained apart, though a common enemy and critical situations should have united them.

2

The threat of a war with Prussia hung over France. Neither Louis Napoleon nor Bismarck tried to reduce tensions, to work out a modus vivendi, for on each side of the frontier dynastic ambitions were at stake. The Prussian dynasty, apart from the aim of uniting Germany under its domination, believed that by defeating a descendant of Bonaparte, who had humiliated it in 1806, it would raise its prestige in Europe. The French Emperor counted on a war to restore his sinking reputation. The opposition at home was mounting. Economic conditions were far from bright, for the fear of war made business men hesitate to invest.

Napoleon sought confirmation for his regime in plebiscites, but the negative vote steadily increased. Liberal republicans, radicals, trade unionists and Internationalists seem to have temporarily found common ground.

The year 1870 opened unhappily for the government. A large strike at Creusot led to a battle with troops and to casualities. There were protests all over France. In the same month Prince Pierre Bonaparte, a royal ruffian, killed Victor Noir, a radical journalist on the staff of *Marseillaise*. The funeral was a vast demonstration. Perhaps a sign of the trend of opinion was the daily sale of more than 100,000 copies of *Marseillaise* that publicized the doings and doctrines of the International. Reports from Procureurs généraux told of growing unrest in the provinces: there was a slump in business; the Creusot strike had awakened wide sympathy for the strikers; the behavior of Pierre Bonaparte was none too flattering for the dynasty. Uncertain about the outcome of the strike movement and troubled by the agitation in the capital, political factions of the upper social strata rallied around the imperial regime.

The government looked upon the International as the fomenter of the trouble and as the most formidable obstacle to its plans for war. Congresses of the International had taken a resolute position against it, going so far as to recommend a general strike to prevent it, without studying, however, the many grave difficulties the method might encounter. Considering the weakness of the trade unions, the recommendation was not likely to have an effect on policy. Of greater consequence was the exchange of addresses among Internationalists. In December 1869 Germans and Frenchmen exchanged manifestoes for the defense of 8,000 striking miners in Waldenbourg, Germany.[17] The following month the section of the International in Brussels voted its congratulations to the French workers in general and in particular to Henri Rochefort, editor of *Marseillaise*, for their firm stand in the affair of Victor Noir.[18] These expressions of workers' solidarity were sufficient to convince Napoleon's government that French Internationalists were obeying commands from abroad in order to weaken France.

Orders of the Minister of the Interior, dispatched by telegram, resulted in the arrest of many Internationalists throughout the country. Despite wide protests, thirty-eight were put on trial in Paris on the charge of conspiring against the regime. They were accused of being in league with foreign organizations in order to bring down the established order. Save for four, the rest were sentenced to fines and imprisonment. Trials in other French cities ended in similar verdicts, but several trials, in Lyons for instance, were interrupted by the Franco-Prussian War.

Their general effect was to disorganize the already loose sections of the International in France.

Thus, by the time the War started, the Association was in effect weaker than before. Important leaders were in jail or hiding. Its sections were skeleton groups; its members, scattered. In aim, it was as many tongued as the Tower of Babel. The allegedly strong Association with millions of followers, ready to respond to a call to arms, was incapable of interfering with Napoleon's drive towards war.

The Franco-Prussian War felled the French Second Empire. Its armies were unprepared; the provinces lacked enthusiasm. When the Parisians learned of Napoleon's capitulation at Sedan on September 2, 1870, they replaced the Empire with a republic.

The republican Government of National Defense did not represent a radical break with the old political forms. Save for two of its members, Léon Gambetta and Henri Rochefort, the rest were defenders either of existing institutions, minus an emperor, or were closely allied to the fallen Empire. Though the government declared it would wage war to the end it was disposed to negotiate an armistice. But large sections of the urban population, of the Parisian in particular, were differently minded. Swayed by French revolutionary traditions, they called for an all-out war against the invader. From September 1870 to March 1871, demonstrations succeeded one another, each with an object of opposing an armistice. Three were particularly menacing to the government. Workers and National Guardsmen protested in September against any negotiations with the enemy.[19] On October 31 demonstrators invaded city hall and set up a new provisional government with Blanqui at its head. It lasted but a few hours, because the Proudhonists, one observer concluded, had abandoned the cause.[20] Another attempt on January 22, 1871, to overthrow the government equally failed.[21]

There were imitations of the capital in provincial towns, notably in Brest, Marseilles and Lyons. They were all as unsuccessful. The most spectacular and reckless of these risings was in Lyons, where Michael Bakunin, the Russian anarchist, had seized power and proclaimed the abolition of the state. The National Guard quickly quashed the uprising and sent Bakunin scurrying to Geneva.

3

What was the policy, or, to be more accurate, what were the policies of the International in France during the Franco-Prussian War? We have seen it badly injured by the series of trials begun in June and continuing through September 1870. Branches, however, carried on the fight against the Empire and the War.

Anti-war manifestoes were legion. Early in July, shortly before the

French declaration of war, almost 200 French Internationalists addressed themselves "To the Workers of all Countries," denouncing what they called "a war for superiority and a dynastic war." Whether it was fought under the pretext "of European equilibrium or of national honor," it was "a criminal absurdity," a means of awakening savage instincts. They predicted that its results would be the destruction of humanity, the burning up of the wealth labor produced, and the suppression of civil liberties.[22]

The manifesto won the applause of other French Internationalists and inspired the writing of addresses. Sections in Rouen, Lyons and Marseilles, no less than in Paris, professed the solidarity of labor against the solidarity of despots. Replies to French manifestoes from Switzerland, Belgium, Spain and Germany[23] reechoed the same sentiments. The German Social Democratic Party answered that "the workers of all countries are our friends; the despots, our enemies." Sections in Barcelona said the difference between the International and the warring powers was the same as that between vitality and decadence. The manifesto of the section in Brussels declared that, without the overthrow of the existing social system, peace could never be secured.

All the manifestoes were in keeping with the stand the International had taken at its congresses and with appeals the General Council had issued from London. In view of the broad anti-war feeling the Council issued on July 26, 1870, its first address on the Franco-Prussian War, imputing it to the treachery of Napoleon and Bismarck. The absolute systems on both sides of the Rhine, said the Council, merited the reprobation of the workers whose exchange of fraternal greetings was a token of a better future.[24]

The altered character of the war as a result of the establishment of a republic in France caused Internationalists to shift their position. One of the first fruits of the political change was a decree of amnesty, setting free leading French Internationalists. A number tried to revive the labor organizations; others set about organizing relief for bereaved families. Under their direction, too, old sections came to life, and new ones sprang up. French Internationalists desired to defend the republic against monarchy and the nation against the invader. To these ends, many organized committees of safety and security in imitation of the Jacobins. The less imitative met emergencies with organizations best suited for the occasion. But such differences were not unusual. For the absence of a common program and strategy had been a special quality of the International in France. Sections in separate localities, judging by their pronunciamentos, were more or less internationalist in outlook or chauvinist.

The Paris sections seem at first to have exhibited comparative calmness. The evening of September 4 their Federal Council issued an appeal to the German people, urging them to withdraw to their own country. The French wanted peace without the sacrifice of territory. Instead of making war on each other, the two peoples should forge fraternal bonds and cooperate for the extinction of international hatred.[25] The sections in Rouen fully shared the views of this manifesto,[26] but sections in Marseilles drafted another that had little of the international spirit.[27]

Sections in the provinces looked to Paris for directives. Shortly after releasing the above manifesto, the Council of the Paris Federation found itself under obligation to lay down the policy of French Internationalists during the War. They were to be guided by two objectives: the defense of Paris; and vigilance against reaction. The first could best be served through public meetings, republican committees, participation in the work of the municipalities and appeals to the Germans. But as precautions against the return of reaction, vigilance committees had to be set up. The Council epitomized the end of all activity under two heads: the stimulation of patriotism; and the adoption of measures calculated at once to defeat reaction and to introduce the beginnings of communes.[28]

Actually the Paris Council was providing French Internationalists with an immediate program that anticipated a bright tomorrow. Perhaps to suggest its underlying aims, the Federal Council demanded that the republican government should abolish the repressive legislation of the Empire, arm the National Guard, separate church and state, guarantee the freedom of the press and the right of labor to organize.[29]

German socialists and Internationalists also desired peace without annexation. The day after the declaration of the French republic, the Central Committee of the German Socialist Democratic Workmen's Party addressed itself to the German people, maintaining the necessity of an honorable peace. The German workers should state firmly that they would not tolerate any injury to the French people. If Germany annexed Alsace-Lorraine, it would make war a European institution, and compel France to seek an alliance with Russia. A just peace, on the other hand, would permit the free development of the Continent. For these reasons, the central committee protested against Germany's intentions of adding the provinces to the new Empire. In conclusion it appealed to German workers to stand faithfully by the workers "in all civilized countries for the common cause of labor."[30] Following the release of the manifesto the members of the central committee were arrested, chained and sent to a fortress.

French and German Internationalists, therefore, had a common peace program. They were totally in agreement that a new political situation in France made the continuance of the war and the annexation of French territory a thoroughly criminal policy that workers everywhere should denounce. With this object in view, the Paris Federal Committee appealed to the General Council in London to issue an address to Internationalists in all countries.

The debate at the General Council's meeting of September 6, 1870, disclosed a division on the nature of the address. British labor representatives were inclined to be critical of the French. They should sue for peace. After all, it was Napoleon who had started the war. A British member of the Council was ready to let Germany have Alsace-Lorraine, provided the inhabitants were consulted. Marx was the principal defender of the French. He pointed out that only the court party, aristocracy, and middle class wanted the provinces. Not a single workingmen's meeting had favored annexation. The unpublished minutes report Marx concluding as follows: "We had said in our first address that the death-knell of the Second Empire had sounded and that it would end by a parody that had already come to pass. We had also foreseen that the war might lose its defensive character and told the Germans if they allowed that victory or defeat would be alike disastrous. We had only to stick to what we had said already and appeal to the German working class to guard themselves against the Prussian government who had assumed another tone. The annexation would furnish a reason why Europe should keep armed. Russia and France would prepare for new wars to revenge the present war."[31]

The policy Marx had outlined became a cardinal theme in the General Council's second address on the Franco-Prussian War. It refuted the military considerations behind the German demand for Alsace-Lorraine. It would but cause a new war in which Russia would be the partner of France. The Address went on to say that the German workers, having borne the brunt of the war, desired guarantees that victory would not be turned into a defeat. The first guarantee they demanded was *"an honourable peace for France,* and the *recognition of the French republic."* Turning to the French workers, the Address cautioned them against any attempt to overthrow the republican government. They should instead perform their civic duties and utilize their new liberties to build stronger organizations. And they should also avoid being swayed by French revolutionary souvenirs. To repeat the past would prevent them from looking to the future.[32]

With the publication of the second address the agitation against the annexation of Alsace-Lorraine went into international gear. In England there was a movement for the recognition of the French Republic. Public meetings and delegations to prime minister Gladstone tried to force the government's hand. There was even a demand for British military intervention on the side of France.[33] But the agitation was powerless to impose a change of British policy. Besides English labor leaders themselves, in charge of the movement, did not push it vigorously enough.

Workers' activity in Germany in behalf of the French Republic brought them persecution. The Committee of the Socialist Democratic Workmen's Party was arrested, it has been said, for issuing a manifesto against annexation. A workers' demonstration in Leipzig was suppressed; and in Mayence four were expelled from the city for having agitated against the Prussian policy. There were protests in Berlin, Augsburg and Nuremberg, but the government was ruthless. *Volksstaat*, the organ of the Party, was in danger of being silenced. Bismarck called the socialists the nation's enemies, the allies of the International that was plotting to establish the universal republic.[34]

Germany's aim at aggrandizement aroused protests and meetings in the United States. The two sections of the International in New York, comparatively recent in origin, drew up a manifesto, denouncing Louis Napoleon and Germany's contemplated annexation of Alsace-Lorraine.[35] A large mass meeting, initiated by the two sections, was held in New York on November 19, 1870. An attendance of approximately 2,000 voted a series of resolutions condemning the war and annexation. The American Republic was requested to use its influence in behalf of France.[36]

4

A full balance sheet on the effect of the Franco-Prussian War on the International as a whole cannot be drawn up with the presently available data. Clearly while the organization benefited in certain countries it lost in others. If it gained new recruits in the United States its numbers were reduced in Germany, Austria and certainly in France. In the last country, its ranks were in confusion. Paul Lafargue reported from Bordeaux that it had made some advance in that city, but it had to face strong opposition from the officialdom. A report to the General Council from Rouen said that the old Bonapartist bureaucracy was harassing members and leaders. Aubry, the reporter, completely mistrusted the men at the head of the republic. News from Brest told the dismal story that the entire committee was under arrest on the charge of conspiracy. Some members had been sentenced to long terms of imprisonment. The section itself had dwindled in size.[37]

Division and bewilderment were also present among Internationalists in the capital. Here Auguste Serraillier served as envoy and observer for the General Council. He was a shoemaker by trade who had established himself in London. The account he later gave the Council on the state of the International in Paris was gloomy indeed. We shall follow it here.

Having arrived in the capital several days after the proclamation of the republic, Serraillier found the local branch disorganized and many of its members thoroughgoing chauvinists. Neither federal council nor sections were to be seen. Members were either in prison or in the regiments. According to his story, "Some were in the regular army, some in the National Guard, some in the Garde Mobile. The association was broken up." He met Charles Longuet, future son-in-law of Marx, and asked if the second address could be published in some newspaper. Apparently Longuet was not helpful. Félix Pyat, a journalist, an old Jacobin, and an enemy of the General Council, refused "because it was too Prussian." The *Réveil,* edited by Charles Delescluze, whose ideas had remained fixed since 1848, also refused to print the document. Serraillier then met Combault, "who was always a good man, but when I spoke of the International he replied: 'If you speak of the Germans as our equals I shall shoot you down. We can only talk of the Germans as the enemies on our soil.' "

At the demonstration of October 8, Serraillier continued, "all our members were present, but only as individuals, not as an association. There was no concerted action, they did nothing. Then I tried to get a meeting of the federal council to take some steps for the next demonstration which was to come off on the 31st of October, but they said they could not connect politics with the International. So the day was lost again. Blanqui was the only man who stuck to his post to the last; all the other great gods slipped off. The Internationals declined to support Blanqui. Had they done so, things would stand different with France today. Varlin, like the rest, declared that the International could not act politically as an association in this way. At every new attempt we must lose the day again."

Seeing he could not get the sections to elect a new federal council, because "the names of the familiars . . . were an obstacle to doing anything," Serraillier proceeded to set up a new branch in Paris. Eleven sections answered his appeal to send delegates. The new federal council's manifesto stirred the old federal council to summon the sections together in opposition to the new one. Apparently the existence of a rival body awakened the old guard from its lethargy, but only for a short time. Although they said they were ready to help in the demonstration of January 22, 1871, they failed to bring out the sections at the decisive moment. Only Malon appeared with his two sections. "We had everything in our hands, but the members of the government were allowed to get away, and then we were literally kicked out."

The conflict between the two Parisian branches became acute during the elections in February 1871. Several months of siege, in the midst of a hard winter, had exposed the incapacity of the Government of

National Defense. Paris was closely beset, but France had not yet been defeated. People suspected defeatism in the upper ruling set. Suffering and privation were not likely to make them tolerant of those they believed were wanting in patriotism. Then there was talk among workers of the social republic that might be theirs if present rulers were swept aside and a campaign begun in earnest against the invader. But towards the end of January 1871, representatives of France and Germany signed an armistice. A National Assembly had to be elected to decide on the question of war or peace. Serraillier proposed that the two federal councils present one list of candidates, of whom the new council would nominate but thirteen. The old leaders refused, first because Blanqui was one of Serraillier's nominees; second because the new council wanted the candidates to be endorsed by all the sections; third because the same council rejected an alliance with radical groups. Unable to come to terms, Parisian Internationalists entered the election with opposing candidates. Some Internationalists such as Malon, Tolain, and Varlin appeared on both lists.[38] The nominees of the new council were all defeated. Blanqui received only 52,000 votes. But Malon and Tolain were elected from the list of the old council.

The election on February 8, 1871, gave victory to the monarchists. Two-thirds of the new Assembly were royalists; and they were ready to accept Bismarck's terms. Nearly 100 deputies were conservative republicans, while twenty belonged to the extreme Left. Most of these had been chosen in Paris.

Serraillier was bitter against several Parisian Internationalists. "All that Tolain has done for the last three years [he said] was to go to the congress once a year and make a speech. He has made alliances with the bourgeoisie. He is said to represent the International but he does nothing for it. He has undeceived the bourgeoisie of the danger of the socialists. They can make anything they like of him. Malon, they say, is dreaming. Murat gave orders to arrest the two commandants, Piazza and Brunet, who were going to prevent the capitulation of Paris. He is quite with the middle class and has signed all the orders that were made in favor of the middle class." Serraillier promised to prefer charges against them at the next international congress.[39]

After his departure from Paris the two federal councils came together.

Serraillier's observations on the International in Paris are confirmed by the brief minutes of the meetings of its Federal Council for the months of January through March 1871. Its finances were so poor it could not found its own paper. Its dues had fallen off since September 4, 1870, according to Varlin; it had lost communication with the provinces; and it was negligent in its appeals to sections, according to

Frankel. The workers were not with the International, members acknowledged. Unemployment and their concern for the welfare of their families had inactivized them. The trade unions were feeble, and for the same reasons. Moreover, many were devoting themselves to the vigilance committees that had sprung up.[40] Attendance at council meetings was fairly poor. Out of an approximate thirty sections twenty-two had delegates at only one meeting, and that represented the maximum.

In the middle of February, the attempt was made to reorganize the Federal Council. Frankel believed the International had moral force. If a strong organization were created, its material strength would make it quite influential and give it an ascendancy over public opinion. There was general agreement on the objective, but how was reorganization to be effected? The first step, insisted Serraillier, who was still in Paris, was to end the breach among Internationalists. A committee was finally appointed to look into the status of each section.[41] From what is known the organization did not make progress. Promises and recommendations were not wanting; and the Council adopted revised statutes in the middle of March 1871. But they remained mere records of intentions.

Other problems were pressing. Food was far from plentiful; prices exceeded all bounds. Workers were restless, uncertain of tomorrow, troubled with debts and with arrears in rent. Then the question of a dual power was injected into the disturbed atmosphere, for in February 1871 the battalions of the National Guard in the capital formed a federation and elected a central committee to which the Federal Council delegated four of its members.[42] The Council recognized that it could not isolate itself from the largest organization in the city. Here it might have influence. But as an independent body it was powerless to have its policies accepted. The International in Paris could only follow events. It was incapable of directing them, as the Paris Commune demonstrated.

THE PARIS COMMUNE

SIX and a half months intervened between the proclamation of the republic on September 4, 1870 and the rise of the Commune on March 18, 1871. A fresco of the period would represent military disaster and invasion, irate patriotism, popular discontent and unsuccessful insurrections. An earlier essay attempted to show that the Franco-Prussian War had disordered the trade unions that had grown up in the preceding decade. Their unifying force, the First International, had been no less damaged. Its ranks had thinned, in spots had melted; its press, never its greatest asset, had virtually ceased to exist. A breach in the Paris branch, lasting several months, divided old style Proudhonists and new, more active, Internationalists. The breach was closed in February 1871. But a move in March to reorganize and strengthen the branch had brought little improvement. Actually it was beyond repair.

Everything conspired to provoke the Parisian populace. The War had dislocated industry and caused unemployment. Those who had enrolled in the National Guard were drawing a franc and a half a day, a pittance, too meager to pay for bare necessities. The siege had made food scarce and prices high. In workers' homes there was a struggle against starvation. The payment of rent had been postponed during the siege, but that, even in good times, had generally figured less prominently in a Parisian workers' budget than the price level. This had risen more rapidly than wages during the sixties; and rents, too, had been raised thanks to the rebuiding of the capital. The Empire that had sought to secure itself against the workers of Paris, had gone down in military defeat. Napoleon had been the cause of his undoing. The Government of National Defense, constituted thereafter, had as much reason to fear the plain Parisians. They were restless, pressed by primary

150

needs, their national pride wounded by disaster and a long siege of their historic city. Many had shown their resentment by following radical leaders and clubs in the numerous demonstrations against the government.

Towards the end of January 1871 an armistice was signed, providing for the election of a National Assembly to settle the issue of war and peace. The news affronted the capital's inhabitants. A large number had come to believe with Louis Auguste Blanqui that the nation could be defended and defeat turned into victory by recruiting men and resources without regard to private interests. Others, less programmatic and equally patriotic, trusted to sansculottic élan, calling for the type of war their ancestors had fought in 1793 to rid the country of invaders.

The armistice caused indignation in Paris. People charged that it had been motivated by the government's sense of insecurity. Never, since 1848, had the buttresses of the social order been in so much danger of giving way. Peace was necessary in order to strengthen them, according to current reasoning. As supporting evidence, men pointed out the speed with which the election was called. And the fact that the enemy occupied almost one-third of the nation's territory might be an advantage to the peace party.

The election on February 8, 1871, resulted in a monarchist victory. Fear coupled with defiance spread in urban areas, especially in Paris. Would another crowned head impose himself on the nation and erase the democratic liberties recently earned after years of oppression? The question naturally forced itself on people, so real was the threat to republican hopes and popular aims. Men believed there was a plot against the republic in the high echelons of government. After all, the imperial generals, not the capital, had capitulated to the enemy. Paris had held out. The signers of the armistice surrendered it by permitting the Germans to occupy a portion of the city. The insult was felt deeply. Thanks to the determination of the central committee of the National Guard Federation, bloodshed was prevented. Upon its orders the city was in mourning when the goose-stepping conquerors marched in: statues veiled in black; crape hanging from shut doors and windows; the streets deserted. But barricades had arisen along the line of march. The spectacle was at once frightening and majestic.

1

The central committee was potentially the strongest rival of the government. The Federation it represented had had its origin in the February election. Company delegates had come together at first with the restricted aim of agreeing on candidates. The election over, the delegates looked to new horizons. There was the republic to defend, and elemental rights, too, now that the National Assembly had a strong royalist majority. Towards the end of February, statutes, drafted for the Federation of the National Guard of the Seine, were adopted at a meeting attended by 2,000 guardsmen. Its central committee, made up of delegates chosen by the companies, had the duty of defending the people's rights and of taking measures to develop the general welfare and the safety of the republic. The assignment was so broad that the challenge to authority was at best only implicit. But the authors of the statutes erased all doubts about the Federation's real purpose. Their reporter concluded his remarks at the large meeting of guardsmen with an appeal to the departments to do what the Department of the Seine had done. By expanding to national dimensions, the Federation would replace the standing army. The army was the instrument of despotism; a national militia, on the other hand, would open the way "to the replacement of human exploitation by universal fraternity and solidarity." That was the high objective of the Federation, according to the statutes.[1]

The central committee was a cross section of the radical political factions. Four of its twenty-eight members were from the Paris Federal Council of the First International. The rest were neo-Jacobins, Blanquists or just trade unionists.[2] Its first act was to announce, on the eve of the Germans' entrance into Paris, that any attempt to disarm the National Guard would be met by armed resistance. Further, at its meeting on March 3, it voted unanimously the resolution, submitted by Eugène Varlin, the Internationalist, that the Federation alone had the right to choose and dismiss its leaders.[3]

The committee, called into being in the overcast, threatening atmosphere of February 1871, was indeed a dual power. It had the obedience of an armed militia, composed of enlisted workers; it gave orders, patrolled the capital and, what was most disturbing to the government, it counted on becoming the sole military authority in the nation. Beginning in March signs of rivalry for power between committee and government were sufficiently in evidence.

The National Assembly, headed by Adolphe Thiers, did everything possible to make itself unpopular in Paris. It ordered the court-martial of Blanqui and Gustave Flourens, an Internationalist, for having led the demonstration of October 31, 1870, despite the stipulation after the event that there would be no reprisals. The Assembly alienated small traders by a law on overdue bills whereby their holders could demand payment after March 13, though business was practically paralyzed. Nothing could have made shopkeepers more friendly to workers. As if further to tighten their bonds the Assembly had before it a decree ordering the payment of rents that had been postponed during the siege.[4] The decree never became law, but it revealed the intentions of the government. The apprehension it caused turned many Parisians to the side of the radicals.

The irritating legislation exemplified what appeared to be a policy of provocation. The monarchist Assembly, perhaps fearing the pressure of opinion in the capital, decided to make Versailles the center of government. Parisians interpreted the return to the old Bourbon seat of power as an earnest bid to restore royalty. The committee of the National Guard, for its part, anticipating the move, had decided to canvass popular opinion on the desirability of declaring Paris an independent republic.[5] Then, in the first week of March, Thiers announced that the commander of the National Guard would be General d'Aurelle de Paladines, a Napoleonic officer, disliked by the guardsmen. The appointment slighted the declaration of the central committee that the National Guard alone could choose its commanders. The committee defiantly gave notice, in its report of March 10, that the men would disregard the new commander's orders.[6] The commander, on the other hand, made it known that he would suppress energetically any breach of the peace.[7] A sample of what the government was planning to do was an order of the commanding general of the Paris army, suppressing six radical newspapers, several of them with large circulations.

A clash between the two sides was fast approaching. Versailles called on the Parisians, on the National Guard in particular, to disown the central committee. The militia had arms and a good supply of munitions; and it had moved the cannon guarding the city to the hill of Montmartre in order to prevent them from becoming German booty. There were attempts to negotiate a peaceful arrangement. But Thiers and the men around him at Versailles were impatient. They could not brook a challenge for power from the nation's first city that had been an exemplar for other French cities since 1789. The monarchist dominated Assembly might be the cause of republican defiance elsewhere, that would give allies to the capital and make it the leader of a powerful, perhaps triumphant movement. Versailles acted to disarm Paris.

During the night of March 17, an official bulletin, posted throughout the city, gave notice that action would be taken against the committee. Its men, according to the proclamation, were criminals and conspirators.[8] The government of Versailles did not plan to move to Paris. It merely aimed to disarm the capital and then subdue it, in the manner of a conqueror.

The attempt was made in the early hours of March 18. The operations at first moved ahead with vigor and without opposition. Word spread among the people of Montmartre and in the National Guard. A dense and surging crowd stopped the convoys with the cannon. National Guardsmen arrived, followed by civilian folk; their intermingling with regular soldiers broke discipline. Fresh troops equally succumbed to friendship and allurement. Paris became untenable. Towards the afternoon, Thiers hurriedly left for Versailles. While he was in flight, two of his generals, Lecomte and Thomas, prisoners in Montmartre, were shot by their own soldiers, despite the efforts of the vigilance committee and of officers of the National Guard to stay the execution. Finally an order came from Versailles "to evacuate City Hall and all points occupied by the Army in Paris."[9]

2

Power fell to the central committee practically without a struggle. The men in the new government of the capital were of lowly origin and obscure. The majority of them were manual and white collar workers or shopkeepers. Politically they belonged to different radical factions; but exposed to a common threat, and bewildered by their sudden rise to undisputed authority in the city, they acted in concert. On March 19 the committee occupied the centers of administration and instructed General Charles Lullier, commander of the National Guard, to occupy the forts around the city. The Versailles government, however, already held Mont Valérien, the highest fortified point, and that proved to be very costly to the Commune.

The central committee seems to have been totally in the dark about the significance of the triumph. Nor was it aware of its new responsibilities. Instead of taking up the tasks of government, or of ordering the pursuit of the straggling and discouraged troops of Versailles, it concerned itself with declarations to answer charges emanating from there. Unexpected was its call for the election of a communal government. As the official journal of Paris said three days after the victory: "There is no example in history of a provisional government so eager to turn over its mandate to those chosen by universal suffrage."[10] A small minority of the committee argued that before all the National Guard had to "march on Versailles, disperse the Assembly and appeal to France,"[11] but it failed to persuade others. Seen retrospectively, the military situation of the National Assembly seems to have vindicated the position of the minority, for the Versailles troops were undisciplined, unwilling to fight. Thiers later admitted that had his army been attacked, directly after March 18, it could not have resisted.[12] But the central committee spent time talking, meeting, and getting involved in debates with local mayors and deputies.

The union of mayors and deputies, aware of a dismay in Paris, on account of the uncertainty of the future, believed it could compel the committee to accept a compromise. Headed by Georges Clemenceau and Louis Blanc, mayors and deputies professed to be the sole authority in the capital. When the committee refused to surrender its power, Louis Blanc exclaimed: "You are the insurgents against a most freely elected Assembly. We the regular mandatories, we cannot avow a transaction with insurgents. We should be willing to prevent a civil war, but not to appear as your auxiliaries in the eyes of France."[13] The committee finally decided to remain at its post.

The committee also had to contend with local resistance to the new regime. First, it issued a stern warning to twenty-eight newspapers that had counseled the voters to boycott the forthcoming communal elections.[14] Then it dispersed from 800 to 1,000 hostile demonstrators at the place Vendôme whose slogans "Down with the committee!" "Long live the National Assembly!" left little doubt about their intentions.[15]

For the present the committee was the uncontested authority in Paris. Labor and radical groups responded to its summons to the polls, among them the Federal Council of the local sections of the International. Its program during the Commune is best left over to other pages of this essay. All we can say at this point is that its manifesto of March 23, appealing to the people to show their faith in the changed situation by registering their votes for the Commune, was Proudhonist from start to finish. It looked to "liberty, equality and solidarity" for "the reorganization of labor," and it, above all, reasserted its confidence in "credit, exchange and association to secure the worker the full proceeds of his labor."[16]

The election was on March 26. Of the ninety-two councilors elected, twenty-one were moderate and radical Republicans, forty-four were neo-Jacobins and Blanquists, and eighteen were members of the International. The remaining nine were either double elections or unfilled seats, such as those of Blanqui, who had again been arrested on March 17, and of Garibaldi, who was in Italy. By-elections, on April 16, to fill thirty-one seats made vacant for one reason or another, gave most of the seats to neo-Jacobins, Blanquists, and Internationalists, one of them Auguste Serraillier whom the General Council in London had once more sent to Paris. By the end of April there were two major groups in the council of the Commune: a majority of neo-Jacobins and Blanquists, and a minority of Internationalists.

The council's personnel was without distinguished names, save perhaps Blanqui's and Gustave Courbet's. But the first, a well-guarded prisoner, could not serve. A large number of the councilors were men with calloused hands, railroad employees, printers, carpenters, hatmakers, dyers, bookbinders, shoemakers, and jewelry workers. A number of others were white-collar workers such as office clerks, teachers, artists, and journalists. There was also a sprinkling of physicians, veterinarians, lawyers, and even of former curés. Many in the council had either been under the observation of the imperial police or had spent time in a political prison. Among them might be counted those who had taken up arms against the Government of National Defense. Dividing lines were conspicuously clear between the council so constituted and the Assembly in Versailles with an overwhelming majority of conservatives, Bourbons, Orleanists and Bonapartists. The outlooks and aspirations of the two were totally different. A contemporary observed: "Paris is more than a thousand leagues from Versailles; Versailles is more than a thousand leagues from Paris. To go from one town to the other is like entering a new hemisphere."[17]

The communal council of Paris was far from being a politically homogeneous body. Controversies between Jacobins, Blanquists and Proudhonists frequently interrupted its business. The first were graybeards, harking back to the Mountainists of 1793 and 1848. They had no social program, but only revolutionary relics. Several among them, Charles Delescluze for instance, distinguished themselves by their devotion to the Commune. Others, such as Félix Pyat and Pierre Vésinier, caused confusion by their unseasonable proposals and blatant formulas. They were forever at feud with the International. In 1868 they had helped set up in London a rival French branch that called for the assassination of Louis Napoleon. The General Council had to disclaim any responsibility for the pronouncements of the branch, for it did not belong to the International.[18] Pyat and Vésinier went on attacking it during the Commune, and did what they could to prevent Serraillier from entering the government.[19]

Though the Blanquists often cooperated with the Jacobins, they formed a group apart. In general, they were younger men, given to action. The preceding essay already outlined the patterns of their thought and organization. Here it can be restated that they counted on a small group of bold men to capture political power and wield it for the achievement of vaguely defined ends. For they were political revolutionists with a sentimental socialism, and with little support among the workers. Whatever strength they had was in Paris. Blanquists were military leaders under the Commune and in control of its police.

The Proudhonists were inclined to specialize in the social and economic questions of the Commune, for their experience had derived from organizing and leading trade unions. They were Internationalists who had wholly committed labor's future to free credit, made available through a people's bank. That alone could liberate the workers from capitalism and the farmers from the financial hierarchy. The disciples of Proudhon, it has been shown elsewhere, had at first considered labor's political action less important for their final aim than the organization of producers' cooperatives. Strikes were frowned upon. Their theories and the events, however, did not mix. They found themselves leading strikes and involved in political action. But they remained loyal to their social and economic tenets. Reference has been made to the Parisian Internationalists' manifesto of March 23, 1871, in which they took their stand on credit, cooperation and the free exchange of the products of labor. These panaceas they counted on to return to the workers what they had produced were in line with Proudhon's mutualism which continued to animate Paris Internationalists. Whatever formal program the Commune had was their making. If the authors of its "Declaration to the French People" of April 19 subordinated production, credit and exchange to communal autonomy,[20] that was because they considered the economic changes best attainable under federalism. The two were thoroughly consistent with the Proudhonist creed. Serraillier reported to London in the middle of April that in policy making groups they "talk only of a plan for a people's bank, exchange, etc. In short, each day a new scheme is pulled out of the works of the great master."[21]

The disputes among Jacobins, Blanquists and Proudhonists might well have contributed to the Commune's defeat. Friction became sharper after the by-elections of April 16. Blanquists and Jacobins demanded the appointment of a Committee of Public Safety, somewhat akin to that of 1793. Proudhonist Internationalists strongly resisted the proposal, refusing to give up the right to debate at length immediate and ultimate issues. That was the period in the history of the Commune when the military situation took a critical turn. But neither side would yield. The first made a principle of an anachronism; the second believed they could settle accounts with generalities.

Factionalism encouraged other rival groups to come into the open. Thus the old central committee that had ceremoniously surrendered its authority to the elected council on March 28, reappeared to demand a commanding place in the government. The contest between the civil and military branches became further complicated after the creation of a Committee of Public Safety that claimed full power for itself. The three bodies competed for supremacy almost to the end.

3

The word, commune, brought to mind the Commune of 1793. That of 1871, however, was different, and for two cardinal reasons: first, the majority of its council consisted either of workers or of their representatives; second, the same council was at once a legislative and an executive body. The councilmen, revocable by the electorate, were both legislators of the Commune, administrators in their respective districts, and members of commissions that drafted legislation. Laws were first worked out with the assistance of professional or labor groups. The Commune seems to have been free from political careerism, and in essence was incompatible with the division of labor that was characteristic of western representative governments. It was inimical to a high-priced officialdom. Four days after its inauguration it decreed that the maximum wage of civil employees was to be but 6,000 francs a year, on the ground that "in a really democratic republic there could be neither sinecures nor exaggerated salaries."[22] Symptomatic of the government's objectives was the replacement of the standing army by the National Guard.[23] A later decree confiscated all military weapons in the hands of enemies.[24] A member of the council was at the head of the police. Thus the Commune controlled all the instruments of political power. But it did not take over the Bank of France.

The main force behind the Commune was the workers and small shopkeepers. The legislation of the communal council on rent and over-due bills won the favor of the second. The workers themselves drew up regulations for the operation of abandoned workshops; they enrolled in the National Guard, worked on the construction of barricades and de-fended them. A few examples may illustrate their basic sincerities. A National Guardsman from Brittany, who had enlisted in the service of the Commune, wrote to his father on April 11, after attending the funeral of thirty-six comrades, killed in battle:

"To see thirty-six corpses buried alongside one another makes your hair stand on end. People wept when the members of the Commune spoke. These are courageous men. Day and night they are seen on the battlefield, encouraging the workers. They are not afraid to die like the Versailles cowards. . . . Yesterday we buried Colonel Bourgouin who at half past three said to the National Guardsmen: 'Let my life belong to the Commune!' At twenty minutes before four he died on the barri-cade of the bridge of Neuilly. He was only thirty-two years old and he left two small children. In the name of his children who were present, we took an oath: 'We shall avenge you, citizen! Death to Versailles! Death to the assassins!' . . . Dear father, married men are leaving their wives and children and are coming with us. I have seen women with rifles fighting in our ranks and shouting: 'Long live the Commune!' . . . My eyes are filled with tears as I write this letter. It is eleven o'clock. I am going to sleep, but from my room can be seen the light of the cannon, firing at least ten shots a minute. It is perhaps the last time I shall write you. But, if I die, you will at least be able to say: 'My son died for the universal republic.' "[25]

Such complete attachment to the Paris Commune was not unique. A surgeon said to Gustave Lefrançais, a member of the council, who asked about the state of the wounded: "I do not share your opinions, and I cannot desire the triumph of your cause; but I have never seen wounded men show more calm and *sang-froid* during operations. I attribute this courage to the power of their convictions."[26]

Workers regarded the Commune as theirs. Letters that have been made available affirm their warm interest in policies and their impatience with drawbacks. The letters to the editors of *Père Duchêne*, a popular newspaper, mirror the discussions that must have gone on daily in workers' quarters. One worker was disturbed by expressions of reaction in fashionable sections of Paris and asked: "Why is the Commune so wanting in firmness?" "A little energy," is a common refrain in the letters. One correspondent made up in vigorous phraseology what he lacked in orthography, "Don't cease to shake up the members of the Commune. Don't let them fall asleep on their seats and fail to execute the decrees," he urged the editors of *Père Duchêne*. "Tell them to avoid personalities. More harmony will gift them with greater force to defend the Commune rather than their persons." A railroad worker, inspired by the law abolishing night work in bakeries, took occasion to describe the miserable lot of the employees in his industry and requested the editors to recommend improvements. He was willing to wait, however, until the military situation was less pressing. A white-collar worker, who had acquainted himself with the aims of the Commune, ventured this prophecy:

"A day will come, and the day is not far off, when all peoples will understand that each should live by honest, remunerative labor. No more exorbitant salaries, but to each according to his work. The class that suffers must not waste itself for the advantage of an exploiting class. The republic cannot permit its partisans to die of hunger while infamous traitors gorge themselves with the products of painful labor. All workers should produce. It is immoral that property today should bring a return of 27 per cent."

And then he continued: "The day is coming when our present oppressors, the Prussian people, will find it necessary to shake off their yoke. We, the oppressed, must promise to support them, but only when they shall have freed themselves from this degrading domination."[27]

The Commune had the services of intellectuals, physicians, students, artists, actors and musicians. Prompted by Edouard Vaillant, chief of the Education Commission, the few medical professors who remained in Paris—the great majority had fled to Versailles—medical students and physicians met on April 23 to draw up a plan for reorganizing medical education. Several projects were under consideration at subsequent meetings. But nothing final emerged from the deliberations, for physicians and medical students were preoccupied with the wounded.

Artists, in response to Vaillant's request, offered to protect and organize exhibitions of the art treasures of Paris and to draw up a curriculum for art instruction to children and adults. On April 13, on the initiative of Courbet,[28] they established a federation and issued a program on the role of the artist. In a democratic society, art was socially responsible, they held. "Art through freedom" was one of the aims of the federation. It took over the care of public buildings, the preparation of plans and catalogues, and the supervision of art teaching in the schools and at public lectures. On its executive committee served such celebrated painters as Courbet, Corot, Daumier, Manet and Millet; the sculptors Dalou and Ottin; the lithographers Flameng and Gil; and the industrial artist Pottier.[29] The last one, Eugène Pottier, later wrote the *International* and was a political refugee in the United States.

Inspired by the example of the artists, 600 actors, musicians, and dancers federated in April. They proceeded at once to plan concerts, plays and festivals, for the benefit of the wounded, widows and orphans of the Commune. Several concerts and plays were all that the federation had time to give. The concert on May 9 in the Palais des Tuilleries was so well attended that many could not get admission; and three special concerts had to be scheduled for May 11 to meet the demand. The federation's aid to the Commune went beyond stage-performances. On April 18 it formed its own company to defend the Commune on the military front.[30]

Women had a heroic part in the Commune. Most of them came from the working class; a minority, however, was middle class in origin. Their services were many and varied. They nursed the wounded, encouraged their husbands and sons, brought them fresh linen and hot soup at the front, sewed sandbags to plug up breaches in the forts and barricades, organized women's clubs and trade unions, addressed meetings, edited newspapers, wrote manifestoes, taught school, shouldered rifles, created their own battalion and fought in the front lines. Here were the observations of an eye-witness:

"Armed with rifles, a revolver stuck in the belt and a red scarf thrown from shoulder to waist, some of them incite and accompany combatants. In their patriotic, or rather revolutionary zeal, they are seen in the role of policemen, stopping lukewarm or recalcitrant citizens. Others mount the pulpit in churches and proclaim the advent of human reason."[31]

The women were impressive both by their earnestness and number. They were more than 10,000 in the service of the Commune. At their head stood Nathalie Le Mel, a friend of Varlin and an organizer of cooperatives;[32] André Léo, a novelist, a journalist and a champion of women's rights; and Paule Minck, a veteran propagandist of labor's cause, a worker in the ambulance corps and, after the Commune, a founder of the French Labor Party. Two outstanding leaders were Louise Michel[33] and Elisabeth Dmitrieff.[34] The first, a school-teacher in Paris, earned prominence by her activity among the women of Montmartre. Dressed in the uniform of the National Guard, she was like a modern Joan of Arc, always at the most dangerous points of the battle, inspiring men with her courage, sleeping in trenches, holding a barricade while comrades were falling about her. Finally, after having been led to Versailles amid insults from *élégantes,* she faced a court martial with these words: "I belong entirely to the social revolution and I wish to accept responsibility for all my deeds. . . . I am told that I am party to the Commune. Definitely, for the Commune aimed above all at a social revolution, and social revolution is my deepest desire. I deem it an honor to have been one of its partisans."[35] The second, Elisabeth Dmitrieff, young and attractive, of Russian noble origin, had been in Switzerland where she had joined the Russian section of the International, that opposed Michael Bakunin's teachings. The story has it that, while in London in 1870, she was Marx's personal secretary. She had come to Paris almost at the same time as Serraillier and kept the General Council informed of events. "The Russian lady," as Elisabeth was referred to in the Council's still unpublished minutes, had lost no time in assuming direction of the women's groups, despite poor health. On April 11 she held a large meeting to coordinate their work in the wards and founded a large organization, the Women's Union for the Defense of Paris.[36] Its manifestoes hailed the Commune as the rule of labor over capital, denounced the inequality between the sexes as an instrument for maintaining in power the privileged classes, rejected any conciliation with Versailles and acclaimed the universal republic.[37] The Union performed many functions. It directed bureaus, constructed barricades, assisted the ambulance corps, held twenty-four public meetings in a little more than a month, organized women workers into trade unions, and formed several military detachments that went to the front. Elisabeth Dmitrieff must have been impressive as she moved about in either a scarlet or black velvet dress with pistols hanging from the belt. Her letter of April 24 to the General Council in London gave some idea of the work the Union was doing.

"I am very sick; I have bronchitis and fever. I have been working a great deal and we are rousing all the women in Paris. I have been addressing public meetings. We have set up defense committees in all the wards and in addition a central committee, all of it for the purpose of organizing the Women's Union for the Defense of Paris and of caring for the wounded. We have been working with the government, and I believe that the organization and work will continue. But what a great deal of time has been lost and what trouble it has cost me. I have to speak every evening and write a great deal, with the result that my illness gets worse. If the Commune triumphs, our organization will cease to be political and become social. We expect to form international sections. The idea is taking hold very well. In general, my international propaganda aimed at showing that all countries, Germany included, are on the eve of a social revolution, and the women appreciate it very much. From three to four thousand women attend these meetings. Unfortunately I am sick and there is no one to take my place. The Commune is progressing; but many mistakes were made at the beginning. C[luseret] was named fifteen to twenty days ago, against all my arguments; but M[alon] is already tearing his hair for not having listened to me. *One of these days Clus[eret] will be arrested.*"[38]

A measure of the women's share in the fighting is to be had in the casualties and in the prisoners taken by Versailles. Of the 20,000 Parisians killed in and around Paris during the last week of the Commune many were women. More than a thousand others were arrested; hundreds of them were dragged to Versailles and condemned to prison or deportation.

4

The Communards were quite aware of the importance of the provinces in their conflict with Versailles. The above letter by Dmitrieff said emphatically: "The provinces must be agitated at all cost to have them come to our aid." But the military side of the contest so occupied the Commune that its propaganda in the departments took a secondary place. Its feeble efforts to rally sentiment behind it were either neutralized by the counter propaganda of Versailles or rendered powerless by the blockade around the capital.

Still Paris had considerable sympathy in other cities of France, if we are to judge by the many urban risings. Lyons was shaken by two insurrections, in each of which the workers succeeded in installing provisional governments. But the absence of contact with Paris as well as factional friction caused the movements to go to pieces. Similar risings disturbed Marseilles, Toulouse, Bordeaux, Saint-Etienne, Grenoble, Narbonne, Limoges and Creusot. In the last town the red flag was hoisted over the City Hall when news arrived from the capital that the central committee had taken over power. Here, again, as in the other towns, the insurrection went under for lack of aid from without. Paris had simply failed, for one reason or another, to unite these movements with its own. All it could do was to issue appeals to the provinces.[39]

The isolation of the Commune, even more than its indecision, may be considered a fundamental cause of its defeat. Communication with the outer world grew extremely difficult as the ring around Paris was tightened. The Commune's delayed manifesto to the peasants, urging an alliance of town and country, had to be scattered from balloons.[40]

With a *cordon sanitaire* around the capital, the Prussians assisting, Versailles had a free hand to present to the world its side of the conflict. But it was not distinguished for its veracity. It painted the Communards as pillagers, assassins, incendiaries, terrorists, and foreigners whose object it was to break up France. What surprised visitors to the capital was the peacefulness and good behavior of the citizens. The American journalist, John Russell Young, for example, wrote that he had never seen "a more orderly city. . . . I saw no drunkenness, no ruffianism, no pillage,"[41] despite the fact that he saw no police. The Communards were strict moralists, believers in the sanctity of the family. Hence, they decreed the closing of the houses of prostitution. Even though Versailles tried to cause disorder and sabotage through former jailbirds and spies, even in official departments of the Commune, only one assassination occurred during the life of the Commune.[42] Its treatment of hostile newspapers was generous. Not until the creation of the Committee of Public Safety was a severe policy begun against the press. Spies whose guilt was proved were not subjected to the rules of war. The Commune made at most from 1,300 to 1,400 arrests, two-thirds of whom were detained but a few days.[43] The unfortunate shooting of the Commune's hostages was a final act of desperation in the last week, when the Versailles troops in their fury killed around 20,000 men, women and children. Thiers could have saved the prominent hostages had he agreed to exchange them for Blanqui.[44] Two reasons might explain Thiers's callousness: he believed that the release of his prized prisoner would put a first-rate head on the movement; and he desired to drive the Communards to acts of folly so that an aroused public opinion would condone the ruthless suppression he was premeditating.

Actually Thiers had miscalculated both the value Blanqui might have had for the movement and the ability of the Communards in general. Blanqui, as leader of the movement, might have divided it even more than it was. And his estimate of the Communards had proved erroneous. For he had counted on leaving the city thoroughly disorganized once its administrators had retired to Versailles as he had ordered them to do on pain of dismissal. A number of them disobeyed and gave their services to the Commune. Other posts were quickly filled. Instead of the anarchy Thiers had looked for, Paris was the best and cheapest-governed city in France. Considering the pressing problems of the Commune, its administration functioned with extraordinary smoothness. The day after his arrival in the French capital Serraillier reported to London:

"What a difference between the Paris I see and the one that has been depicted to us. Everything is quiet. Everyone accepts the Commune as an accomplished fact. Better still, people show a certain zeal in serving it. If Versailles weren't there, everything would go well. . . . What is more astonishing is that all are performing their duties as if it were the most natural thing in the world." Again more than two weeks later: "Concerning the administration, one can only be astonished to see how all of it is progressing. Nothing is languishing save the post office whose region does not go beyond the ramparts."[45]

The administration consisted of nine commissions, drawn from the communal council. Whatever reforms the Commune adopted had first been worked out by them with the help of professional or labor groups. There were commissions on war, finance, justice, food supply, foreign affairs, public service, police, education and labor. The Commission on Education, directed by the trained Edouard Vaillant, met with teachers and parents to reorganize instruction, and planned a curriculum for children and adults that would provide for elementary, art and technical training.[46] Before the events terminated the project the Commune had decreed the secularization of education. The reform complemented another decree that separated church and state and nationalized all church property.[47]

The commission on trade and labor was the Commune's pledge of resolving the workers' problems. Frankel was its chairman, and under him served the Internationalists, Serraillier, Theisz, Malon and Longuet. The commission stimulated the organization of trade unions and cooperatives and, through the Women's Union, led by Elisabeth Dmitrieff, the unionization of female workers.[48] It summoned the labor societies to constitute a committee for the sake of inquiring into the state of the factories employers had abandoned. The committee had to report when these shops could be put into operation, "no longer by the deserters who have abandoned them, but by the cooperative association of the workers employed in them."[49] The plan, like that on education, was never carried out. It merely lifted the veil on the ultimate designs of the Commune.

The labor and social reforms were of a practical character. Together they might be regarded as the minimum program of the Commune and the initial steps to more fundamental changes. It remitted rents for the period of the Franco-Prussian War, legislated for the relief of debtors, took widows and orphans under its care, permitted the free withdrawal of essential articles from pawnshops, fixed the price of bread, requisitioned vacant apartments to house the homeless, abolished fines on labor, prohibited night work in bakeries, departed from the system of municipal contracts by authorizing the Commission of Trade and Labor to treat directly with the labor organizations, and accepted a plan for the arms factory of the Louvre, that permitted the workers to participate in its management. The Commune also demolished the Vendôme Column, already proposed by Courbet in September 1870.[50] The monument to Bonaparte was held to be "a symbol of brute force and false glory, an affirmation of militarism, a negation of international law and a permanent insult of the conqueror to the conquered. . . ."[51]

Many foreigners served the Commune. An estimate given to the National Assembly in 1875 had it that of the 36,309 arrested, 1,725 belonged to national groups other than French. Belgians made up the largest number with 737. Then there were 215 Italians, 201 Swiss, 154 Dutch and 110 Poles. Germans, Spaniards and Russians were 81, 30 and 23 respectively; 27 belonged to England and 17 to the United States. The rest came from such places as Africa, Asia, Luxembourg, Greece, Sweden, Turkey and Austria. Denmark and Brazil had two each, and Ireland one.[52] In sum, the support for the Commune was international. If the number of foreigners killed in action and those who escaped were added to the above figure, the total would probably be above 2,000.

Most of the foreigners were in the armed forces of the Commune. Among its best generals were the Poles, Jaroslaw Dombrowski and Walery Wroblewski, and the Italian La Cecilia, formerly with Garibaldi. Other foreigners, such as Dmitrieff, a Russian, and Frankel, a Hungarian, were organizers and administrators.

The Commune also had defenders in many countries, in England, on the Continent and in the United States. Addresses by Italians and Swiss expressed their solidarity with Paris. In Hanover, Germany, 3,000 persons hailed the Parisians as "the proletariat struggling for the rights of man."[53] A mass meeting in Hyde Park, London, extended its sympathy to the Paris workers. To a well attended meeting in New York City on July 2, 1871, the Communards were the champions of human rights and of a great cause.[54]

5

The most active defender of the Commune was the General Council of the International Workingmen's Association. The International had had no hand in starting the Paris Revolution, or as Engels wrote to Sorge, "the International did not lift a finger to produce it." But it "was without any doubt the child of the International intellectually."[55] From the very beginning of the conflict the Council in London was in contact with Internationalists in Paris. After the middle of April, however, lines of communication were broken between the two cities, so that when information reached London it was usually old.[56] During the first month of the Commune, the Council kept abreast of events and assessed them judiciously. When it learned in April of the first military reverses of the Commune, Engels, who was no tyro as a military analyst, ascribed them to want of resolution in the first days. He told the Council that "the time for action against Versailles had been when it was weak, but that opportunity had been lost; and now it seemed that Versailles was getting the upper hand and driving the Parisians back. People would not put up long with being led into defeat." The Communards, he continued, were losing ground, spending ammunition and consuming provisions. But "they could not be starved into submission as long as one side of Paris was open." The war, he was fairly certain, would not be terminated as rapidly as in June 1848, for the 200,000 Parisian workmen were "far better organized than at any former insurrection."[57] An English delegate believed that the situation called for a public statement by the Council.

For the press in Europe and in the United States was publishing fantastic accounts of the Commune and the International. Judging by the daily stories that besieged the public, one was tempted to conclude that reason had to wage a bitter struggle for survival. Actually many tales were so extravagant that they lost all credibility; but they had a vast reading public and a wide persuasion. People were told that the Commune was begotten by the monster, the International. The offspring with its reign of terror, with its love of destruction and carnage was a sample of what the parent had in store for western civilization. According to the narratives, the International had world revolution in view in order to erase private property, suppress all faiths, level all institutions and make men the obedient servants of its top directorate. Frenchmen said it was German in origin; Germans argued that the revolutions in France since 1789 had reared it; and the Pope attributed it to the materialist philosophy that had taken root in the eighteenth century. All agreed that, whatever its source, it and its progeny had to be exterminated, or it would continue to beguile innocent people. But it was difficult to uproot the International, for it was a mysterious, underground society, reaching out everywhere, starting strikes, hatching plots, waiting for the day when it would call out its hordes for an all-out war against legally constituted authority. It was enormously wealthy, stories had it, with millions of followers distributed in the many countries.

These reports, for the most part, were funneled by Versailles and its envoys throughout Europe and America. And they were probably further embroidered in the retelling, so that the final portrayals must have been quite ghastly. Engels' old mother, hearing some of them, was simply shocked. She firmly believed that her fifty-one year old boy would never have been party to such mischief had it not been for his satanic friend.[58]

Marx was inclined to hold the English press more culpable than that of other countries. But the press of France, Germany and of the United States printed similar accounts, as if they had copied one another. Yet the record of the International had been public knowledge since its foundation in 1864. Its congresses had been reported by correspondents; its manifestoes had been widely distributed; meetings of the General Council had been summarized in newspapers. Everyone who had followed the history of the Association from its inception knew that the allegedly plotting, sinister, wealthy, all-pervading society was a heterogeneous, slow-moving, poor organization that had come out of the Franco-Prussian War weaker than it had been. It had often been helpless in its effort to fulfill an important purpose of its establishment: to prevent manufacturers from importing foreign labor. Why then did the press convert the International into an ogre? Marx believed the purpose was "to justify any action" against it. "The upper classes were afraid of the principles of the International," he said at a meeting of the Council.[59] The best the General Council could do was to reply by letters to the press and by an occasional article.

The Council could justly be credited with an international agitation in behalf of the Commune. Mass meetings in Germany, Italy, Switzerland and the United States endorsed the principles of the International and made the cause of the Commune their own. In England the Council participated in public meetings that were induced to adopt resolutions in defense of the Communards. On March 28 it voted to issue an address to the Parisians, and Marx was asked to write it. But in view of the events in the French capital it was postponed. Further delays prevented its drafting. Finally, on May 30th, Marx read to the Council the *Address on the Civil War in France*. The General Council adopted it unanimously and ordered the printing of 1,000 copies.[60]

The *Address* was completed while the Versailles troops were wreaking vengeance on their adversaries, making no exception of women and children. Writing as reports of mass slaughter were reaching him, Marx did not aim to produce a historical critique of the Commune, but a passionate defense of its combatants. The result was perhaps the greatest polemic he ever composed, and the one that caused more controversy than any other piece of writing on the Paris Commune. It is not the intention here to enumerate the particulars of Marx's brief. All that need be said within the given space is that he juxtaposed Versailles and Paris as the symbols of different social systems: the one, headed by an assembly of specimens of defunct regimes and bent on perpetuating the rule of the bourgeoisie; the other, "essentially a working class government," aiming at the emancipation of labor.

The *Address* won an immediate audience in several languages. Naturally, it had its critics and enthusiasts. Internationalists everywhere promoted its sale and defended its principles. Several English members of the General Council, finding it too radical, resigned. In the United States, it had a wider circulation than had been anticipated. Sections of the International issued special editions. *The Workingman's Advocate* in Chicago and *Woodhull & Claflin's Weekly* in New York republished the entire text; and the New York *World*, nearly all of it. Thereafter it received editorial comment throughout the nation.

It lifted to prominence its author and the organization it stemmed from. Journalists sought interviews with Marx; and the International was the subject of many articles, pamphlets and books. A whole new literature, international in scope, grew up around the Association, most of it as full of calumny and extravaganza as the accounts on the Commune.

Better than that, the police forces of several countries exchanged dossiers on the International and the great powers planned a new Holy Alliance against it. The Commune had been defeated, they argued, but its diabolical fomenter, the International, was there, with designs of other Communes. It had to be exorcized and crushed. Apparently men in power had fallen victim to an obsession. They believed in ghosts. The fact was the defeat of the Commune had drained the International of much of its vitality and closed an era in the history of labor.

THE AMERICAN PRESS VIEWS THE COMMUNE

SENSITIVITY of Americans to political and social movements abroad is hardly a recent development. Without going too far back in history, we may recall the excitement and the party alignments produced by the first French Revolution. In an earlier essay we showed how that great event became a vital domestic issue for Jefferson and other Americans, not to mention its effect on American foreign policy. No other European happenings of the nineteenth century, before the Paris Commune, evoked as much controversy or interest in the United States.

This is not to suggest that other episodes or occurrences were without their flurries in America. For example, the danger of war between England and the United States over the Oregon territory brought forth the Chartist "Address to the Working Classes of America," calling upon them "as brethren" with identical interests to prevent war that could only jeopardize all rights and liberties. We are told on good authority that the Address circulated widely in both countries and won the praise of a portion of the press in England and America.[1] The contemporary press also informs us that at the news of the Revolution of 1830 in France workers in Philadelphia and New York City held large meetings to voice their admiration of the French people for the masterly way they had restored the nation to its rights. The turnout in New York City was estimated to have been around 250,000.[2] The European Revolutions of 1848 had the effect of renewing agitation for reform. Again workers' meetings in large cities of the East saluted the English Chartists and the French workers, this time paying them the tribute of having inspired deeper aims in American labor.[3] But these events, however outstanding in the canvas of the nineteenth century, aroused less emotion in the United States than either the Revolution of 1789 or the Paris Commune of 1871. A plausible explanation was that both in 1789 and

169

1871 the challenge to the received concept of property and of the institutions surrounding it went to the heart of the matter.

The preceding essay depicted how the Paris Revolution, the sequel of the Franco-Prussian War, represented a sharp departure from anything France had known since its Great Revolution. What had been a dual power in the capital, starting in the last week of February, became its governing authority on March 18, 1871. The central committee of the National Guard, holding the reins of government, was made up of comparatively unknown men. They were workers, socialists or revolutionists who had fought against the Second Empire. While the committee had no defined program, a number of its members were imbued with objectives in which the welfare of labor was central. The vehicles for attaining it might have terminated in futility, but the proclaimed final end was out of harmony with the existing order. The same type of men were in the Commune's council. Here, too, though the final aims were far from marked out, the tendency was in the direction of what many of its members held to be the emancipation of labor.

The Paris Commune was essentially a workers' government. Whatever legislation came out of it, its traits were proletarian, secularist and anti-militarist. This character of the Commune alarmed its antagonists both in France and abroad as much as did its ability to stay in power more than two months and the imitations it inspired in other French cities. Disquieting, too, was the assistance it had from foreign revolutionists. Many served it in a military capacity or as civil servants. A great many in other countries stood up for its principles, deplored its weakness and defended it after its demise.

The Paris Commune had international significance. If socialists and anarchists in other countries recognized it as a symbol of their particular aspirations, partisans of the existing social order considered it an abomination. The accounts of it in the press were sufficiently removed from fact to make them pure fantasy. Perhaps the cardinal purpose of that was so to disfigure the Revolution in Paris as to make it hideous in the public eye. Yet in the process of making it terrifying several of its features remained visible. It was possible to see that behind the Commune were plain, simple folk who loved their country, desired it democratic and republican in the face of the monarchist dominated National Assembly, and dreamed of having a better life than they had had under Louis Napoleon's regime. Then there were a number of journalists and writers who, after a good deal of searching, decided that the picture in the press was a caricature, and ended by drawing another they considered to be in keeping with the facts. All in all the Paris Commune was taken very seriously by friends and enemies alike, both in Europe and in the United States. It is not our intention to survey European

opinion on the Commune. That is far too ambitious. Our concern here
is with the way Americans regarded it. Even within these limits we must
confine ourselves to the press as far as possible.

1

In general, American newspapers and periodicals aligned themselves with Versailles against Paris. That was not so different from what
newspapers in England were doing.[4] Restricting ourselves to the American press, we can say that it systematically and persistently hurled
calumny at the Commune. Its combatants were presented as savages or
bandits, as enemies of family, property, religion and organized government, to whom no quarter was to be given. Though several American
papers had their correspondents in France, the main source of the reports they printed, as of the reports in European papers, was either the
English press, or the officially inspired French press or the information
given out by Versailles and its foreign envoys. There is no way of measuring the share the press had in shaping American opinion on the Commune. We may safely assume that the steady fire of charges and epithets
inflamed many to hate it and hold it in horror.

The picture began to take form with the early cables after March
18, 1871. The flight of Thiers, generals and civil servants from Paris
must have caused a panic in the offices of the large press in New York
City, if the headlines were any indication. Every important metropolitan
newspaper, from the *Times* and *Tribune* to the *Evening Telegram*, the
World and the *Herald*, believed that the bonds of organized existence
had snapped. Anarchy, assassination, terror, slaughter, gutters filled with
human blood—this successive series of frightening scenes was monoto-
nously served up by the press. It forebodingly predicted the return of
1793 with its Guillotine, the shadows of Marat and Robespierre and the
inevitable, screaming mob that only heads of the rich could satiate.

Metropolitan newspapers outside of New York by and large took
their cue from the press of the big city. To the Cincinnati *Daily Gazette*
Paris was still the "den of wild beasts" it had been in the Great Revolution.[5] That was also the viewpoint of the Chicago *Tribune*.[6] The terms,
"mob rule" and "reign of terror," were to be found in the Wisconsin
State Journal.[7] The *Morning Bulletin* and *Evening Bulletin* of San Francisco were convinced that Paris, dominated by "violent reds, was destroying genuine republicanism and individual liberty, and reviving the
worst events of the first Revolution."[8] The contention of Versailles that
the Commune was but the start of a general conflagration, plotted by
the First International, was echoed by the Washington *Star*.[9] Also in
the nation's capital Frederick Douglass' weekly accused the Communards
of mobocracy, vandalism and terrorism akin to that of 1792.[10] The re-

porting in the Philadelphia *Ledger*[11] and the Pittsburgh *Daily Gazette*[12] followed the usual pattern. The Parisians, according to their accounts, were bent on destruction and bloodshed, in imitation of their ancestors of 1789. In sum, American journalists spread the notion that the Commune was re-enacting what was commonly believed to have been frequent scenes in the first Revolution.

Since on the question of the Commune the New York metropolitan press served more or less as the source for newspapers elsewhere in the country, we must dwell on it from now on. Major contemporary newspapers seem to have derived four main conclusions from the Paris Commune. They may be formulated as follows: 1. the plain people in France were unfit for popular government; 2. the socialist nature of the Commune made violence inevitable; 3. the Communards were communists, dominated by a foreign organization; 4. their ruthless suppression should be welcomed for the Commune might happen here. We shall consider the four conclusions in their order.

1. The mere existence of the Commune by means of alleged terror and bloodshed, ran the argument, was ample proof that the French people could not live in a democratic republic. The New York *Tribune* showed disdain for the ability of the common people to rule. The Commune, it said, exemplified "the unreason and caprice of the gentlemen of leisure who live in the gutters."[13] Other newspapers, pursuing the same logic still further, regretted the overthrow of Louis Napoleon. With all his faults he had at least kept off "the universal republic," commented the New York *Times*.[14] The Bonapartes alone were "the proper doctors" for Paris, according to the New York *Herald*.[15] The *Evening Telegram*[16] and the *Journal of Commerce*[17] were thoroughly convinced that the Emperor, if released by the Germans and allowed to march on Paris, would be the best alternative to the socialistic republic. Failing that, a good portion of the press added, the Germans should intervene.

Several dailies and weeklies, however, did not accept the verdict that democracy was something alien to the French. Claiming Jefferson as their authority and teacher, they held that the rise of the Commune had demonstrated the failure of absolutism and the centralized apparatus of government it had built up. The only possible escape from it, said the *Evening Post*, was "by convulsively dashing the machine itself to pieces."[18] The Commune had done just that. The solution, however, the *Post* went on, was not a Bonapartist strait-jacket, but municipal autonomy or decentralization. This bent for federalism was shared by the New York *World* and the New York *Sun* and by several weeklies, notably *Frank Leslie's Illustrated Newspaper*, the *Weekly New York Democrat* and the *Golden Age*. And federalism was the only principle of the Communards these publications considered reasonable, in the belief that local government was calculated better to secure the rights of the individual. The *Sun,* followed by the *Weekly Democrat* committed the heresy of finding justification for such enactments of the Commune as secular education, separation of church and state, the abolition of conscription, the moratorium on rent and the taxation of property.[19] They were, however, but a tiny minority. The bulk of the press rejected the Commune outright as a threat to the foundations of the social structure.

2. For since the Commune was socialistic, they reasoned, its aims could never be achieved without bloodshed. Socialism and violence were indistinguishable and inseparable, they argued. No one seems to have understood what socialist aims the Communards had in view. The *Herald* equated socialism with anarchy, and its understanding of anarchy might have shocked students of social theory. It defined anarchy as "Everything for everybody; everything in common; no work but a general carousal, till everything on hand is eaten, and then a sale of the national palaces to raise the wind, and so on."[20] Correspondents reported various socialist plans being introduced. Some believed the Fourierist phalanx would be ushered in. The available evidence, however, does not show a single Fourierist in the Commune's government. Others thought Saint-Simonism was the objective, even though that school of thought had been dead nearly forty years. Still others suggested that Marx was the real inspiration. Yet, not a single Communard, with the possible exception of Auguste Serraillier, was either a Marxist or, as far as we know, understood his theories, although several respected him highly. Whatever reforms the Commune adopted could at best be regarded as its minimum socialist program. The New York *Sun,* we showed, found reasonable ground for a number of the reforms that were already common practice in many communities of the United States. The vital and disturbing difference, however, was that a workers' government had voted them. And since plain people were not credited with administrative wisdom, violence was their only method, according to the press. Workers in power were the best premise that heads would fall. Moreover the red emblem on public buildings and ramparts, said editorial writers, was a warning that the obligation of contracts and the theory of natural rights on which private property rested were in great jeopardy. Correspondents visiting Paris were meanwhile finding out that the inhabitants were courteous and orderly, respecters of property and churches. These observations were conceded subsequently. For the present the Communards were presented as "political bohemians," "the savage mob," and "fanatical ruffians."[21] And to lend authority to their portraits, metropolitan newspapers republished all or part of Joseph Mazzini's blistering attacks on the Commune and the International from *Roma del popolo* and the *Contemporary Review.*[22]

3. In keeping with these dreadful descriptions, the press equated the Communards with communists. It was so easy to slip from the one into the other. Despite the fact that the word, commune, meant local self-government to its partisans, journalists made it synonymous with destruction and the partition of property. That was their conception of communism, though in reality they were confusing it, on a social and economic level, with what had passed in the eighteenth century for egalitarianism. We pointed out in an earlier essay that three main groups made up the Communards: Jacobins, Blanquists and Proudhonists. The first were political actionists, sustained by souvenirs. The second were loyal to their imprisoned leader; and save for a few who were coming closer to the International, the socialism they professed was hazy and sentimental. The third, trade unionists for the most part—a few, such as Frankel and Varlin, were beginning to look out on less cloudy horizons—had objectives that were not very different from what an American labor leader like William Sylvis had aimed at. In brief, the term, communism, was a misnomer as a description of the Commune's program. Besides, the term had often been applied in America to the aims of certain Utopian communities. All the efforts of French Internationalists in New York to bring some clarity into the general confusion were to no avail.[23] The equation between Commune and communism gained currency and was applied indiscriminately in labor disputes. The expression, Commune, became a bugbear. The *Evening Post* referred to a coal miners' strike in Pennsylvania as "The Commune of Pennsylvania."[24] And the Washington *Evening Star* followed the New York *Times* in drawing a likeness between the strikers and the Communards.[25] During the railroad strike of 1877 one heard of the "Reign of the Commune," the "Commune in Pittsburgh," the "Commune in Reading," the "Commune in St. Louis," the "Commune in Chicago," the "Commune in Philadelphia," and the "Commune in New York."[26] To all intents and purposes Communard became identical with communist.

The confusion became all the greater because the press and polemical literature made Communards and Internationalists uniformly the same. We have already shown elsewhere that the International came to the assistance of the Commune after its start. But the organization had done nothing to bring it about. Within the Commune itself, the Internationalists were a minority whose influence on policies waned as the military situation worsened. Still, the American press repeated the legend, started by Versailles, of a world-wide plot against governments, headed by the General Council of the First International. The Commune was the first attempt of the plotters, the story had it, in fact a test of their master-plan. The whole conception was appalling. Almost overnight, the International became a well-advertised society, the subject of numerous articles, pamphlets and books. The literature on the organization grew comparatively large both in Europe and in America. Though little of it could stand the test of comparison with the documentary evidence, it performed its purpose.

The International became a conspiratorial, anti-national body, with disciplined cohorts in every land and with incalculable resources. No country was safe from it, and no one knew where it would strike next. A new alchemy transmuted legend into fact. Yet every leading newspaper that had reported the meetings of the organization knew that it had never been strong. Moreover the defeat of the Commune fairly staggered it, and it never recovered from the blow. Five years later it quietly passed out of existence in a small meeting room in Philadelphia, with only its intimates present. Nevertheless, press and police, in Europe and in the United States, continued to credit it with vast armies Bonaparte had never dreamed of, and with storehouses of gold Midas himself might have envied. The hand of the International was seen in every disturbance, demonstration and strike. In the railroad strike of 1877, the story made the rounds that the International had started it to establish Communes in America. But the small remains of the International had been quietly buried the previous year. Its followers in the United States had never amounted to much more than 5,000 in its heyday, that is in the first half of 1872. Yet the records of the French police on the International in America gave it around 1,400,000 in April 1876,[27] less than three months before the delegates of its last 600 or 700 members administered the final rites.

4. Now such wild and extravagant stories were already abundant at the time of the Commune. The conclusion to be derived from them was perfectly manifest. For if the Commune was an international menace, promoted by the Internationalists—and American newspapers let it be known that that was beyond question—the United States was just as much threatened by revolution as any country in Europe. The Commune might rise again, this time in America, in a shape more terrible than before. Twilight would then descend on civilization.

When news arrived that the Versailles troops had put down the Commune with a mass slaughter, the metropolitan press of New York condoned it with a feeling of relief. The *Tribune,* though at first shocked by the vengeance, could not forbear "a cry of thankfulness that the beast has been conquered."[28] In the opinion of the New York *Standard,* Paris needed the "terrible purgation."[29] The carnage so horrified the *Evening Telegram* that it called for moderation, but only the week before it had demanded severity "to deter their allies in other cities from trying the game of rebellion again."[30] The *Star* wrote that "The conduct of the Communist leaders has in fact been so atrocious that they must not hope for mercy."[31] The *Journal of Commerce* looked to the total extermination of the Communards;[32] and the *Herald* wrote that clemency "would be mistaken kindness." It recommended that the Communards "and their friends all over the world ought to be picked up and summarily disposed of."[33] To the *Times* the massacre signified that the underlying moral forces had written out "a history of retribution, as plain as if it were written on the midnight sky in miracle letters of fire." It was "the hand of Providence."[34] Only a small number of newspapers, among them the *Sun,* held back from calling for more blood. But the *Evening Post,* though it reproached Thiers on one day for having inspired his troops with bitter hatred and "exaggerated the cruelty of the Communists," concluded on another: "All nations, indeed, rejoice with France at the suppression of a revolt which was blind, aimless, and hopeless."[35]

Because the Commune was said to be the legitimate and planned offspring of the International, it was regarded as a problem to all nations. For the International was a hydra, they said, with tentacles everywhere, in the United States, too. Their contention was true to the extent that the organization had been in existence in America in a small way since 1869. By May 1871, it had had around eight or nine sections, most of them in the East. Several had been in Chicago, and others had been in the process of formation in San Francisco and New Orleans. There was a difference, however, between the American sections and the European, for example in Belgium or France. There the International had established itself among indigenous workers. Most of its members in the United States, however, were immigrants. Perhaps its greatest source of weakness in this country was its inability to take root among native workers, or among the Irish who made up a good portion of the labor force. Its American enemies, however, cared little about its character in their own country. The mere presence of its sections and its stout defense of the Commune was their best evidence of its standing threat to the United States. In confirmation of their thesis, they pointed to the Communards who had sought asylum in America. Compared with their number in England or Switzerland, those in America were too few to be considered a disturbing factor. But some of them joined American sections of the International, and continued to uphold the cause of the Commune. To champions of the status quo ex-Communards and sections of the International on American soil were final proof of the universal menace of the Commune.

It could happen here, the press warned. Several newspapers even recorded their sympathy with extradition,[36] as Versailles had demanded. The *World*[37] and the *Star,*[38] however, vindicated the right of asylum. The second was one of the few metropolitan sheets that did not share the current opinion that the Commune was a permanent threat to society. It argued that Paris had "vaccinated the world."[39] The leading papers thoroughly disagreed with that. Society as a whole had not heard the last of the Commune, they said. American cities sheltered a restless proletariat; trade unions had grown to national dimensions; capital and labor eyed each other as enemies; Internationalists aided strikers; reformers and socialists moved about, agitating for their particular programs. These were all signs of imminent conflicts, of potential disorders that might jeopardize the economic system. "Let us keep our eyes open," was the advice of the *Herald*.[40] The American army should get more training and the soldiers' condition improved, was the recommendation of the *Evening Telegram*.[41] A coal miner's strike in Pennsylvania was, in the opinion of the *Evening Post*, a rehearsal for another Commune.[42] The *Nation*, edited by Edwin L. Godkin, ventured the prediction that the ideas of the Paris Commune "will live and grow." They will not cease to spread "until they have made one great attempt for the conquest of modern society, and have in that attempt shaken our present civilization to its foundation."[43]

The New York *Times* was an untiring Cassandra. True, the teachings of the Commune, it conceded, did not present an immediate danger to the American republic. But the future was not reassuring. Only about a year and a half earlier, the *Times* had reported a disturbing increase in pauperism in New York City. One of every thirteen inhabitants was either on temporary or permanent relief.[44] Consequently, insisted the paper, it was a mistake to regard the Commune as peculiar to France. The materials that gave it sustenance were seething in every large city. New York, like Paris, the *Times* gave notice, had "a volcano of deep passions and explosive social forces." And while the pressure on American workers was less heavy than on the European, while workers in the United States could expect to become capitalists, the danger was always there. Socialists and communists were disseminating their principles among workers; American trade unions were becoming allies of the European unions. If the opportunity that had existed in Paris presented itself in New York, the *Times* was convinced, "we should see a sudden storm of communistic revolution . . . such as would astonish all who do not know these classes."[45]

A mine was beneath every large city, the *Times* believed and others agreed, needing but some theory to set it off. What was the precaution? The classes that bred communists should be helped, was a general answer. Instead of going West, which would only transfer the problem to another area, the *Times* saw merit in the Rochedale cooperative plan and in some form of profit sharing as likely measures for offsetting strikes

and socialist teachings. Free schooling, lower taxes and religious indoctrination were also reliable antidotes, it held.[46]

Every editor had his own preventive. The *Herald* had full confidence in the teaching of religion. It was the "saving essential for man,
both in the present and for the hereafter."[47] The *Tribune* put complete
trust in the untrammeled laws of economics to remove social friction.
The avenues to wealth and distinction had to be kept open to allow
frugal and industrious workers to rise to the class of capitalists.[48] The
Standard was partial to the remedies of the *Times;*[49] and the *World*
held with the *Tribune* in the efficacy of economic freedom, provided
the national government maintained possession of the national domain.[50]
The only methods for restoring the balance between capital and labor,
according to the *Evening Post,* was to reduce taxes, reform the civil
service and return to specie payment.[51]

In fine, after having done what was possible to distort the Commune and to put it beyond the pale of humanity, the metropolitan press
recommended its quarantine. It might infect the United States. The
cures emanating from editorial offices differed superficially from one
another. At bottom they were quite similar, for in no instance was the
remedy calculated to shake faith in the accepted order of things.

2

A survey of the metropolitan press on the Commune must necessarily take account of the small number of papers that either did not
move with the tide of opinion or showed restraint in judgment. There
was the *Weekly New York Democrat* that considered the political demands of the Commune worthy of being incorporated in the Constitution of the United States. The underlying significance of the workers'
government escaped the *Weekly.* But it rejected the charges of terror.
If there were excesses, it reasoned, they were unavoidable in civil
dissension.[52]

The New York *World* tried to balance between Paris and Versailles.
The result was a mixture of fact and falsehood. Still it consciously strove
to hold a middle position. If it published Jules Favre's circular to foreign governments, calling for the extradition of Communards,[53] it also
believed the demand was "one of the most outstanding pieces of ef-
frontery which even our day . . . has brought to view."[54] If it excerpted
Mazzini's indictments of the Commune,[55] it set against them interviews
with leading Communards and Internationalists, among them Charles
Longuet, Léo Frankel and Karl Marx.[56] The long interview with Marx,
on July 3, 1871, highly valued by Internationalists, was republished by
Woodhull & Claflin's Weekly.[57]

Radicals were also grateful to the *World* for having published nearly all of the *Address on the Civil War in France*.[58] Thereafter editorial writers could not avoid noticing it. The weeklies, the *Golden Age* and the *Nation*, found in it confirmation of their respective forecasts: the one, that the Commune was a patriotic and laudable attempt at self-government; the other, that the Commune would increase the audacity of the International and push back the horizon of the future.[59] Both weeklies, however, regarded the *Address* with great respect. The *Golden Age* described it as "a pungent, angry and manly defence of the Paris Commune."

Each of the three New York dailies that commented on the *Address* drew a different meaning from it. For the *Star* it dispelled all doubts that the Commune aimed at absolute state control of all goods, and this angered the editor.[60] The *Times* discovered in the *Address* a verification of its foreboding that the struggle of the Commune heralded greater conflicts in order to achieve "a new order of society."[61] The *World* appraised the *Address* as a frank presentation of what the Commune was and what it meant to be. Apart from the content, said the paper, the statement had great literary merit. In its opinion, "No clearer, stronger, or more fervent piece of political writing, in the hortatory way, has ever appeared." But the *World* had also read the *Address* as a warning to statesmen and men of property. No country was immune to the electric waves of popular movements. Their impact could be cushioned if the government was frugal with its unoccupied lands.[62] That was the favorite panacea of the *World*.

The press comments on the *Address* were a gauge of the interest the Commune had stirred in the United States. Journalists were inclined to take the General Council's pronunciamento as an official declaration of what the Commune had aimed at, and hoisted the danger signal. Still, the *Address* won a wide audience in America. According to *Woodhull & Claflin's Weekly*, "No public document has ever been more sought after. . . . Hundreds of thousands have been circulated upon the Continent, and nearly as many in the United States."[63] The metropolitan press could well have claimed some of the credit for the success of its circulation.

Feeling on the Commune ran high in American cities. Opinion weighed heavily against it, if the press and pulpit were any guide. The large press, we have seen, presented it in a frightening form. The pulpit assisted by charging it with impiety and atheism. Catholic priests likened it to Satan, said it was the direct descendant of materialism and the French Revolution. And Protestant divines, including the eloquent, popular and highly paid Henry Ward Beecher, called the Communards a Godless lot. Since America, in their belief, was less vulnerable than Europe, they were not unduly alarmed over the possible effects of the

Commune on Americans. Nevertheless, they demanded systematic, religious indoctrination.

The denunciations of the Paris Revolution, often detailing the same alleged horrors, make monotonous reading. Accounts that departed from the accepted pattern or were incompatible with it were indeed uncommon, and their authors inevitably singled themselves out. There were Frank M. Pixley of the San Francisco *Chronicle* and William Huntington of the Cincinnati *Commercial* who described the Communards as noble defenders of democracy against monarchism. And there was George Wilkes whose stories in the New York *Herald*, subsequent to the event, presented the Commune as a government of moderation and decency, guarding public morals, respecting religion and protecting property. What he said was the direct contrary of what the *Herald* had printed.

To the same category of journalists belonged John Russell Young of the New York *Standard*. His long story from Paris, that shocked colleagues of the press, showed that the Communards had been libeled. Arriving in the French capital, during a confidential mission for the State Department, he observed that its inhabitants were neither the infidels, nor the pillagers nor the débris of human nature they had been painted, neither drunkards, nor ruffians, nor dividers of property. He saw instead peaceful and orderly citizens, and a marked absence of police. The picture, needless to say, was quite the reverse of what the people had been given to see.[64] His reply to newspaper editors who reproved him for his exposé merits citation:

"It would have been so much easier, so much more popular, so much more acceptable, to home people, to have united in the chorus of anger that seemed to come from the English written press; to have shared the agitations of correspondents, who looked at Paris from the terrace of St. Germain and telegraphed their emotions to New York; to have written a wild article or two, freshened up with the rhetoric of the Reign of Terror. But what we saw and what we heard and what impressions they made upon us—a stranger in a strange and deeply interesting land, among people whose history we had read with affection and deep emotion—we felt called upon to write and print. In that shape truth came to us, and we spoke it."[65]

Wendell Phillips, after reading Young's report, declared it was "the ablest, most brilliant and searching of all essays on the Commune."[66]

Phillips was the eminent representative of a tiny group of American intellectuals in whom the Commune, for one reason or another, struck sympathetic chords. Intellectuals generally seem to have been indifferent to it, or joined the body of its accusers. Such were also the attitudes of a great many of them in Europe, including France. Phillips, much as Frederic Harrison in England, was among the exceptions, who rejected the current opinion and attributed the printed nightmares to diseased minds. With him was W. J. Linton, a former English Chartist. He made the *Tribune* the object of his polemic, not because its calumnies were more offensive than in other leading dailies, but because it had been haloed for its integrity and authority.[87]

Inspired by Linton's series of articles, and possibly by the *Address* of the General Council, Phillips embarked on a defense of the Paris Commune. His position was in keeping with the essence of his thought as it had taken form after the Civil War. For he had moved in the direction of the labor movement, and rested his hopes on it to complete an unfinished revolution. The scope of this essay does not allow an inquiry into his social and political philosophy. We can, however, say that he was a Jeffersonian democrat with socialist leanings. His vision, or rather the terminal point of his social philosophy, was a small community that was free from the extremes of wealth and poverty. That was also the ideal of the artisan and small owner. The wage system was as repellent to Phillips as it was to the artisan. And for its abolition he had come to regard expectingly the international unity of labor and its contemporary embodiment, the First International. Perhaps therein was his reason for affiliating with it.

His understanding of the Paris Commune was not the same as is to be found in the *Address* of the General Council. For example, he did not appraise it as a new type of government that would be instrumental in the attainment of labor's ends. His estimation of it was in line with democracy and humanitarianism as then understood by Americans.

His mind shuttled from the present to the past. Americans, in judging the Commune, he advised, should not repeat the mistakes of their ancestors with regard to the French Revolution. Contemporaries, urged Phillips, should take a broad view, consider the Commune in its real historical setting, see it as a noble attempt to regenerate France after a long, demoralizing reign. The defeat of the Commune was in itself a pledge of the final triumph of its mission. The world would then rank it with the grand movements of history.

Phillips refused to lend credence to the alleged crimes of the Communards. Their movement was a popular one and orderly, he said. Even the Bourse declined to close. And the pillagers? Those arrested, he replied, were poor; and those who had escaped, equally so. If they were guilty of bloodshed, he reasoned, the blame was Thiers's. He had set the example; he had rejected the exchange of prisoners, and had shot captured soldiers. The Communards, continued Phillips, were patriots who had not made peace with Napoleon, but who had spent their lives "in noble protest against a cruel and sensual despot, while Thiers basked in his smiles. . . ." Phillips chided American journalism for catering to prejudice. The truth was, he said, the Communards fought for a cause similar to that of the American revolutionists in 1776. "The Commune," he believed, "is one end of the telegraph wire of Liberty; the United States are the other."[68]

People promptly took note of Phillips's articles. The *Times* tried to minimize their value by saying that they rested on half-truths.[69] On the other hand, French Internationalists in the United States rated them highly, and sent him their thanks.[70]

Phillips clung to his faith in the Paris Commune. Seven years later he was as convinced of the righteousness of its aim as he had been in 1871. It "had some of the ablest men in the world," he told a reporter in an interview, "men of the purest character, highest motives, and of the staunchest honesty. History will vindicate them and the cause for which they struggled."[71]

American supporters of the Commune were a comparatively small minority. Labor papers by and large were unsympathetic, even hostile. They believed the horror scenes in the big press. Even the *Workingman's Advocate* of Chicago, that had regularly published friendly reports from a European correspondent, finally accepted the colored versions or reprinted painfully astonishing stories from English newspapers. The Commune had steadfast partisans in American Internationalists. If their press was too weak to stem the influence of the large newspapers, they voiced their opinions at meetings and demonstrations. But they reached only a fraction of American labor. English speaking workers generally were either apathetic or antagonistic to the Paris Commune.

THE FIRST INTERNATIONAL AND A
NEW HOLY ALLIANCE

A SURVEY of the vast literature on the International Workingmen's Association which appeared in the four or five years after the Franco-Prussian War would be an independent essay. Most of it added nothing but heat to the passions aroused by the Paris Commune and the International.[1] The significance of these publications was their international character and a similarity of their themes, as if they had derived from the same source. Publicists painted the International as an immense conspiracy with a full treasury and with countless forces. They held it responsible for strikes and labor disturbances; and they regarded it as the sworn enemy of national interests. Journalists and statesmen charged it had a master plan for bringing down the entire social structure. The Commune, they said, was the creature of the International. The powers should agree on a modus vivendi, or the International would achieve its plan through a European War. Never before had a workingmen's association been the focus of so much emotionalism.

The purpose of this essay is not to sketch the general history of the First International, but to draw attention to a chapter its historians have neglected: namely, its effect on European chancelleries. Yet it is worth inquiring briefly whether the fear it had engendered had any basis. It was true that, since its foundation in 1864, the International Workingmen's Association had built up a large following, but it never had the vast numbers with which enemies credited it. Its weakness was apparent to all who had followed its proceedings before the Franco-Prussian War.[2] They revealed sharp divisions on every important question. French Proudhonists vied with Belgian Colinsists[3] or British trade unionists; German socialists took issue with Swiss federalists; and Bakuninists clashed with Marxists. Finally, the attempts of the Bakuninists and Blanquists to capture the organization and to turn it into a conspir-

183

acy led Marx and his followers to expel the former and move its head-quarters to the United States.

Nor was the International a wealthy organization, as its antagonists believed. It was forever in need of funds, and the dues from sections were constantly in arrears. The unpublished minutes of the General Council testify that it often could not pay rent on its modest quarters or the publication of important manifestoes. It was accused of sending abundant aid to strikers; but if aid there was, it came from trade unions at the request of the General Council. The First International did not organize strikes, as it was held. Once they broke out, however, the Council called for assistance and did what was possible to prevent the importation of strike-breakers. Its success in checking wage reductions, in reducing the working day, in organizing some of the most underpaid workers, was a cardinal factor behind the assaults on the International.

The attacks turned into an all-out offensive with the rise of the Paris Commune. Though its program was far from clear, it nevertheless had a working class character corresponding to the state of develop-ment of the Parisian workers. That individual Internationalists had shared in the establishment and administration of the Commune is a matter of record. Also on record is the Council's advice to the Parisians not to take up arms against the republic.[4] However, when the Com-mune arose, it received the entire backing of the International. Hence its enemies regarded the Paris Revolution as its design. The strike move-ment during the sixties, that culminated in the Commune, was said to be in character with the master plan of the organization for seizing power everywhere. It was like eating an artichoke, first leaf by leaf and finally the whole head.

The facts prove that fear of the International was groundless. It was neither rich, nor powerful, nor a conspiracy. It was a workers' asso-ciation whose meetings and decisions were public knowledge. The charge of conspiracy was a specious reason for persecuting it. Behind the charge was the larger purpose of wiping out workers' associations.

Much of the ephemeral literature on the International, after the Commune, lacks sincerity and astuteness, not to mention reliability. There is no way of measuring the persuasive power these hostile publications had, for no polls were taken. It is safe to assume that many credited the accounts they had read. Propagandists themselves became a prey to their own hallucinations; and police officials, too. The general effect was a hysteria over the First International, that eventually reached into the highest strata of government, as is revealed in documents we have found in the French National Archives and especially in the Archives of the Belgian Ministry of Foreign Affairs.[5] So great was the concern about the Association, that statesmen called into being a new Holy Alliance to combat it.[6]

1

The interest of governments in the First International was not a novelty in 1871. Its first congress in Geneva, in 1866, received ample publicity in the controlled French press. According to information received by the General Council in autumn of that year, the French and Prussian Governments were intercepting the mail of the International.[7] That was not surprising. For contrary to the wishes of French Proudhonists, it championed the rights of subject peoples, and called on the workers to resist the warlike policies of their governments.[8]

To European capitalists, the International was a mysterious power that intruded impertinently to prevent them from employing labor on their own terms. Conflicts between capital and labor grew steadily more bitter after 1865, resulting in skirmishes between workers and troops. To hold the International responsible for the violence in time became proper and convenient, and no European ruler was as prompt in presenting charges as was Napoleon III, the self-appointed patron of labor. His prestige was ebbing after the failure of his plans in Mexico and on the European Continent. Twice in 1868 the Paris bureau of the Association had to stand trial for the alleged crime of conspiracy. It was not long before the governments of Belgium and Austria-Hungary followed Napoleon's example.

Statesmen had not yet arrived at a common policy on the international. This is not to suggest that there was no collaboration on lower levels. Available documents show that before the Paris Commune French and Swiss police, for example, were assisting each other against the organization.[9] The Belgian police cooperated with Napoleon III by expelling French political exiles and Internationalists.[10]

Increasing European rivalry and the unstable economic situation, during the four years before the Franco-Prussian War, disposed government officials to observe the International more closely. Already, after its Congress at Basel in 1869, a French Attorney General wrote to the Minister of Justice: "Prudent and observant minds see in this menacing organization, that has been growing larger and stronger, the big black spot of the future, and they are asking whether governments will not soon feel the need of drawing closer and uniting to defend themselves against the common threat from these formidable leagues."[11] And a high ranking Swiss official, who claimed to have a plan for combating strikes and the International, offered to share it with the Belgian Government. The Belgian Minister of the Interior, however, still relied on private initiative to take the necessary measures.[12]

The Paris Commune impelled statesmen and business men to take common action against Communards and Internationalists. For the Commune was the most dangerous alternative the existing order had yet had. Governments watched uneasily the outcome of the struggle in France. Shortly after its start the Belgian Foreign Minister wrote to his colleagues in the government that, in view of "the gravity of the situation in Paris and the numerous ramifications of the International in Belgium," exceptional vigilance was necessary in the workers' centers, "so that we may be in a position to act efficiently at the first sign."[13] The Prussians threatened to intervene, but Bismarck vetoed it lest it cause Thiers's fall from power. The Chancellor was reported to have said: "Thiers was the suitable man." And while he reserved the right to interfere, if the Commune were to triumph, he also encouraged Versailles to assemble the largest possible number of troops, even aided it by releasing French prisoners of war. Officials in Vienna feared that the triumph of the Commune would increase the membership of the International in Austria.[14] Evidence that the International had nine sections in Portugal disquieted police officials and ministers in Madrid and Lisbon.[15]

The defeat of Paris gave a sense of relief to the monarchies of Europe. Thiers received congratulatory messages from the Governments of Sweden, Holland, Spain, Belgium and Russia.[16] The Vatican, sharing the general contentment, regarded the Commune as a form of retribution for the diffusion of rationalism. According to the Belgian representative in Rome, Vatican spokesmen were saying that since Paris had been the laboratory of this doctrine "God wanted to show in this center of progress what man-made institutions result in when they do not rest on Christian ethics. On the whole, the consensus of opinion in the territory of the Pope seems to attribute all present evils in France to the influence of the principles arising from the Revolution of 1789."[17] People in high rank were also uneasy lest the Commune and the International inspire a violent conflict between the Italian and Papal parties over the Roman Question. As a precaution, the government, headed by Thiers made plans to build in Corsica a comfortable refuge for the Papal court.[18]

2

Versailles, considering itself the successor to Napoleon as the guardian of order and property, called on governments to extradite refugees and Internationalists. A circular, addressed on May 26, 1871, by Jules Favre, the Foreign Minister, to French foreign envoys, charged Communards with premeditated assassination, theft and incendiarism. Their continued residence abroad, he wrote, "would be both a shame and a danger."[19]

There is ample evidence to show that Versailles used every suitable method to achieve its purpose.[20] It sent secret agents abroad "to spy on insurgents"; it bombarded its embassies with telegrams and circulars; and it briefed the press. The instructions dwelt on conditions in France, calculated to make it a bulwark against the International. France, according to the directions, had a large class of small landed proprietors; its workers had every opportunity to climb the social ladder; its soldiers, sons of peasants and workers, would never jeopardize their future by treating with Internationalists. In fine, France was so rooted in conservatism that it was a stabilizing power in Europe.

Perhaps behind this neat picture of France was the object of building up public opinion for the projected domestic loan of two billion francs. But there was no doubt about the purpose of Favre's Circular of June 6, 1871, to diplomatic agents abroad.[21] The document was in keeping with earlier messages. The Commune, it declared, was the net result of demoralization under the Second Empire. The depressed feeling stemming from the Franco-Prussian War had inspired extravagant thinking that a small political group had exploited to establish the Commune. Nowhere in the document was there reference to the measures of Versailles that had alienated Parisians, or to the monarchist threat of the National Assembly. With utter irreverence for the facts, Favre went on to say that the International, as an integral part of the group that had risen to power in Paris, was far stronger and more dangerous than its accomplices. It had numbers and discipline. Citing anarchist sources, he tried to establish that it preached atheism and communism, that its aim was to impose a frightful despotism. He then directed the envoys to impress foreign statesmen with the gravity of the situation. "Governments cannot afford indifference and inertia," he wrote. "They would be guilty, after the recent lessons, if they remained unconcerned over the destruction of laws protecting morality and the prosperity of peoples."

The General Council of the International, in London, issued a reply that appeared in the *Times* and the *Eastern Post*. It pointed to Favre's errors, his misuse of documents and his distortion of the principles of the International. Favre, for example, presented the program of Bakunin's Alliance of Socialist Democracy as that of the International, though the General Council had opposed it. The Council disclosed that Favre, though a sworn enemy of the organization, had approached it to agitate in behalf of the Government of National Defense. But in vain. The Council had forewarned the Paris workers against him and his colleagues in the government.[22]

Favre's request for international action against Communards and the International had a varied reception abroad. Dispatches reveal that where governments were sensitive to surviving traditions and public opinion, they were inclined to be cautious in making commitments. English officials, mindful of the tradition of asylum, could not give the French ambassador any hope of conforming with Favre's request. This did not mean that a number of them were not in sympathy with it. The Home Secretary, for instance, offered the services of the London metropolitan police to watch dangerous Communards and tolerated the activity of French spies for the same purpose.[23]

A demand to have the English Government join the crusade against the International was made in the House of Commons in March 1872 by Mr. Baillie Cochrane, from the Isle of Wight. With a copy of the *Address on The Civil War in France* in his hand he argued that the International and the Commune were identical. He praised George Odger and Benjamin Lucraft, English trade union leaders and members of the General Council, for having withdrawn their names from the *Address*. He, too, made Bakunin's declarations on atheism, family and inheritance the guiding principles of the International. For additional authority, he leaned on Mazzini's venomous attack on the organization in *Roma del popolo*.[24] Mr. Cochrane, however, had little support in Parliament.

The speech of Mr. Henry Fawcett, a member for Brighton, was a measure of the knowledge Parliamentarians had of the Association. Mr. Fawcett, a champion of laissez-faire economics, interpreted the International's program as state intervention. Yet he had claimed in his opening remarks to have "devoted considerable attention to the subject under notice." State interference, he feared, gave workers false hopes and intensified their misery. They should be taught instead to rely on their own efforts.[25]

The sharp reply of the General Council, written by Marx, credited Mr. Cochrane with falsehood and ignorance, and Mr. Fawcett with "scientific nullity."[26]

In Switzerland, as in England, the right of asylum was an established tradition. Answering Favre's request for extradition, the Swiss Federal Council took the position that a distinction could be made between political and criminal refugees. In that event the right of asylum might have to be refused to persons of the second category.[27] Since the policy did not draw a clear demarcation between the two, the Swiss Government might have yielded to pressure and surrendered a number of ex-Communards if public opinion had not been aroused. A petition emanating from the National Labor Association of Geneva received wide circulation.[28] The petition called on the Swiss Federal Council to preserve unimpaired the right of asylum. "At the same time," as the French Minister in Berne wrote to his government, "the radical and socialist press in all of Switzerland has seized upon the question, treating it from a point of view favorable to the refugees. Meetings have been organized in several places, in Geneva, in Zurich, in Saint-Gall and elsewhere in favor of the right of asylum. The conservative press is keeping silent."[29] The Swiss government, yielding to popular pressure, set free the refugees it had arrested.

Switzerland followed a somewhat similar course on the International. The Swiss President's reply to the French said that his government had never given any attention to the International Association. Its aim, he continued, had never been a threat to the security of his country, and the government had never inquired whether it had many partisans. Recent events in Paris, he concluded, "would in no way change the government's line of conduct."

The Belgian minister believed that the President was telling the truth, for the radical strength in the Swiss Federal Council would prevent interference in the affairs of the International.[30] But the Swiss police cooperated with the Belgian, just as they had cooperated with the police of the Second Empire. The chief of the Department of Justice and Police in Geneva readily agreed to show his dossier on the International to the Belgian Consul, hoping at the same time for an international agreement on a mutual exchange of intelligence.[31]

The desire for an understanding among governments expressed by the Geneva Chief of Police probably got warm acceptance from the Belgian Consul. For his Foreign Minister, in a conversation with the French representative had already urged an entente of the powers for the suppression of the International. He promised that his cabinet would welcome any overtures with that end in view.[32] He knew the International was far from strong in Belgium. His own Minister of Justice had written him: "I have often been able to ascertain that the French greatly exaggerate the forces of the International in Belgium and that they willingly take their own desires and aspirations for reality."[33] But since the International had had a hand in the strikes in Belgium at the end of the Franco-Prussian War,[34] its destruction was held to be the preliminary to the weakening of the trade unions.

The Belgian Foreign Minister had already astonished liberals and progressives by his announcement in the Belgian Chamber of Deputies that he would not treat Communards as political refugees.[35] That was clearly inconsistent with the country's established policy, particularly of the right of asylum that had protected such eminent political figures as Buonarroti, an Italian, Marx, a German, Lelewel, a Pole, and Blanqui, a Frenchman. Internationalists in Belgium at once called meetings of protest, and Victor Hugo, then residing in Brussels, wrote a letter to L'Indépendance belge,[36] stating his indignation. The celebrated man of letters made it known that, while he neither shared the views of the

Communards nor condoned their acts, he considered the right of asylum sufficiently sacred to defy authority if it tried to remove a refugee from his home. He furthermore declared:

"If they come to my home to arrest a fugitive of the Commune, they will have to take me, too. If they surrender him, I shall follow him to the witness chair. And, in defense of the cause, the republican Bonaparte had outlawed will place himself by the side of the Communard the Versailles Assembly has taken captive." An unsigned note in the Belgian Foreign Archives, appended to the letter, says that in view of Hugo's resistance to the policy "we think it our duty to take with regard to the red bandits, it seems to me we must not hesitate a moment. We must turn him out."[37] The government expelled him from the country on May 30, 1871.

The Belgian authorities cooperated with Versailles. Two dossiers in the Belgian Foreign Archives contain lists and photographs of Communards, labelled, "Foreigners who are forbidden entrance into Belgium." Both lists and photographs, supplied by the Versailles police, were designed to help the Belgian secret service identify escaping victims of the terror.[38] It is clear from the documents that the Belgian police circulated the lists in the principal centers along the French frontier and in ports with strict orders to arrest those who were recognized. Similarly mayors and local administrators got instructions "to watch out for foreigners."[39] So certain was Versailles of Belgian compliance with its demand for extradition that its minister in Brussels had prepared warrants for the arrest of designated Communards.[40]

The Belgian course of action was unpopular, but diplomats were grateful. The Belgian Minister in Rome reported on June 3, 1871, "the highly favorable impression the determined attitude of the King's government towards the insurgents of Paris has had on all honest people. My diplomatic colleagues, the Pontifical authorities and many distinguished persons of this city have abandoned reserve in the chorus of praise I was happy to hear from them."[41]

3

Though the continental powers did not reach an understanding on the International before 1873, they were already exchanging information in 1871. The Geneva Police Commissioner, we have remarked, turned over to the Belgians his dossier on the International; the Belgian authorities acted as policemen for Versailles; the London police kept French refugees under surveillance; and the British Home Secretary privately permitted French spies to follow the movements of "dangerous" individuals. In this connection, the French ambassador in London recommended the revival of the French secret service in England as it had existed under Napoleon III.[42] Probably this revived service had the assignment of reporting on Marx and Engels. If its reports are a measure of its calibre, it must have been either incompetent or dishonest. The dossier on Marx seems to have assembled all the myths about him and the International, that the daily press gave out.[43]

The French government ordered its embassies to send it data on the International abroad. The representative in Denmark wrote that the strength of the International there could not be established. Some said it had 3,000 members, but the estimate of competent observers was only 300. From Stockholm arrived a report that the International had little influence in Sweden. Workers there were inclined to favor cooperatives, mutual aid and credit societies, rather than revolutionary organizations. Nevertheless, the chief of police in Stockholm decided to visit the Prefect of Police in Paris to study the problem with him. Similarly, the head of the Belgian detective force visited the Parisian Prefect to draft a common plan of action against the International. A dispatch from Russia had it that the French could count on full Tsarist support to root out the International Workingmen's Association.[44]

This mutual exchange of information may account for the existence of several important documents on the International in the French National Archives. Thus, the French consul in Frankfort sent his government a report on the private conference of the International in London in September 1871. The report, probably received from the German police, was accurate in the main, although it erred in several respects.[45] Together with the report is a copy of a secret circular Premier Sagasta of Spain addressed to the provincial governors on January 16, 1872. Sagasta's understanding of the principles of the International was on a par with Favre's or with Cochrane's, though Francisco Mora, secretary of the Spanish Federal Council of the International, had written many illuminating articles on the organization.[46] All three made Bakuninism the program of the International; and they all equally saw it as a gigantic conspiracy. Sagasta considered the International "a challenge to the integrity and security of the country." But behind the grandiloquence was the design of stopping workers from organizing and of putting into practice what he held to be "the sound traditions of the liberal school." The natural law of supply and demand could not be interfered with. "The intervention of authority becomes both legitimate and indispensable for the protection of the freedom of all." In the language of economic liberalism, Sagasta stated the fundamental reason why the Spanish and other governments had transformed the International into an antediluvian monster.

The Spanish authorities were among the first to accede to Favre's request for extradition. As early as May 30, 1871, the Spanish consul in Marseilles gave local police the right to search Spanish ships in the harbor for refugees.[47] Also, at the request of the Prefect of Toulouse, Spanish police tried to arrest Paul Lafargue, Marx's son-in-law, who had crossed the frontier to escape French police.[48]

The Spanish government in time became the victim of an illusion. It was ready to introduce a law against the International, modeled on the one voted in France on March 14, 1872. But it first desired the co-operation of the powers. Great Britain's reply was in line with its answer to Favre's circular. "Despite its revolutionary doctrines," answered the British Foreign Minister, the Association "aimed at serving as the center of communication among the workers of different nationalities . . . restricting its action, especially in England, to giving advice on strikes." After reminding the Spanish ambassador of the British right of asylum, the Foreign Minister concluded that, under existing conditions, there was no ground for changing the laws regarding foreigners in England.

The other powers, according to an inquiry by the Portuguese Foreign Minister, had no clear and definite principles on which to base an accord. Their decisions on the question would necessarily depend on their particular political and economic situations. For example, Portugal, he noted, because of its distance from the center of things and its undeveloped industry, was less open to the propaganda of the International. Neither the Portuguese Parliament nor public opinion, he continued, "would accept, without great reluctance," a law similar to that in France.[49]

The Portuguese government was inclined to eye favorably the course taken by France and Spain. The increasing number of strikes in Portugal in 1872 persuaded the authorities to regard the International as the instigator. For the present they preferred to rely on the influence of the Church and on international police action to stem its power. Thus the Foreign Minister said to one of the foreign representatives: "We must above all avoid weakening the religious feelings of the people. It is the most solid defense against the brutal and unholy desires the International has been trying to stimulate among us."[50] The police of Lisbon welcomed a representative of the Prefecture in Paris, whose purpose in coming was to study the International and the labor movement in Portugal. Thanks to the French minister in Portugal, his Belgian colleague was permitted to copy the findings. We lack the necessary documentation for checking their accuracy. The papers of F. A. Sorge, who was General Secretary of the International from 1872 to 1874, contain only few references to Portugal. From these we can surmise that as late as May 1873 the International was still active in the Portuguese trade unions.[51] This is in accord with information gathered by the French police investigator. According to his report, the International in Portugal had its greatest prosperity during the period immediately after the Paris Commune. Its membership, however, never exceeded 1,000. It had authority in the trade unions through the Workers Fraternity that came into existence early in 1872. But a series of unsuccessful strikes towards the end of the year exhausted its treasury and caused its ruin. Its final collapse brought down with it sections of the International. By the middle of 1873 they were as moribund in Portugal as in Europe generally.[52]

The weakness of the organization disarmed neither employers of labor nor governments. For while the official International, inspired by Marx, was falling apart in the United States, an anarchist International, led by Bakunin, Guillaume and others, dating from September 1872, was proclaiming its existence in fiery articles and manifestoes. Its revolutionary revolutionism was not likely to silence the foes of organized labor.

Industrialists and big landowners continued to ride the tidal crest of hysteria after the Paris Commune. The cigar manufacturers of Antwerp and Brussels, who had combined to resist demands for higher wages, called for war on the International. They appealed to their government to have their workers deported from France where they had taken jobs on the advice of the International.[53] For the enlightenment of the Belgian higher officialdom, their minister at the Hague sent his government the programs of two organizations Dutch industrialists had created. Their purpose was to dissuade workers from joining the International; and the methods for achieving it were philanthropic measures and directions "that can contribute to the harmony and mutual confidence of the different classes of society."[54] The Society for Public Service in Geneva, for its part, announced in January 1872 the formation of a committee for "the study of ways best calculated to combat the progress of the doctrines of the International Workingmen's Association." The committee set store by profit sharing, consumers' and producers' cooperatives, and instruction in the principles of classical economics. Finally, it recommended the organization of an "International Association of Friends of the Social Order."[55]

One month after the establishment of the committee in Geneva, military leaders, lawyers, landowners, bankers, merchants, manufacturers, rentiers and civil servants met in Paris to found a society they properly called "The Counter-International." The name itself was a program. The object was "the maintenance of order and the respect of individual freedom, property and family." To attain these ends the Counter-Internationalists said they would imitate the International; that is, they would "enlighten the workers, improve their conditions and assist them during strikes, distress, sickness and unemployment." Their declaration, however, also promised "aid to employers, especially during strikes

brought about by the maneuvers of the International."[56] Actually, the
raison d'être of the Counter-International was to keep things as they
were, and to protect employers, with funds if necessary, against organized labor. Underneath was the assumption of the mysterious International Workingmen's Association.

4

Associations against the International, though far-reaching in aims,
do not seem to have extended themselves beyond national frontiers. Belgian dispatches, however, provide evidence that Count von Beust, Austrian Chancellor, and Prince Bismarck, German Chancellor, tried to correct this deficiency by planning to erect a European Association against
the International. There are suggestions that the two Chancellors discussed the plan at their meetings in Gastein and Salzburg in August and
September 1871.

For Favre's circular of June 6, 1871, had made the International
a diplomatic question. It was a cause for consultations between the
French, English and Russian ambassadors and the Austrian and German Foreign Ministers. Bismarck proposed to Beust an exchange of information for combating the organization. In a conversation with the
Belgian Minister in July 1871, Count von Beust said that he had not
yet settled on a method for checking the propaganda of the International. Certain that coercive measures were insufficient, he conceived a
defensive association of European industrialists, "a sort of mutual insurance to indemnify those who were the victims of strikes or whose
plants were damaged or destroyed." According to the Belgian representative, Austria's slowness in taking a stand was due to its favorable economic situation. There was a labor shortage; and socialism in Austria
had not yet become an organized movement. The government "wished
to avoid giving the International an importance it has not yet gained
in Austria." But this policy did not prevent it from indicting socialists
or expelling foreigners reputed to be members of the International.[57]

Disturbed by the rise of socialism in Germany,[58] Bismarck met in
conference, at the end of 1871, with delegates from the German states
and Austria. The Austrian Chancellor offered to submit a memoir on
the problem, and Bismarck in turn promised to study proposals that
might pave the way for a mutual understanding. If the two powers
arrived at a common program, he would communicate it to the other
governments as the basis of a European agreement.[59] Beust had nothing
new to offer. His memoir was a variation of the plan he had presented
earlier, which seems to have been acceptable to the German Chancellor.
Both statesmen, according to a Belgian dispatch from Stuttgart, believed
that the first step was "the creation of an international society of capital-

ists, having as its aim the struggle against the tendencies of the International Workingmen's Association." And since the English government had turned down offers for a common offensive, Beust counted on making a special appeal to English industrialists in the hope of inducing them to join.[60]

We do not know to what extent Beust and Bismarck furthered the plan. It is certain that it remained on paper. The task of achieving harmony among European industrialists raised insoluble issues, at least in the foreseeable future. A number of leading diplomats, however, agreed with Favre that the International should be suppressed. For example, Count Andrássy, Minister of Austria, who was prosecuting Internationalists in Pesth, was eager to join other governments, first on preventive measures and then in an entente.[61] Still more convinced of the need for a pact was the Tsarist government. We have seen that diplomats and officials in different countries had on occasion called for a European agreement to stamp out the International. If we are to believe what the King of Wurttemberg confided to the Belgian Minister, this idea had first originated at the summit, with the Russian Tsar. He is said to have left with the German Emperor a written report on the question when he passed through Berlin in September 1871.[62]

The International was not a serious problem in Russia, according to the French ambassador. Socialist ideas, he said, "had yet little influence on its undeveloped working class." The peasants, "forming the greatest part of the factory workers, have not yet had time to change their old ideas by contact with foreigners." Moreover, they were still fanatically attached to the Tsar. But he remarked in another dispatch that nihilism had been gaining ground, thanks to the writings of Alexander Herzen and Nikolai Chernyshevsky.[63]

Other currents, of which the French ambassador was apparently not aware, had converged to give form and content to the Russian revolutionary movement. First, the ill-fated Crimean War had exposed the rottenness of the Russian social structure. Then there was the wretchedness of the peasant who felt cheated by the Act of Emancipation. Third, the insurrection in Poland in 1863, that the Tsar had crushed with ferocity, had convinced intellectuals that the door of peaceful reform had been shut tight. Finally, the examples of Western Europe, the Paris uprising in particular, invigorated the Russian movement. "With the Paris Commune," wrote Stepniak (Kravchinsky) more than a decade later, "Russian Socialism entered upon its belligerent phase, and from the study and the private gathering passed to the workshop and the village."[64] That may explain the full backing Tsar Alexander II gave in Berlin to the request of Thiers for the release of French prisoners of war who were to be used against the Commune.[65]

Russian response to Favre's circular was quick and warm. True the Tsar had nothing to fear from the International either in the old provinces of the empire or in Finland, but it was a dangerous example for Russian revolutionists. To ridicule them at home and abroad his government staged a public trial of Nechaev's followers in July 1871. Poland, however, was a source of anxiety. Polish insurgents had found refuge in London, where the General Council of the International championed their cause.[66] Poles, present at every congress of the International, symbolized the unity between the labor and national questions.

Paris, too, had had its share of Polish refugees. One hundred and ten had served the Paris Commune, most of them in a military capacity. Three had risen to the rank of general and two of them had died for the cause.

The stress on the national question by the International and the heroism of the Poles in the Paris uprising had made the Tsar eager to recapture the reactionary role his government had had on the Continent from the Congress of Vienna to the Crimean War. The problem, however, was different after the Franco-Prussian War and the Commune. In the first place the victory of Germany, causing a shift in the balance of power, impressed upon him the need of a rapprochement with France. Secondly, to secure his western frontier against an invasion from socialism, he had to cooperate with the two large central powers in order to revive the old Holy Alliance. From the Tsar's point of view the two objectives were not incompatible. In fact, they were part of one pattern.

Before establishing cordial relations with France the Tsarist government sought a pledge that the problem of Polish refugees would no longer stand between the two countries. The Paris Commune had not been the first example of French revolutionists fraternizing with Poles. Back in 1831, after the unsuccessful Polish insurrection, French democrats had welcomed Polish refugees. The Revolution of 1848 had inspired Poles to organize a military unit on French soil. And during the Franco-Prussian War Poles had formed a legion to defend France, though the Government of National Defense had refused their services. The Tsar looked upon that as a friendly gesture that had potentiality.

After the Paris Commune, the Tsar raised the question of Poland in a conversation with the French ambassador. Their exchange of views, early in August 1871, is contained in a dispatch of the French ambassador to his government. The Tsar, he wrote, was highly pleased with the service the French army "had rendered to all of society by the energetic suppression of the last insurrection." He then dwelt on the part Poles had had in it. "Here is another question which has cast many doubts and suspicions on our relations," he added. "I hope this question has now been settled between us." The ambassador, having assured his Majesty that Poland had been a source of embarrassment to France, too, concluded with the hope that the two powers might be on the best of terms.[67]

President Thiers replied to the dispatch that the Polish Question "is the real key for opening the door" to an understanding. And he prided himself on having been consistently opposed to the harboring of Polish revolutionists. Now that he was the head of the French state, he was determined to enforce that.[68]

In line with the Tsar's aim of discrediting the Polish cause, his Third Division financed a Polish journalist in France to write articles and pamphlets. The journalist, Apollo Mlochowski, writing under the pseudonym, De Belina, found the Thiers Government cooperative, for it put at his disposal a number of police dossiers of the Second Empire.[69] Mlochowski showed in his *Les Polonais et la Commune de Paris*[70] that he was more interested in pleasing the Tsar's police than in writing scientific history.

The revival of the Holy Alliance seems to have presented fewer obstacles than a Franco-Russian rapprochement. Bismarck who, in common with other diplomats, regarded democracy and socialism as a challenge to the system of order on a monarchical basis, was ready to enter into an understanding with other governments. He also endorsed Beust's scheme of an international association of industrialists. Russia favored a firmer policy than Austria's. For the reasons we have indicated, the Tsar was persuaded that the united action of the powers alone could stem the tide of radicalism.

Meanwhile Count Andrássy had replaced Count von Beust as head of Austrian foreign affairs. The new minister's hope for an alliance with Germany to check Russian penetration in South-Eastern Europe did not prevent him from supporting the demand of Prince Gorchakov, the Tsar's foreign minister, for an entente against the International. Such an entente was reached at the meeting of the Emperors of Germany, Austria-Hungary and Russia and of their foreign ministers in Berlin in September 1872.

The purposes of the meeting were no secret in diplomatic circles. The Belgian minister in Vienna informed his government on August 1, 1872, that, apart from securing peace, the three powers ". . . must seek to erect a dike against European radicalism that has been threatening all thrones and institutions. It must no longer be the Holy Alliance of absolutism, but a union which, while respecting the needs of modern progress, will have to study the obstacles to withstand the subversive doctrines that have been its most inveterate and formidable enemy."[71]

The agreement, known as the *Dreikaiserbund* (League of Three

Emperors), was at first a verbal understanding. It was supplemented by a written accord in May 1873 between the Emperors of Russia and Austria-Hungary. The German Emperor acceded to it in October 1873.[72]

The agreement made no mention of socialism and the International, but they were implied in the following clause: "Their Majesties are determined to prevent anyone from succeeding in separating them on those principles which they regard as alone capable of assuring and, if need be, of imposing the maintenance of peace in Europe against all upheavals, from whatever quarter they may come."

This was the old Holy Alliance refurbished.

Reports, written shortly after the meeting in Berlin, show that the International was an important subject in the negotiations. The essence of what Gorchakov thought on the question was sent by the British ambassador to his Foreign Secretary.

"Your Lordship's dispatch to the Spanish Government on the subject [wrote the ambassador] left the impression on his [Gorchakov's] mind that H.M. Government underrated the power of the International to sap the foundations of society. Germany, but especially Austria, would suffer much from the revolutionary and subversive action of the International. Russia, thanks to her police regulations, was still free from it; but in the interests of order and morality in Central Europe he would cooperate in crushing the International by every means in his power."

Gorchakov hoped England would not withhold its cooperation in bringing about a reconciliation between capital and labor.[73]

Andrássy was no less impatient to put an end to the International. According to the Russian Foreign Minister's communication to the Tsar on September 9, 1872:

"Count Andrássy indicated a measure which he considers it indispensable to embody in the agreement to be reached, i.e., the prohibition of congresses at which the 'International' poses as a cosmopolitan government, issues decrees, etc.

"To such a measure, agreed upon by the three Courts, the other European Powers would be invited to give their adhesion, and he believes that even Switzerland would then be unable to hold aloof."[74]

There is some indication that a representative of the Tsar, in January 1873, endeavored to persuade the English government to line up with the powers against the International.[75] But England was more interested in settling its colonial differences with Russia than in boxing with shadows. The headquarters of the International had been moved from London to New York. Its sections in England were disintegrating, and its decline in other countries went on simultaneously.

The saving of Europe from revolution, and that was one of the purposes of the League of Three Emperors, actually had no basis in

1872. As time went on, this purpose was completely submerged by other diplomatic issues which were behind the formation of the League.[76] The phantom that deluded journalists and statesmen was losing its haunting power. The official International quietly passed away unnoticed in 1876. After the Congress of Ghent in 1877, where the anarchists were outvoted on the question of political action, the anarchist International also sank into oblivion.

The hysteria after the Paris Commune died slowly. Thus, French police, on hints from Italian and Spanish consuls, searched for Internationalists as late as 1879 and 1880.[77] Also in 1879, the Belgian Chargé d'Affaires in Berne attributed to the International every demand workers made, including the demand for jobs.[78]

Legislation and police measures undoubtedly hastened the break up of the International Workingmen's Association. Apart from that the organization was rapidly losing numbers and influence. That mattered as little to governments as it did to capitalists, for the object was to arrest the organization of labor and to subdue the movement for democratic rights. Again they underestimated labor's potential and the depth of popular resentment.

Colonial and diplomatic problems overshadowed the interest of the powers in the First International. History, moreover, placed the issue between capital and labor on a new level. Socialist parties in various countries made labor's independent political action the keystone of their program. German socialists polled 340,000 votes in 1874 and won nine seats in the Reichstag. The following year Lassalleans and Eisenachers united in one socialist party. The reawakened labor movement in France took the same path. Eight years after the Paris Commune the third labor congress in Marseilles voted that the workers could achieve socialism only by their independent political activity. In essence the program of the International had the same end and, for its achievement, counted on the same means.

NOTES

MARAT, FRIEND OF THE PEOPLE

1. One example, among others, of the manner in which Marat was introduced to English readers was the brief biographic sketch of him, published in 1797 and reprinted in 1799. The opening words were characteristic of the entire piece: "Short in stature, deformed in person, and hideous in face." *Biographical Anecdotes of the Founders of the French Republic and Other Eminent Characters Who Have Distinguished Themselves During the Progress of the Revolution* (London, 1799), I, 231 f. Fourteen years later another volume of short biographies was translated from the French. The eight pages on Marat were filled with abuse and hatred. He was described as follows: "his face was hideous, his character of countenance horrible, and his head monstrous for his size. From nature he derived a daring mind, an ungoverned imagination, a vindictive temper, and a ferocious heart, and the mode of life he pursued till the Revolution, added yet more to his natural wildness and cruelty." *Biographie moderne. Lives of Remarkable Characters who have Distinguished Themselves from the Commencement of the French Revolution to the Present Time* (London, 1811), II, 348-356.

2. Louis R. Gottschalk, *Jean Paul Marat* (New York, 1927), 10 f.

3. *Le publiciste de la république française*, no. 147.

4. Published in English in London in 1774, it had three subsequent French editions.

5. Published in Neuchâtel in 1780. Two other editions appeared in Paris in 1790 and 1794.

6. *L'Ami du peuple*, no. 448.

7. *Les chaînes de l'esclavage* (Paris, 1833), 25 ff., 72 ff.; *Plan de législation criminelle* (Paris, 1790), 13 ff., 19 ff., 22 ff.

8. *Les chaînes de l'esclavage*, 158, 174 ff., 187 f.

9. *Ibid.*, 143, 195, 197, 203.

10. *Ibid.*, 229 ff., 236 f., 241.

11. Among the many programs of reform was one by Babeuf, the future organizer of the Babouvist Party, who proposed a more equal distribution of wealth to solve the problems of poverty and unemployment. See his *Cadastre perpétuel* (Paris, 1789), "Discours préliminaire." A strong plea in favor of the workers and a plan for eradicating poverty came from Linguet, author of the famous *Théoria des loix civiles*, in his pamphlet, *Point de Banqueroute* (1789).

12. John Wilkes, outlawed in absentia for his attack on the prime minister of George III, was later elected to parliament in 1768. His imprisonment, following his surrender, evoked sympathy from vast masses. His repeated expulsions from parliament after repeated reelections stirred up artisans and lower classes

generally to strike and riot. With the slogan "Wilkes and Liberty," they forced
his release and ultimately his election to the Lord Mayoralty in 1774.

13. Charles Vellay, ed., *La Correspondance de Marat* (Paris, 1908), 142;
Charles Vellay, ed., *Les pamphlets de Marat* (Paris, 1911), 2-35.

14. *Les pamphlets de Marat*, 37-70.

15. *L'Ami du peuple*, nos. 18 and 36.

16. *Les pamphlets de Marat*, 118, n.

17. *La constitution ou projet de déclaration des droits de l'homme et du
citoyen, suivi d'un plan de constitution juste, sage et libre* (Paris, 1789), 13 ff.,
and 60 n.

18. The prospectus of the paper first appeared under the title, *Le publiciste
parisien, journal politique, libre et impartial.* Beginning September 12, 1789, the
title was *L'ami du peuple ou le publiciste parisien.* It was a daily, eight page
pamphlet; sometimes Marat increased it to sixteen pages.

19. *L'Ami du peuple*, nos. 11-12.

20. *Ibid*, nos. 14, 40.

21. *Lettre de Marat, l'ami du peuple, à M. Joly, avocat aux conseils,
membre et secrétaire de l'Assemblée générale des représentants de la commune et
l'un des soixante administrateurs de la municipalité* (Versailles, 1789).

22. *L'Ami du peuple*, nos. 29-30, 37, 40; Gérard Walter, *Marat* (Paris,
1933), 15 ff.

23. *L'Ami du peuple*, nos. 13, 28, 52.

24. *Ibid.*, nos. 34-35.

25. *Ibid.*, no. 221.

26. Marat stated his case against Necker not only in numerous issues of
L'Ami du peuple, but also in two pamphlets, *Dénonciation contre Necker*. Both
were republished in *Les pamphlets de Marat*, 72-120, 165-196. According to
Marat, ten different printers refused to handle the first pamphlet. It was finally
set up, in January 1790, in Marat's own printing shop.

27. *L'Ami du peuple*, nos. 21, 84-85, 89-91, 147, 251.

28. *Ibid.*, nos. 155, 292, 320, 390, 414, 419.

29. *Ibid.*, nos. 222, 238, 248, 255-256, 283, 365, 371, 381, 439-442.

30. *Ibid.*, nos. 75, 189, 205, 223, 232, 263, 453, 463, 468, 534.

31. *Ibid.*, nos. 159, 457.

32. *Ibid.*, nos. 249, 334, 414, 549, 610.

33. Robespierre was supported in the Assembly by the abbé Grégoire and
Adrien Duport. In the press, Marat's defense of the propertyless was seconded
by Camille Desmoulins in scattered pages of his *Révolutions de France et de
Brabant*, by Nicholas de Bonneville in *Cercle social*, 1790, no. 24, 148 ff., and by
Abbé Fauchet in *La bouche de fer*, no. 1. One of the best pleas in behalf of the
poor was by an obscure writer in Lyons, L'Ange, *Plaintes et observations d'un
citoyen décrété passif aux citoyens décrétés actifs* (Lyon, 1790).

34. In 1791 there were 4,298,360 active citizens out of a total population
of approximately 26,000,000.

35. *L'Ami du peuple*, nos. 137, 150, 172-174, 264.

36. *Ibid.*, no. 149.

37. *Ibid.*, no. 159.

38. *Ibid.*, nos. 162-163.

39. *Ibid.*, no. 165.

40. *Ibid.*, nos. 462, 558, 624.

41. See the essay on Babeuf, *infra*.

42. *L'Ami du peuple*, nos. 201, 205-206, 208, 211, 213, 215-216; also
Marat's two pamphlets on the Nancy Affair, *Les pamphlets de Marat*, 237-253.

43. *L'Ami du peuple*, nos. 120, 130, 133, 413.

44. *Ibid.*, nos. 285, 487.

45. For this document see *Le moniteur universel*, April 29, 1791. It is re-

printed in Buchez and Roux, *Histoire parlementaire de la révolution française* (Paris, 1834-38), IX, 444 f.

46. Sigismond Lacroix, *Actes de la commune de Paris* (Paris, 1894), second series, IV, 123 f.

47. *Ibid.*, IV, 351 ff.; *L'Ami du peuple*, no. 487.

48. For the full text of the Le Chapelier report and law see *Archives parlementaires*, first series, XXVII, 210 f.

49. *L'Ami du peuple*, nos. 401-402.

50. *Ibid.*, no. 493.

51. *Ibid.*, no. 298.

52. *Ibid.*, nos. 473, 475.

53. *Ibid.*, no. 467.

54. *Ibid.*, nos. 175, 342, 477.

55. *Ibid.*, no. 364. See also Albert Mathiez, "Marat, 'père des sociétés fraternelles,' " *Annales révolutionnaires*, 1908, I, 660-64.

56. *Le club des Cordeliers* (Paris, 1913), 22.

57. For details of Marat's persecutions see *L'Ami du peuple*, nos. 224, 316, 331, 334, 336, 338, 358, 448, 473, 571. See also *Révolutions de France et de Brabant*, no. 34, 479.

58. *Les pamphlets de Marat*, 201-209.

59. *Ibid.*, 212-217.

60. On this incident, see *L'Ami du peuple*, nos. 180-183, 193, 196.

61. *Révolutions de France et de Brabant*, no. 37, 601 ff.

62. *La Correspondance de Marat*, 162 f.; *L'Ami du peuple*, no. 193.

63. *La Correspondance de Marat*, 203; *L'Ami du peuple*, no. 449.

64. Walter, 199.

65. Published by Mathiez in *Annales révolutionnaires*, 1911, IV, 666 ff.

ROBESPIERRE ON THE PROBLEM OF WAR

1. *L'Ami du peuple*, no. 556.

2. H. Chassagne, *Coblence 1789-1792* (Paris, 1939), 112.

3. *Ibid.*, 91.

4. *Ibid.*, 115 f.

5. Albert Laponneraye, ed., *Oeuvres de Maximilien Robespierre* (Paris, 1840), I, 131 f.

6. *L'Ami du peuple*, no. 412.

7. Louis R. Gottschalk, *Jean Paul Marat, A Study in Radicalism* (New York, 1927), 111.

8. Jean Jaurès, *Histoire socialiste de la révolution française* (Paris, 1922), III, 61.

9. Georges Michon, *Robespierre et la guerre révolutionnaire* (Paris, 1937), 16.

10. Chassagne, 171 ff., 178 ff.

11. See his *Recherches philosophiques sur le droit de propriété considéré dans la nature* ([Chartres], 1780); also *Observations d'un républicain sur les différents systèmes d'administrations provinciales* (1787), published in [Dupont de Nemours], ed., *Oeuvres posthumes de M. Turgot* (Lausanne, 1787), 135, 145, 146.

12. *De la France et des Etats-Unis, ou de l'importance de la révolution en Amérique pour le bonheur de la France* (Londres, 1787).

13. Jaurès, III, 50 ff.

14. *Ibid.*, 98 ff., 132 ff., 148 ff.; Michon, 24 ff., 36 ff.

15. Laponneraye, I, 185.

16. *Ibid.*, I, 166.

17. *Ibid.*, I, 82 ff.

18. *Ibid.*, I, 46 ff.

19. G. Hardy, "Robespierre et la question noire," *Annales révolutionnaires*, 1920, XII, 357-382.
20. Laponneraye, I, 384 ff.
21. See O. G. de Heidenstam, ed., *The letters of Marie Antoinette, Fersen and Barnave* (New York, 1926), 85 ff., 114 ff.
22. See *e.g.* his "Introduction a la revolution française," *Oeuvres*, (Paris, 1843), I.
23. Ernest Hamel, *Histoire de Robespierre* (Paris, 1866), II, 40 ff.
24. Cited in Michon, 40.
25. Laponneraye, I, 246.
26. *Ibid.*, 227.
27. *Ibid.*, 237 ff.
28. For Robespierre's two famous speeches against war see *ibid.*, I, 235-290.
29. See his *Danton et la paix* (Paris, 1919), 16 f.
30. Charles Vellay, ed., *La correspondance de Marat* (Paris, 1908), 203.
31. Michon, 39, n. 2.
32. See *e.g.* *L'Ami du peuple*, nos. 627 and 628.
33. *Ibid.*, no. 648.
34. F. A. Aulard, *La société des Jacobins: recueil de documents pour l'histoire des Jacobins de Paris* (Paris, 1892), III, 518 ff.

BRITISH JACOBINISM

1. See my *Buonarroti* (Paris, 1949), 68 ff.
2. Maurice Dobb, *Studies in the Development of Capitalism* (New York, 1947), 239.
3. Carl B. Cone, *Torchbearer of Freedom. The Influence of Richard Price in Eighteenth Century Thought* (Lexington, Ky., 1952), chs. 8-9.
4. See Minnie Clare Yarborough, *John Horne Tooke* (New York, 1926); also James E. Thorold Rogers, *Historical Gleanings* (London, 1870), 188-247.
5. See F. D. Cartwright, ed., *The Life and Correspondence of Major Cartwright* (London, 1826).
6. Appeared in many editions.
7. Joel Barlow, *Political Writings* (New York, 1796), 253 ff.
8. Appeared in many editions.
9. Moncure Daniel Conway, ed., *The Writings of Thomas Paine* (New York, 1895), III, 322-344. The text published by M. Beer, ed., *The Pioneers of Land Reform* (New York, 1920), 179-206, omits Paine's important prefatory letter to the Legislature and Directory.
10. Copy in New York Public Library, manuscript division.
11. Home Office Papers, cited in Victor Clyde Miller, *Joel Barlow: Revolutionist, London, 1791-92* (Hamburg, 1922), 4, n. 13.
12. Part I, consisting of the first four chapters written at the end of 1791, was published anonymously in London in February 1792 and was suppressed in November of the same year, after the publication of a second edition. Editions also appeared in 1792 in Paris and New York. Part II appeared first in Paris in 1793. It was published subsequently in New York in 1794 and in London in 1795. A German edition of Part I appeared in London in 1792.
13. The major part of his papers are in the Harvard University Library and in the Pequot Library, Southport, Conn.
14. Miller, *op. cit.*, 27-29, 34-45; *Le moniteur* (réimpression), XIV, 592 ff.; *Discours à l'Assemblée nationale, prononcé par William Henry Vernon, au nom des citoyens unis de l'Amérique, séance du 10 juillet 1790*. Only a summary of this address appeared in the Assembly's minutes.
15. Each of these publications had several subsequent editions. The first appeared in London in 1792. The French Convention ordered its translation into

French. Partly on the strength of this *Letter*, the Convention admitted Barlow to French citizenship. The resolution signed by the Convention's diplomatic committee is in the Barlow MSS., Pequot Library, Southport, Conn. The other *Letter*, written in December 1792 at the suggestion of the abbé Grégoire (See H. Carnot, ed., *Mémoires de Grégoire* (Paris, 1840), I, 422.), was first published in French in 1793 and then in Italian in the same year. An English translation, by the author, was published in New York in 1795.

16. Cited in Miller, *op. cit.*, 27, n. 79.

17. The most detailed and critical biography is Ralph M. Wardle's *Mary Wollstonecraft* (Lawrence, Kansas, 1951).

18. See Charles Cestre, *La révolution française et les poètes anglais* (Paris, 1906).

19. *An Enquiry Concerning Political Justice and its Influence on Virtue and Happiness* (New York, 1926), Introduction, xx, ed., Raymond A. Preston. We have followed this edition.

20. *Ibid.*, II, Book viii, contains his discussion on property.

21. *Ibid.*, II, 237 f., 249 f.

22. See *e.g.* his letters to John Thelwall in Charles Cestre, *John Thelwall, A Pioneer of Democracy and Social Reform in England during the French Revolution* (London, 1906), Appendix, 201-204.

23. See the letter of the Friends of the People to the London Corresponding Society, February 15, 1793, *Second Report from the Committee of Secrecy* (London, 1794), Appendix E.

24. *Proceedings of the Society of Friends of the People in the year 1792* (London, 1793); *An Abstract of the History and Proceedings of the Revolution Society in London* (London, 1789).

25. *The Correspondence of the Revolution Society, with the National Assembly, and with Various Societies of the Friends of Liberty in France and England* (London, 1792), 3.

26. *Second Report from the Committee of Secrecy of the House of Commons*, Appendix C. See also George S. Veitch, *The Genesis of Parliamentary Reform* (London, 1913), 200 ff.

27. The most recent and best account of the Society is that of Henry Collins, "The London Corresponding Society," in John Saville, ed., *Democracy and the Labour Movement* (London, 1954), 103-134; see also Veitch, *op. cit.*, 191 ff., 205 ff., 216 ff., 220 ff., 275 ff., 299 ff.

28. *London Corresponding Society's Addresses and Resolutions* (1792), a pamphlet containing three addresses; also *A Vindication of the London Corresponding Society* (London, [1796?]).

29. Here are the titles of some of the pamphlets: *Liberty and Equality Treated of in a Short History Addressed from a Poor Man to his Equals* (London, 1792); *Equality as Consistent with the British Constitution* (London, 1792); *Letters, etc., from Friends of the People, or the Last Words and Dying Advice of a Weaver to his Children* (n. p., 1792); *Village Politics Addressed to all Mechanics, Journeymen and Day Labourers in Great Britain* (London, 1793); *An Address to the Yeomanry of Great Britain* (Edinburgh, 1792); *Plain and Earnest Address to Britons, Especially Farmers on the Interesting State of Public Affairs in Great Britain and France* (London, 1792); *Short Hints upon Levelling* (London, 1792); *Liberty and Equality Weighed in the Balance and Found Wanting* (Edinburgh, 1793); *A Poor Man's Friend: An Address to the Industrious and Manufacturing Part of Great Britain* (Edinburgh, 1793); *A Whipper for Levelling Tommy* (London, 1793).

30. For the Association's aims see *The Annual Register*, 1792, 92-96; also *Parliamentary Register*, 1792-93, XXXIV, 26 ff., 39 f.

31. The general title of the series was *Liberty and Property Preserved against Republicans and Levellers: A Collection of Tracts.*

32. William Eden, Lord Auckland, *Journal and Correspondence* (London, 1861), II, 463.

33. *Political Curiosities, Including an Account of the State of Political Affairs in Europe* (1795), a collection of nineteen of his pamphlets.

34. *The Rights of Swine: An Address to the Poor* (1793?), a four-page tract.

35. *Husks for Swine, Dedicated to the Swine of England, the Rabble of Scotland and the Wretches of Ireland, by One of the Herd, for the Benefit of the Grumbletonians* (1794).

36. *Pig's Meat; or Lessons for the Swinish Multitude*, 1793-95, 3 vols.

37. *Hog's Wash; or, A Salmagundy for Swine.* With its seventh number the title changed to *Politics for the People; or Hog's Wash.* Sixty numbers appeared.

38. On Spence's life and thought see Olive D. Rudkin, *Thomas Spence and his Connections* (New York, 1927). See also Christopher Hill, "The Norman Yoke," in Saville, *op. cit.*, 51-53.

39. Christopher Hill, "The English Revolution and the Brotherhood of Man," *Science & Society*, 1954, XVIII, 289-309.

40. *A Collection of Addresses Transmitted by Certain English Clubs and Societies to the National Convention of France* (London, 1793), contains the addresses of many English Societies, including (p. 15-18) the address of the London Corresponding Society, subscribed to by four others; also *Second Report from the Committee of Secrecy of the House of Commons*, Appendix C; The address of the London Corresponding Society was republished by Thomas Hardy, *Memoir* (London, 1832), 20 ff.

41. *A Collection of Addresses*, 164-165.

42. *Second Report from the Committee of Secrecy of the House of Commons*, Appendix E.

43. *Ibid.*

44. *Ibid.*, Appendix F, no. 10.

45. Hardy, *op. cit.*, 30.

46. *An Account of the Proceedings of the British Convention, Held in Edinburgh, the 19th of November, 1793, by a member;* also *Second Report from the Committee of Secrecy of the House of Commons*, Appendix F.

47. *Second Report from the Committee of Secrecy of the House of Commons*, Appendix H.

48. *Ibid.*, 14-21, 24-27; also *Addresses to the Nation, from the London Corresponding Society on the Subject of a Thorough Parliamentary Reform* (1793-94), Address of Jan. 20, 1794.

49. Collins, *op. cit.*, 132.

50. Hardy, *op. cit.*, Preface.

JEFFERSON ON THE FRENCH REVOLUTION

1. *Voyage de M. le Chevalier de Chastellux en Amérique* ([Cassel], 1785), 145.

2. See *e.g.*, his *De la félicité publique, ou considération sur le sort des hommes dans les différentes époques de l'histoire.* Published in 1772, it was reprinted in an augmented form in 1776. Another edition in two volumes appeared in 1822.

3. See M. Beer, ed., *The Pioneers of Land Reform: Spence, Ogilvie and Paine* (New York, 1920); and William Godwin, *An Enquiry Concerning Political Justice.* First published in 1793, it had subsequent editions in 1796, both in England and in America, and in 1798.

4. See his "Supplément au voyage de Bougainville," in J. Assézat, ed., *Oeuvres complètes de Diderot* (Paris, 1875), II, 207-250.

5. *Rapports sur les principes de morale politique qui doivent guider la*

Convention Nationale, 18 pluviôse, an 2, 4, cited in R. R. Palmer, *Twelve Who Ruled: The Committee of Public Safety during the Terror* (Princeton, 1941), 275.

6. *Writings* (Washington, D.C., 1907), VI, 393 f., ed., Albert Ellery Bergh.
7. *Ibid.*, V, 93.
8. *Ibid.*, XIV, 391. It should not be implied, as Gilbert Chinard has done, *The Correspondence of Jefferson and Dupont de Nemours* (Baltimore, 1931), xi, that Jefferson drew the main body of his thought from the Physiocrats. True, Jefferson, as many others, held in common with the Physiocrats that an agricultural society was preferable to an industrial one, that religious differences should be tolerated and that education was a state function. But these ideas were not peculiarly Physiocratic. The fact is that Jefferson opposed large concentrations in land, advanced by Physiocrats, rejected the "legal despotism" they deemed necessary to guarantee property and watch over the free operation of the economic laws. And there is no indication that he accepted the Physiocratic theory of the net product.
9. Georg Wilhelm Friedrich Hegel, *The Philosophy of History* (New York, 1900) Introduction, 85 f.
10. *Writings*, II, 229.
11. *Ibid.*, I, 207.
12. *Ibid.*, XIV, 119.
13. See above p. 11.
14. *Writings*, XIV, 119.
15. *Ibid.*, XIV, 181, 182.
16. *Ibid.*, X, 438.
17. *Ibid.*, VII, 459.
18. *Ibid.*, XV, 39.
19. *Ibid.*, VI, 57.
20. *Ibid.*, II, 207.
21. *Ibid.*, IX, 307.
22. *Ibid.*, XVI, 182.
23. *Ibid.*, XIV, 491, 492.
24. *Ibid.*, XV, 399.
25. *Ibid.*, VI, 255.
26. *Ibid.*, VII, 76; XIX, iii.
27. *Ibid.*, XI, 224 f.
28. *Ibid.*, I, 34 f.
29. *Ibid.*, II, 226 f.
30. *Ibid.*, V, 4.
31. *Ibid.*, VI, 325 ff.
32. George Jellinek, *The Declaration of the Rights of Man and of Citizens* (New York, 1901), 20, tr. Max Farrand.
33. *Oeuvres complètes* (Paris, 1875), III, 324, ed., J. Assézat.
34. "De l'influence de la révolution de l'Amérique sur l'Europe," *Oeuvres* (Paris, 1847), VIII, 14 ff.
35. *Remarks Concerning the Government and the Laws of the United States of America* (London, 1784), 6.
36. *Oeuvres de Saint-Simon et d'Enfantin* (Paris, 1868), XVIII, 140, 149.
37. *Writings*, VI, 70.
38. *Ibid.*, VI, 387 f.
39. *Ibid.*, XIX, 18.
40. *Ibid.*, V, 80.
41. *Ibid.*, VI, 58.
42. *Ibid.*, VI, 286.
43. *Ibid.*, VII, 19.
44. *Ibid.*, VI, 287.

45. *Letters of Lafayette and Jefferson* (Baltimore, 1929), 125 f., 135 ff., ed., Gilbert Chinard.

46. For the complete document see *Writings*, VII, 372 ff.

47. For Jefferson's estimate of Necker see *ibid.*, VII, 382 ff.

48. *Ibid.*, VII, 405 ff.

49. *Ibid.*, VII, 421.

50. *Adresse d'une société allemande à la Convention nationale* (n. p., 1792).

51. See my *Buonarroti* (Paris, 1949), ch. 1.

52. See *infra*, the essay on British Jacobinism for a summary of the polemics.

53. *Works* (Boston, 1851), IV, 428; VI, 65.

54. *Ibid.*, VI, 279 f.

55. Pseudonym of John Quincy Adams, son of John Adams, who published a series of articles in the *Columbian Centinel* to attack Paine.

56. *Writings*, VIII, 224.

57. *Writings* (New York, 1895), VI, 249, ed., Paul Leicester Ford.

58. *Writings* (Washington, D.C., 1907), VI, 373.

59. *Ibid.*, XVIII, 212.

60. *Ibid.*, VIII, 124.

61. See Louise B. Dunbar, *A Study of "Monarchical" Tendencies in the United States from 1776 to 1801* (Urbana. Ill., 1923), 101 ff.

62. *Writings*, I, 273 ff.

63. *Ibid.*, VIII, 13.

64. *Ibid.*, VIII, 234.

65. *Writings* (New York, 1895), VI, 265, ed., Paul Leicester Ford.

66. *Writings* (Washington, D.C., 1907), IX, 285.

67. *Ibid.*, IX, 7 f.

68. *Ibid.*, I, 196.

69. *Ibid.*, IX, 9 f.

70. *Ibid.*, IX, 300.

71. *Ibid.*, VIII, 444.

72. For the celebrations see C. D. Hazen, *Contemporary American Opinion of the French Revolution* (Baltimore, 1897), 165 ff.

73. Eugene P. Link, *Democratic-Republican Societies, 1790-1800* (New York, 1924), 74 ff., 81.

74. On Genet see Meade Minnegerode, *Jefferson, Friend of France* 1793; *The Career of Edmond Charles Genet* (New York, 1928).

75. For the intrigues behind the plot see Gouverneur Morris, *A Diary of the French Revolution* (Boston, 1939), II, 595 f.; Minnegerode, *op. cit.*, 127 f.

76. Henry Budd, *Citizen Genet's Visit to Philadelphia* (Philadelphia, 1919), 48.

77. See Charles Gayarré, *History of Louisiana* (New Orleans, 1885), III, 337 ff.; also Genet's dispatch to the minister of Foreign Affairs, in C. H. de Witt, *Thomas Jefferson: Etude historique sur la démocratie américaine* (Paris, 1861), 523 f.

78. Samuel Flagg Bemis, *The American Secretaries of State and Their Diplomacy* (New York, 1927), II, 69.

79. *Writings*, III, 227, 242.

80. Budd, *op. cit.*, 59.

81. *Writings*, IX, 180 ff.; see also *ibid.*, I, 389 ff.

82. *Oeuvres de Maximilien Robespierre* (Paris, 1840), III, 455 f., 473 ff., ed., Albert Laponneraye.

83. *Writings*, XIII, 36.

84. *Ibid.*, XIII, 402.

85. *Ibid.*, XIX, iii.

86. Lincoln's complete letter was republished in *ibid.*, I, xv ff. The italics are Lincoln's.

208   ESSAYS IN POLITICAL AND INTELLECTUAL HISTORY

BABEUF AND BABOUVISM

1. Alphonse Aulard, *Paris pendant la réaction thermidorienne et sous le directoire* (Paris, 1898), II, 664; III, 180.

2. Charles Ballot, *L'Introduction du machinisme dans l'industrie française* (Paris, 1923), 24. Emile Levasseur, *Histoire des classes ouvrières et de l'industrie en France de 1789 à 1870* (Paris, 1903), I, 262 ff., 267 and notes 3-5.

3. See *e.g.* Aulard, II, 616; III, 38, 82, 143.

4. E. Levasseur, I, 223; Aulard, II, 271.

5. Aulard, I, 619, 661, 730.

6. *Ibid.*, I, 615; III, 35, 144.

7. See his "Défense générale devant la Haute-Cour de Vendôme," Victor Advielle, *Histoire de Gracchus Babeuf* (Paris, 1884), II, 69.

8. Aulard, II, 623. See also Bayard, *La cause des rentiers présentée au tribunal de l'équité* (Paris, 1795).

9. Aulard, II, 616-617; III, 22, 115, 406.

10. See *e.g.* C. Riffaterre, *Le mouvement anti-jacobin et anti-parisien à Lyon et dans le Rhône-et-Loire en 1793* (Lyon, 1928), I, 346, n. 4; and Albert Mathiez, *Le directoire* (Paris, 1934), 161.

11. Riffaterre, I. 347.

12. Jean Jaurès, *Histoire socialiste de la révolution française* (Paris, 1924), revised edition, VIII, 271-272; Jacques Roux, *Discours sur les moyens de sauver la France et la liberté* [Paris, 1792?]

13. *Le moniteur universel*, April 3, May 23, 1795; F. Dieudonné, "Préliminaires et causes des journées de Prairial, An III," *La révolution française*, 1902, XLIII, 442-465, 504-527; L. Thénard and R. Guyot, *Le conventionnel Goujon* (Paris, 1908), ch. xi.

14. Philippe Buonarroti, *Conspiration pour l'égalité dite de Babeuf* (Bruxelles, 1828), I, 70-72, 81-95.

15. Cited in Mathiez, *Le directoire*, 144.

16. For an account of the cruel treatment she received, see the Babouvist paper, *L'Eclaireur du peuple*, no. 2, and Babeuf's *Le Tribun du peuple*, II, no. 40, 263. See also Etienne Charavay, "Arrestation de la femme de Babeuf," in *La révolution française*, 1881, I, 214-220.

17. For an account of the Pantheon Club see Buonarroti, I, 77 ff.

18. *Le Tribun du peuple*, I, no. 29, 285.

19. Advielle, II, 117-118, 190-195.

20. *Cadastre perpétuel* (Paris, 1789), xxvi-xxxii, xxxiv-xlii, 13-16.

21. Advielle, I, 53-56.

22. *Ibid.*, I, 487 ff., 525-534; Babeuf, *A messieurs du comité des recherches de l'assemblée nationale* (1790).

23. Maurice Dommanget, ed., *Pages choisies de Babeuf* (Paris, 1935), 101-102.

24. *Ibid.*, 93-97, 103-130; Alfred Espinas, *La Philosophie sociale du XVIIIe siècle et de la révolution* (Paris, 1898), 403-412.

25. Gabriel Deville, "Notes inédites de Babeuf sur lui-même," *La révolution française*, 1905, XLIX, 37-44; *Le Tribun du peuple*, no. 29, 285.

26. *Journal de la liberté de la presse*, no. 1, 3-5.

27. Babeuf, *Du système de dépopulation* (An III), 32-36, n.

28. *Journal de la liberté de la presse*, no. 5, 2.

29. *Le Tribun du peuple*, I, no. 23, 8.

30. *Ibid.*, no. 25, 3.

31. *Le Tribun du peuple*, I, no. 28, 234 ff.; no. 29, 263 ff.

32. *Ibid.*, no. 31, 312-321.

33. *Le moniteur*, February 10, 1795.

34. *Haute-Cour de justice: Débats du procès*, IV, 163 ff. The most recent work is by Irving L. Horowitz, *Claude Helvetius* (New York, 1954).

35. What follows has been based on Babeuf's letter to Germain, July 28, 1795. It is one of the important documents in the history of Babouvism. See Dommanget, 207-221.

36. See Linguet, *Théorie des loix civiles* (1767), II, 461-472; Necker, *Sur la législation et le commerce des grains* (1775), 126-151; Graslin, *Essai analytique sur la richesse et sur l'impôt* (1767), 147-148, 152-158, 184-190, 210-214; see also Baudeau et Graslin, *Correspondance sur un des principes fondamentaux de la doctrine de soi-disant philosophes économistes* (1777).

37. See *Code de la nature* (1755).

38. Espinas, 238.

39. Advielle, I, 162, 167-170.

40. See my *Buonarroti* (Paris, 1949), ch. 1.

41. *Le Tribun du peuple*, II, no. 34, 4-52.

42. Aulard, II, 459.

43. See *e.g.*, *Le Tribun du peuple*, II, no. 35, 63-65, 76-77.

44. *Haute-Cour de justice: Débats du procès*, II, 78-79.

45. *Le Tribun du peuple*, II, no. 35, 82-107.

46. Printed in *ibid.*, II, no. 38, 175.

47. On Antonelle's activities during the Revolution see *Débats du procès*, IV, 357 ff. Also his *Observations sur le droit de cité* (Paris, An. III) and *Le Contraste de sentiments* (Paris, An. III).

48. *Pièces saisies*, II, 60-62.

49. *Ibid.*, II, 66-67.

50. Only three small numbers, 41-43, appeared from March 30 to April 24, 1796.

51. For their names see *Pièces saisies*, I, 52; II, 239.

52. *Ibid.*, I, 169-181, 205-206.

53. *Ibid.*, II, 319 ff.; also *Le Tribun du peuple*, II, no. 41, republished as a pamphlet with the title, *Adresse du Tribun du peuple à l'armée de l'intérieur*, and *L'Eclaireur du peuple*, nos. 3-5.

54. *Haute-Cour de justice: Débats du procès*, III, 296, 299.

55. *Pièces saisies*, I, 271-276, 284-285.

56. *Ibid.*, I, 295-296.

57. *Ibid.*, II, 162-163.

58. *Ibid.*, I, 269-270, 333-334.

59. Aulard, III, 114

60. *Haute-Cour de justice: Pièces lues dans le cours de l'exposé fait par l'accusateur national*, 78-80; Aulard, III, 110, 116.

61. The list of subscribers of the *Tribun du peuple* is in Archives nationales, F⁷ 4278 troisième carton; Buonarroti, II, 213-229; for a list of the pamphlets see *Pièces saisies*, II, 243.

62. *Pièces saisies*, I, 159-163; Postgate, *Revolution from 1789 to 1906* (London, 1920), 54-56.

63. See Peter Kropotkin, *The Great French Revolution* (New York, 1927), 489 and Max Nettlau, *Der Forfrühling der Anarchie* (Berlin, 1925), 43 ff. For an apparently complete list of Maréchal's writings see Maurice Dommanget, *Sylvain Maréchal, l'égalitaire* (Paris, 1950), 445-493.

64. *Débats du procès*, IV, 255.

65. *Pièces saisies*, I, 52-53, 133-134; II, 3-9, 41, 78-80; Advielle, I, 205-207.

66. Archives nationales, W³ 562.

67. *Pièces saisies*, I, 221, 224.

68. Archives nationales, W³ 561-563; F⁷ 4276, and 4277 deuxième carton.

69. See my *Buonarroti*, 62-83.

70. Buonarroti, I, 191; Paul Robiquet, "Babeuf et Barras," *Revue de Paris*, March 1, 1896, 192-211.

71. *Le Tribun du peuple*, II, no. 42, 288 ff., 294; *Pièces saisies*, I, 193, 201-203; II, 169-171.

72. La Révellière Lépeaux, *Mémoires* (Paris, 1895), I, 416.
73. Archives nationales, W³ 561.
74. *Pièces saisies*, I, 36-38, 256-257; II, 96-97, 146.
75. *Ibid.*, I, 35-36, 190-191.
76. *Ibid.*, I, 167-169.
77. *Ibid.*, II, 244-252.
78. Buonarroti, I, 155-156.
79. *Haute-Cour de justice*: *Copie de l'instruction personnelle du repré-*
sentant du peuple Drouet, 161.
80. *Débats du procès*, II, 78-79; 89-91; III, 388 ff.
81. Buonarroti, I, 162-163.
82. For a description of their meetings see the account by Grisel in
Débats du procès, II, 92-93, 95-96, 98-101, 103-105, 110-112.
83. Buonarroti, I, 189, n.; *Pièces saisies*, I, 19.
84. *Pièces saisies*, I, 15-18, 25-26.
85. *Ibid.*, I, 55-59.
86. *Ibid.*, I, 238-242.
87. Buonarroti, I, 133.
88. *Ibid.*, I, 134, n.
89. *Pièces saisies*, I, 130-131; II, 52 ff.; *Débats du procès*, II, 241 ff.
90. Buonarroti, I, 199 ff.
91. *Ibid.*, I, 206 ff.; II, 301, 305 ff.
92. *Pièces saisies*, I, 207.
93. For the terms see *ibid.*, I, 63 ff., 81 ff.; also Buonarroti, I, 166 ff.
94. Grisel's letters to Carnot are in Archives nationales, F⁷ 4278. Grisel
wrote under the pseudonym Armand.
95. *Débats du procès*, II, 129 ff.
96. Police report cited by Paul Robiquet, "L'Arrestation de Babeuf,"
La Révolution française, 1895, XXVIII, 308 ff.
97. For the letter see *Pièces saisies*, II, 235-239; *Débats du procès*, II, 204-
207.
98. *Haute-Cour de justice*: *Résumé du président*, IV, 114 ff.
99. Buonarroti, II, 320-322.
100. See my *Buonarroti*, ch. 10.

SAINT-SIMON'S PHILOSOPHY OF HISTORY

1. Marx-Engels, *Selected Works* (New York, 1936), I, 247.
2. *Anti-Dühring* (New York [1935]), 30.
3. *Oeuvres de Saint-Simon et d'Enfantin* (Paris, 1865-78), XVIII, 150 ff.
4. *Précis historique de la révolution française* (Paris, 1792).
5. *Oeuvres* (Paris, 1843), I, 13.
6. *Histoire socialiste de la révolution française* (Paris, 1922), I, 129 f.
7. *Oeuvres*, XV, 55.
8. *Ibid.*, XXXVIII, 119.
9. *Dialectics of Nature* (New York, 1940), 178 f.
10. *Oeuvres*, XV, 15.
11. *Ibid*, 180.
12. *Anti-Dühring*, 292.
13. *Oeuvres*, XV, 242.
14. *Ibid.*, XIX, 43.
15. *Ibid.*, XVIII, 37.
16. *Ibid.*, 50.
17. *Ibid.*, XX, 142, 152.
18. *Ibid.*, XVIII, 53 ff.
19. *Ibid.*, 92.

20. *Ibid.*, XIX, 148.
21. *Ibid.*, XX, 17 ff.
22. Georges and Hubert Bourgin, *Le Régime de l'industrie en France de 1814 à 1830* (Paris, 1912), I, 171, 173, 365.
23. *Oeuvres*, XXXIX, 144 f.
24. *Ibid.*, 158.
25. *Ibid.*, 128 f.
26. *Ibid.*, XX, 197 ff.
27. *Ibid.*, XXXIX, 92; Marx-Engels *Gesamtausgabe*, 1, III, 298.
28. *Oeuvres*, XVIII, 97 f.
29. *Ibid.*, XXII, 254.

FROM SOCIAL UTOPIA TO SOCIAL SCIENCE

1. For the German text of the catechism see Auguste Cornu, *Moses Hess et la gauche hégélienne* (Paris, 1934), 109-18.
2. *La démocratie pacifique*, August 1, 1843.
3. *The Red Republican*, November 9-30, 1850.
4. December 30, 1871.
5. Georg Brandes wrote in his *Ferdinand Lassalle* (English translation, New York, 1925), 115, that the *Communist Manifesto* was "almost a mere translation from Victor Considérant." Different versions of this charge have appeared from time to time. See *e.g.*, Georges Sorel, *La décomposition du marxisme* (Paris, 1910), 32; Morris R. Cohen, *The Faith of a Liberal* (New York, 1946), 111. The charge is also implied in Harold J. Laski, *Karl Marx; an Essay*, reprinted with *The Communist Manifesto* (New York, 1943), 17, by the League for Industrial Democracy. Anarchists joined in the attack. Thus W.Tcherkesoff insisted at one time (*Précurseurs de l'Internationale* (Bruxelles, 1899), 97) that Marx and Engels had stolen their theories from Louis Blanc, and at another (Pierre Ramus, ed., *Die Urheberschaft des Kommunistischen Manifests* (Berlin, 1906), 9-20) that they had taken the essential parts of their *Manifesto* from Considérant. Enrico Labriola endorsed Tcherkesoff's second conclusion. See *ibid.*, 21-24.
6. *Doctrine de Saint-Simon, Exposition. Première année*, 1829 (Paris, 1924), 238-39, eds., C. Bouglé et Elie Halévy.
7. Karl Marx, *Selected Works* (New York, 1936), I, 238.
8. Marx-Engels, *Gesamtausgabe*, 1, II, 438.
9. *Herr Eugen Dühring's Revolution in Science* (*New York*, [1935]), 289-99.
10. *Histoire des doctrines économiques* (Paris, 1925), VI, 86-87; VII, 137-40, 149-52, 179-83, 205-07.
11. *Selected Correspondence* (New York, 1935), 57.
12. *An Inquiry into the Nature and Causes of the Wealth of Nations* (Everyman's), I, 57-78.
13. See *e.g.* [Quesnay], *Tableau économique avec ses explications* (1760).
14. Necker, "Sur la législation et le commerce des grains," *Oeuvres complètes* (Paris, 1820), I, 126 ff. Linguet, *Théorie des loix civiles* (London, 1767), II, 461 ff.
15. *Oeuvres* (Paris, 1843), I, 13.
16. *Bronterre's National Reformer*, 1837, nos. 1-11.
17. *Selected Works*, I, 238-239.
18. Franz Mehring, ed., *Aus dem literarischen Nachlass von Karl Marx, Friedrich Engels und Ferdinand Lassalle* (Stuttgart, 1902), III, 430.
19. *Selected Correspondence*, 475-76.
20. *Ibid.*, 477.
21. *Selected Works*, I, 216, 217.

FRENCH DEMOCRACY AND THE AMERICAN CIVIL WAR

1. See Louis Bernard Schmidt, "The Influence of Wheat and Cotton on Anglo-American Relations During the Civil War," *The Iowa Journal of History and Politics*, 1918, XVI, 426-438.

2. See *e.g.* Robert Arthur Arnold, *The History of the Cotton Famine* (London, 1865), new edition, *passim;* John Watts, *The Facts of the Cotton Famine* (London, 1866), chs. 8-10; Marx-Engels, *The Civil War in the United States* (New York, 1937), 41-54, 123-155, ed., Richard Enmale; Hermann Schlüter, *Lincoln, Labor and Slavery* (New York, 1913), chs. 5-6; Joseph H. Park, "The English Workingman and the American Civil War," *Political Science Quarterly*, 1924, XXIX, 432-457; W. O. Henderson, "The Cotton Famine in Scotland and the Relief of Distress, 1862-64," *Scottish Historical Review*, 1951, XXX, 154-64.

3. Richard Greenleaf, "British Labor Against American Slavery," *Science & Society*, 1953, XVII, 42-58.

4. The article of Louis Martin Sears, "French Opinion of our Civil War," *Mid-West Quarterly*, 1914-15, II, 357-366, considers labor's position on slavery only in a very general way. The book by Donaldson Jordan and Edwin J. Pratt, *Europe and the American Civil War* (Boston and New York, 1931), tells us nothing on the attitude of French labor on the Civil War. The chapter on French opinion does not go beyond what W. Reed West had already said in his dissertation, *Contemporary French Opinion on the American Civil War* (Baltimore, 1924). West's chapter on distress among French workers is useful, but it neglects their attitudes toward Napoleon's pro-slavery policy. The compilation by Lynn M. Case, *French Opinion on the United States and Mexico* (New York, 1936), consists of extracts from the reports of the Procureurs généraux. It is useful to those who cannot examine the originals. It contains many interesting observations on industry, trade and labor conditions.

5. F. Prevost and P. Pecquet, *Le blocus américain, droit des neutres* (Paris, 1862), 16.

6. Earl S. Pomeroy, "French Substitutes for American Cotton," *Journal of Southern History*, 1943, IX, 557.

7. Archives nationales (hereinafter referred to as A.N.), BB[30] 387 Cour de Rouen, April 2, 1862.

8. West, *op. cit.*, 59.

9. *Mémorial de Lille*, January 15, 1863.

10. West, *op. cit.*, 59.

11. A.N., F[1c] III, Seine-Inférieure, 17.

12. For a number of important documents bearing on the campaign for relief see *ibid.*

13. The appeal was published in *L'Opinion nationale*, January 20, 1863.

14. Cited by Karl Marx, "The French Credit Mobilier," New York *Daily Tribune*, July 11, 1856.

15. On labor's declining standard of living in France from 1851 to 1863 see Emile Levasseur, *Histoire des classes ouvrières et de l'industrie en France depuis 1789 jusqu'à nos jours* (Paris, 1867), II, 440.

16. The series is in the National Library, Paris, under the general heading *Brochures ouvrières.*

17. D. Riazanov, "Die Entstehung der internationalen Arbeiterassoziation," *Marx-Engels Archiv.*, I, 154 f.

18. I. Tchernoff, *Le parti républicain au coup d'état et sous le second empire* (Paris, 1906), 403.

19. The Manifesto appeared in *L'Opinion nationale*, February 17, 1864.

20. A.N. BB[30] 374-388.

21. James Watkins, *Production and Price of Cotton for One Hundred Years*

(Washington, 1895), 13; Louis Reybaud, *Le coton, son régime, ses problèmes, son influence en Europe* (Paris, 1863), 7.

22. A collection of articles and pamphlets on the American Civil War, which had appeared in France, is to be found in the National Library, Paris, under the class mark 8⁰ Pb 456.

23. His lectures, delivered after 1848, were published in three volumes, under the title, *Histoire politique des Etats-Unis*, 1620-1789 (Paris, 1855).

24. For a statement of the Committee's aims see the letter of Augustin Cochin to John Bigelow, May 17, 1865, in Bigelow, *Retrospections of an Active Life* (New York, 1909), II, 563.

25. *Les Etats-Unis en 1861: un grand peuple qui se relève* (Paris, 1861).

26. "Le coton et la crise américaine," *Revue des deux mondes*, 1862, XXXVII, 184 f.

27. *Adresse au roi de coton* (Paris, 1863).

28. Cited in West, *op. cit.*, 108 f.

29. Cited in *ibid.*, 109.

30. See *e.g.*, A.N., BB³⁰ 387, Cour de Rouen.

31. See A.N., BB³⁰ 371-389, *passim.*

32. A.N., BB³⁰ 387, Cour de Rouen.

33. The reports of the Procureurs are filled with observations on the mounting opposition to the Mexican expedition. See *e.g.*, A.N., BB³⁰ 379, Cour de Lyon, April 12, 1863; and BB³⁰ 384, Cour de Paris, August 4, 1864.

34. A.N., BB³⁰ 379, June 27, 1863.

35. A.N., BB³⁰ 371, July 8, 1865.

36. Bigelow, *op. cit.*, II, 557 f.

37. *Ibid.*, II, 579.

38. *Ibid.*, II, 558.

39. A.N., BB¹⁸ 1713, A⁴ 2920; Bigelow, *op. cit.*, II, 596 f., and III, 53 f.

40. U.S. State Department, *Diplomatic Correspondence*, 1865 (Washington, 1866), IV, 82 f.

41. *Ibid.*, IV, 88.

42. Bigelow, *op. cit.*, II, 527.

43. *Ibid.*, II, 526.

44. See Taxile Delord, *Histoire du second empire* (Paris, 1869), IV, 18 f.

45. U.S. State Department, *op. cit.*, IV, 85.

46. *Ibid.*, IV, 108.

47. *Ibid.*, IV, 108 f.

48. The correspondent of the New York *Tribune* was in error when he reported that the corresponding members of the International in Paris had endorsed the address of the deputies of the Left in the *Corps Législatif*. See New York *Tribune*, May 16, 1865, 7.

49. Karl Marx and Frederick Engels, *The Civil War in the United States* (New York, 1937), 285.

50. The full address is in Hermann Schlüter, *op. cit.*, 198-201.

THE FIRST INTERNATIONAL IN FRANCE, 1864-1871.

1. For these labor developments we have based ourselves on *La réforme sociale* (Rouen), March 27, April 3, July 3, 1870; *L'Internationale* (Brussels), March 27, 1870. Useful on the congress in March 1870, provided they are used with caution, are the secret police reports in MSS. on the International, Bibliothèque de la ville de Lyon, I², Liasse 55 (hereinafter MSS. Lyon).

2. That was a general observation of workers' delegates to the International Exhibition of 1867. See some of their reports in Archives nationales, F¹² 3109-3121 A; on labor conditions and strikes see F¹² 4651-4652 and F¹ᶜ III, 9, 12, 31.

3. See his *Quelques vérités sur les élections de Paris* (Paris, 1863).

4. A good biography of Varlin is still lacking. See, however, Maurice

Dommanget, *Eugène Varlin* (Saumur, 1926); Maurice Foulon, *Eugène Varlin, relieur et membre de la Commune* (Clermont-Ferrand, 1934); E. Faillet, *Biographie de Varlin* (Paris, 1890); *La vie ouvrière*, 1913, V, no. 87, entirely devoted to Varlin and containing his letters to Aubry; Edouard Dolléans, "Lettres d'Eugène Varlin à Albert Richard," *International Review for Social History*, 1937, II, 178-90. Dolléans omits the important letter of December 1, 1869, in which Varlin announces the formation of a central labor council in Paris and appeals for aid to the striking tawers

5. E. E. Fribourg, *L'Association internationale des travailleurs* (Paris, 1871), is decidedly Proudhonist and does not go beyond his own retirement from the organization. Jules L. Puech, *Le Proudhonisme dans l'association internationale des travailleurs* (Paris, 1907), is superficial and contains a number of errors. It, too, is Proudhonist. The books by Oscar Testut, a spy in the organization, should be used with great caution. If carefully controlled, his two bulky volumes, *L'Internationale et le jacobinisme au ban de l'Europe* (Paris, 1872), may prove useful.

6. MSS. Minutes of the Meetings of the General Council of the International Workingmen's Association (hereinafter referred to as MSS. Minutes), 1866, *passim*.

7. *Congrès ouvrier de l'association internationale des travailleurs, tenu à Genève du 3 au 8 septembre* 1866 (Genève 1866), a pamphlet published by Card [Czwierzakiewicz].

8. *Procès de l'association internationale des travailleurs, première et deuxième commissions du bureau de Paris* (Paris, 1870), 2nd edition.

9. MSS. Minutes, November 30, 1869; MSS. Lyon, I[2], Liasse 56, Aubry's letters to Richard and Bastelica's letters to Richard; Archives du département des Bouches du Rhône, M[6], Liasses 163, 164 and 309 contain a number of important documents on the International and the trade unions in Marseilles.

10. *Revue des deux mondes*, 1868, LXXVI, 453.

11. *Procès de l'association internationale des travailleurs*, etc., 40.

12. *L'Association internationale des travailleurs*, Report of Prosecutor, 3rd trial, 98-99.

13. Albert Thomas, *Le second empire* (Paris, 1907), (*Histoire socialiste*, X, ed. Jean Jaurès), 384.

14. *Histoire du socialisme* (Paris, 1883), II, 679.

15. Blanqui's papers, National Library, Paris, 9590[2] f.355-357; 9594 f.325-26; 9592[2] f.98.

16. *Ibid.*, 9592[2] f.166, 217; 9590[1] f.245, 429-34.

17. *La Marseillaise*, December 30, 1869; January 1, 1870.

18. *Ibid.*, January 24, 1870.

19. Georges Duveau, *Le Siège de Paris* (Paris, 1939), 129 ff. A recent article that has just come to my attention shows that from August 7th to 9th a large popular movement was on foot in Paris to overthrow the Empire, but failed for reasons stemming from the weakness of the French labor movement as a whole. See E. A. Jeloubovskaia, "Les événements révolutionnaires du 7 au 9 août 1870," *Questions d'histoire* (Paris, 1954), II, 170-195.

20. Serraillier's report to the General Council of the First International in MSS. Minutes, February 28, 1871.

21. Louise Michel, *La Commune* (Paris, 1921), 97-108.

22. *Le Réveil*, July 12, 1870; *L'Egalité*, August 13, 1870.

23. *L'Egalité*, August 13, 1870; *Le Réveil*, July 20, 23, 1870.

24. The first address has been republished frequently together with Marx's *Civil War in France*.

25. *Les murailles politiques françaises*, I, 6.

26. "Bulletin de la fédération ouvrière rouennaise," September 11, 1870, issued in copygraph form.

27. *Aux travailleurs allemands*, a handbill, in the National Library, Paris.

28. *Liberté, Egalité, Fraternité: République française. Association internationale des travailleurs,* a poster, in the National Library, Paris.

29. Duveau, *op. cit.,* 62 f.

30. *L'Egalité,* September 22, 1870.

31. MSS. Minutes, September 6, 1870.

32. The address has been published in many editions. The italics are in the text.

33. MSS. Minutes, January 31, February 7, 14, 1871.

34. *Ibid.,* September 20, 27, November 29, 1870.

35. *The Workingman's Advocate,* October 22, 1870.

36. The New York *World,* November 20, 1870. The resolutions were published in English, French and German as a handbill for mass distribution.

37. MSS. Minutes, November 1, 22, 1870.

38. For the list of the old council see *La République des travailleurs,* February 4, 1871; and *Le Vengeur,* February 4, 1871, for that of the new council.

39. A lengthy summary of Serraillier's report is in MSS. Minutes, February 28, 1871.

40. *Procès-verbaux des séances officielles de l'Internationale à Paris pendant le siège et pendant la Commune* (Paris, 1872), 2nd edition, 12, 32, 47.

41. *Ibid.,* 54-69.

42. *Ibid.,* 86. There are useful dossiers on a number of French Internationalists mentioned in this essay. They are in Archives nationales: on André Bastelica, BB[24] 862, S79-5897; on Charles Longuet, BB[18] 1707, A[4] 2264 and BB[24] 863, S 79-5947; on Auguste Serraillier, BB[24] 859, S 79-3337 and BB[30] 487, dossier 5; on Léo Frankel, BB[24] 862, S 79-5166 and BB[30] 487 dossier 5; on Benoît Malon, BB[24] 862, S 79-5177; on Emile Aubry, BB[24] 850, S 78-7537 and BB[30] 389, Cour de Rouen, July 11, 1869, also F[1c] III, 9, Seine-Inférieure, May 1, 1868; on Albert Theisz, BB[24], S 79-3363. The dossier on Varlin in Archives de la préfecture de police B[a]/1291, has some interesting data.

The dossier on the International, specifically in Paris in the Archives de la préfecture de police, D[b]/422 is disappointing, save for a few documents, especially the appeal, in manuscript, of Parisian Internationalists to the French rural workers, dated April 27, 1870.

THE PARIS COMMUNE

1. The commission's report and the statutes were published in what seemed to be the first number of *La Fédération républicaine de la garde nationale* (n. d.), the official organ.

2. The list was published in *ibid.,* March 7, 1871, apparently the second number.

3. *Ibid.,* [nos. 1 and 2].

4. Edmond Lepelletier, *Histoire de la commune de* 1871 (Paris, 1911), I, 281 ff.

5. *La Fédération républicaine de la garde nationale,* March 7, 1871.

6. *Ibid.,* March 12, 1871.

7. Lepelletier, *op. cit.,* I, 279.

8. For this bulletin see Emile Andréoli, ed., *Le gouvernement du 4 septembre et la commune de* 1871 (Paris, 1871), 170 ff.

9. Marc-André Fabre, *Vie et mort de la commune* (Paris, 1939), 52 ff.

10. *Réimpression du journal officiel sous la commune,* March 21, 1871.

11. Prosper Lissagaray, *History of the Commune of* 1871 (New York, 1898), 90.

12. Cited by Louis Fiaux, *Histoire de la guerre civile de* 1871 (Paris, 1879), 179. Paul Gambon, secretary of Jules Ferry, reported that when he arrived at Versailles the first question from Thiers was: "Well, are these men [the

Parisians] marching on Versailles?" When he learned that they were occupied with debates with the mayors he heaved a sigh of relief. Paul Gambon, "Souvenirs du 18 mars 1871," *Revue de Paris*, 1935, année 42, II, 499.

13. Cited in Lissagaray, *op. cit.*, 99.

14. *Réimpression du journal officiel sous la commune*, March 22, 1871.

15. An account of the demonstrations was published in *ibid.*, March 25, 1871. See also G. Lefrançais, *Etude sur le mouvement communaliste à Paris en 1871* (Neuchâtel, 1871), *Pièces justificatives*, no. ix.

16. *Les séances officielles de l'internationale à Paris pendant le siège et pendant la commune* (Paris, 1872), 145 ff.; also published in *Réimpression du journal officiel sous la commune*, March 27, 1871, and in *Les murailles politiques françaises*, II, 52 f.

17. A. M. Blanchecotte, *Tablettes d'une femme pendant la commune* (Paris, 1872), 27.

18. *Les prétendues scissions dans l'internationale* (Geneva, 1872), 16 ff. See the dossiers on Pyat and Vésinier in Archives nationales, BB^{30} 487, dossier 5, and BB^{24} 859, S 79-3403.

19. Jules Rocher, ed., *Lettres de communards et de militants de la première internationale à Marx, Engels et autres* (Paris, 1934), 29 f.

20. *Réimpression du journal officiel sous la commune*, April 20, 1871.

21. Rocher, *op. cit.*, 30 f.

22. *Bulletin des lois de la commune de Paris* (Paris, 1871), 13.

23. *Ibid.*, 12.

24. *Ibid.*, 17.

25. Cited in Fabre, *op. cit.*, 91 ff.

26. Cited in Lissagaray, *op. cit.*, 299.

27. These letters were never published in *Père Duchêne* but appeared for the first time in a pamphlet, *Lettres au "Père Duchêne" pendant la commune de Paris* (Paris, 1934).

28. His *profession de foi* was republished in *La Liberté* (Brussels), April 27, 1871.

29. On the Federation of Artists see Paul Hippeau, *Les fédérations artistiques sous la commune* (Paris, 1890). For the program and executive committee see *Réimpression du journal officiel sous la commune*, April 15, 22, 1871. Its proposed reforms appeared in *ibid.*, May 10, 1871.

30. Hippeau, *op. cit.*, 29 ff.; *Réimpression du journal officiel sous la commune*, April 26, 30, May 10, 20, 1871.

31. Blanchecotte, *op. cit.*, 136 f.

32. Archives nationales, BB^{24} 792, S 73-4380.

33. Archives nationales, BB^{24} 822, S 76-4922.

34. Archives nationales BB^{24} 856, S 79-2382. A brief biographic sketch is given in *Bolshaia Sovetskaia Entsiklopediia* (1935), XXXII, 698 f.

35. Cited in Irma Boyer, *Louise Michel* (Paris, 1927), 98.

36. For its statutes see *La sociale*, April 20, 1871.

37. *Réimpression du journal officiel sous la commune*, April 14, May 8, 1871.

38. Rocher, *op. cit.*, 36. The italicized sentence is in English in the original.

39. Andréoli, *op. cit.*, 185 ff., 251 f., 290 ff.

40. *Ibid.*, 334 ff. Its authors were André Léo and Benoît Malon. The concluding slogan was: "The land to the peasant, the tool to the worker, and work for all."

41. See his long account in the New York *Standard*, June 15, 1871.

42. Ch. Beslay, *La vérité sur la commune* (Bruxelles, 1877), 54 ff. For an example of the activities of Thiers's secret service in Paris see Gesner Raffina, *Une mission secrète à Paris pendant la commune* (Paris, 1871). See also Archives nationales, F^{1c} I, 131, a note by a Versailles agent.

43. Georges Bourgin, *Histoire de la commune* (Paris, 1907), 162 f.

44. B. Flotte, *Blanqui et les otages de 1871, documents historiques* (Paris, 1885); E. B. Washburne, *Recollections of a Minister to France* (New York, 1889), II, 175; Georges Laronze, *Histoire de la commune de 1871* (Paris, 1928), 377, n. 3; also *Réimpression du journal officiel sous la commune,* April 27, 1871.

45. Rocher, *op. cit.,* 18, 31.

46. *Réimpression du journal officiel sous la commune,* April 27, 29; May 7, 8, 12, 13, 18, 1871.

47. *Bulletin des lois de la commune de Paris,* 14.

48. *Réimpression du journal officiel sous la commune,* April 25, 28; May 10, 12, 14, 18, 1871. A useful dossier on Vaillant is in Archives nationales BB²⁴ 853, S 79-880.

49. *Bulletin des lois,* 26.

50. *Le Réveil,* September 28, 1870.

51. *Bulletin des lois,* 22.

52. Figures in *Annales de l'assemblée nationale,* December 1-17, 1875, XLIII, Annexes, 117, "Rapports d'ensemble de M. le général Appert."

53. *Réimpression du journal officiel sous la commune,* April 28, May 2, 8, 1871.

54. MSS. Minutes, April 11, 1871; New York *Tribune,* July 3, 1871.

55. Marx-Engels, *Selected Correspondence* (New York, 1935), 330.

56. MSS. Minutes, April 25, 1871.

57. *Ibid.,* April 11, 1871.

58. Gustav Mayer, *Friedrich Engels* (New York, 1936), 221.

59. MSS. Minutes, June 6, 1871.

60. *Ibid.,* March 28, April 4, 18, 25, May 2, 9, 23, 30, 1871.

THE AMERICAN PRESS VIEWS THE COMMUNE

1. William Lovett, *Life and Struggles* (New York, 1920), II, 325; the address is given, 319-325.

2. *Mechanics' Free Press,* October 2, 1830; *Morning Courier and New York Enquirer,* November 29, 1830.

3. George E. McNeill, *The Labor Movement* (New York, 1888), 114 f.

4. In this connection an observation of Lewis Henry Morgan, author of *Ancient Society,* has relevancy. He noted in his *European Travel Journal:* "It is a singular fact that the English press from day to day urged on the Thiers government to press the capture of Paris, and thus put an end to the Commune, assuming that the latter was wholly in the wrong, and knowing that butchery was to follow. A workingmen's government finds no sympathy in aristocratic England. The 'gentlemen of the pavement' must stand aside and the privileged class must ride. English sympathy is about as unenlightened as Hottentot sympathy and perhaps more so. They are certain to get on the wrong side of all questions arising among foreign nations because they see all things from the aristocratic and nothing from the democratic standpoint. The recent massacres in Paris, after the capture of the city, prove the barbarism of the nation, and the ferocity of the governing class. As it seems to me it is without excuse, and without palliation." Leslie A. White, ed., *Extracts from the European Travel Journal of Lewis H. Morgan* (Rochester, N. Y., 1937), 343 f.

5. April 11, 1871.

6. March 22, 1871.

7. March 28, 1871.

8. *Morning Bulletin,* March 21 and 30, 1871; *Evening Bulletin,* April 18 and 22, May 20, 1871.

9. April 15, 1871.

10. *New National Era,* May 4, 18, June 1 and 22, 1871.

11. April 7, 1871.

12. April 14, 1871.
13. May 3, 1871.
14. April 4, 1871.
15. April 1, 1871.
16. May 24, 1871.
17. April 4, 1871.
18. April 14, 1871.
19. The *Sun*, April 15, 1871; *Weekly New York Democrat*, March 31, 1871.
20. April 13, 1871.
21. See *e.g.*, the New York *Times*, March 21, 24, April 12, 1871.
22. *E.g.*, the *Herald*, August 12, 1871; the *World*, June 15, 1871; the *Times*, June 16, 1871.
23. See *e.g.*, the interview given by Claude Pelletier in the *World*, April 21, 1871.
24. April 24, 1871.
25. *Times*, April 8, 1871; *Evening Star*, June 6, 1871.
26. J. A. Dacus, *Annals of the Great Strikes* (Chicago, 1877), *passim*.
27. Archives de la préfecture de police, dossier, "L'Internationale en Amérique, 1867-1877."
28. June 24, 1871.
29. May 30, 1871.
30. May 23 and 29, 1871.
31. May 27, 1871.
32. June 1, 1871
33. May 24 and June 4, 1871.
34. May 30, 1871.
35. May 25 and 29, 1871.
36. *Tribune*, June 24, 1871; *Herald*, June 4, 1871; *Journal of Commerce*, June 1, 1871.
37. July 29, 1871.
38. May 30, 1871.
39. July 12, 1871.
40. June 4, 1871.
41. March 20, 1871.
42. April 24, 1871.
43. June 1, 1871, XII, 375.
44. January 9, 1870.
45. April 17, June 2, 18, 1871.
46. April 13, July 6, 1871.
47. February 20, 1871.
48. May 11, August 26, 1871.
49. September 20, 25, 1871.
50. July 1, 1871.
51. December 7, 1871.
52. March 26, April 7, 21, May 5, 1871.
53. June 23, 1871.
54. June 16, 1871.
55. June 15, August 4, 1871.
56. July 18, September 21, 24, 1871.
57. August 12, 1871.
58. June 29, 1871.
59. *Golden Age*, cited in the *Workingman's Advocate*, September 23, 1871; the *Nation*, July 6, 1871, XIII, 2.
60. July 5, 1871.
61. June 29, 1871.
62. July 1, 1871.
63. August 19, 1871.

64. Young's long story appeared in the New York *Standard*, June 15, 1871. It was republished in his *Men and Memories: Personal Reminiscences* (New York, 1901), 166-207.

65. New York *Standard*, November 8, 1871.

66. *National Standard*, August 26, 1871.

67. His articles against the *Tribune*, first published in the *National Standard*, were assembled in a pamphlet, *The Paris Commune* (Boston, 1871).

68. *National Standard*, July 8, August 19, 26, 1871.

69. July 8, 1871.

70. *Bulletin de l'union républicaine de langue française*, July 15, August 1, 1871; *Le socialiste*, January 27, 1872.

71. *The National Socialist*, June 29, 1878.

THE FIRST INTERNATIONAL AND A NEW HOLY ALLIANCE

1. Several of these publications are still useful. Among them are: Benoît Malon, *L'Internationale, son histoire et ses principes* (Lyon, 1872); Edmond Villetard, *Histoire de l'Internationale* (Paris, 1872); Rudolf Meyer, *Der Emancipationskampf des vierten Standes* (Berlin, 1874-75), I, 111-193 and II, 527-741; and, if used with extreme caution, the books by Oscar Testut, particularly *L'Internationale* (Paris, 1871) and *L'Internationale et le jacobinisme au ban de l'Europe* (Paris, 1872).

2. Its four congresses were: Geneva, 1866; Lausanne, 1867; Brussels, 1868; Basel, 1869.

3. Followers of Baron Colins, author of twenty volumes on social science, who held that individual ownership of land was the prime source of poverty. In the Colinsist program collective ownership of the land was heavily underscored. See my *The Beginnings of Marxian Socialism in France* (New York, 1933), 105 f.

4. Second Address on the Franco-Prussian War, Karl Marx, *The Civil War in France* (New York, 1940), 28 f.

5. We express our thanks to Mr. Pierre Durye and Miss Jacqueline Chaumié of the French National Archives, and to Mr. Alphonse-Henri Lambotte and his two assistants, Mr. Georges Colle and Miss Simone Brasseur of the Archives of the Ministry of Foreign Affairs, Belgium, for facilitating research and for their generous help in locating valuable documents.

6. Some of the French documents on the International, in the Archives of the French Ministry of Foreign Affairs, have been published by Georges Bourgin, "La lutte du gouvernement français contre la première internationale," *International Review for Social History*, 1939, IV, 39-138.

7. MSS. Minutes, November 27, 1866.

8. For a documented study of the policy of the First International on the war question see N. Riazanoff, "Die auswärtige Politik der alten Internationale und ihre Stellungnahme zum Krieg," *Die Neue Zeit*, 1915, Jahrg. 33, II, 329-334, 360-369, 438-443, 463-469, 509-519.

9. Archives nationales (hereinafter cited as AN), BB[30] 379, Cour de Lyon, reports of August 27, 1866, and March 28, 1867.

10. Archives du royaume, Bruxelles, dossiers 191,021 and 191,733. See also the pamphlet, *Expulsion de M. Rogeard* (Bruxelles, 1865).

11. AN, BB[30] 389, Cour de Nancy, report of October 18, 1869.

12. Archives, Ministère des affaires étrangères, Belgique (hereinafter cited as AAEB), dossier 1248, Pt. I, Minister of the Interior to the Minister of Foreign Affairs, January 26, 1869.

13. *Ibid.*, Minister of Foreign Affairs to the Ministers of War, Interior and Justice, March 20, 1871.

14. AN, F[1c] I, 131, a note from a secret foreign agent; AAEB, Dossier 1248, Pt. I, Belgian Legation, Vienna, to the Minister of Foreign Affairs, April 6, 1871.

15. AAEB, Belgian Legation, Lisbon, to the Minister of Foreign Affairs, April 11, 1871.

16. The messages are in *ibid.*, "Commune de Paris, 1871," Liasse I, 1856, and in Correspondance politique, Réfugiés, 1871-86, X, pièce 14.

17. *Ibid.*, Correspondance politique, Légations, Sainte-Siège, 1871. XIV, pièce 37 *bis.*

18. *Ibid.*, pièce 39.

19. Gaston da Costa, *La commune vécue* (Paris, 1905), III, 186 f.

20. AN, BB³⁰ 488; Bourgin, *op. cit.*, 44 f., 57 f.

21. See *Journal officiel*, June 7, 1871.

22. The text appears in MSS. Minutes, July 13, 1871. It is republished in Karl Marx, *Letters to Dr. Kugelmann* (New York, 1934), 126 f. There are a few verbal differences between the two texts.

23. See Bourgin, *op. cit.*, 73 f.

24. *Hansard's Parliamentary Debates*, CCX, 1184 f.

25. *Ibid.*, 1198 f.

26. The reply was published under the title: *The International Working Men's Association—Declaration* (1872). Also MSS. Minutes, April 16, 1872.

27. AAEB, Correspondance politique, Réfugiés, IX, pièce 171; AN, BB³⁰ 488, "Poursuites contre les insurgés de la Commune."

28. *Le droit d'asile et le traité d'extradition entre la Suisse et la France: Pétition au Conseil fédéral et mémoire addressé aux autorités fédérales et cantonales de la Confédération politique ouvrière nationale de Genève* (Genève, 1871). A copy of this rare pamphlet is in the library of the University of Geneva.

29. AN, BB³⁰ 488, 'Poursuites contre les insurgés de la Commune," Dispatch of August 18, 1871.

30. AAEB, Correspondance politique, Légations, Suisse, 1871-73, VII, pièce 33.

31. *Ibid.*, pièces 37 supplément and 38 supplément.

32. Bourgin, *op. cit.*, 60.

33. AAEB, dossier 1248, Pt. I, June 3, 1871.

34. Hélène Dajch, "Les associations professionnelles à Bruxelles à l'époque de la première internationale," 1950, ch. iv. unpublished dissertation, University of Brussels.

35. AAEB, Correspondance politique, Réfugiés, 1858-1871, IX, pièce 165.

36. May 28, 1871.

37. AAEB, Correspondance politique, Réfugiés, 1858-71, IX, pièce 169 *bis.*

38. I have found almost identical copies of these lists in departmental archives in France, *e.g.* in Toulouse, Marseilles and Saint-Etienne.

39. The two dossiers are in AAEB, Commune de Paris, 1856, Pts. I and II.

40. *Ibid.*, Correspondance politique, Réfugiés, 1871-86, X, pièces 12-13, 48.

41. *Ibid.*, Correspondance politique, Légations, Sainte-Siège, 1871, XIV, pièce 39.

42. Bourgin, *op. cit.*, 74 f.

43. The dossier on Engels, considerably thinned, is still in Archives de la Préfecture de Police, Paris, B a/1065. The dossier on Marx can no longer be consulted. According to the archivist it has been lost. It was classified under the name Williams, Marx's pseudonym, and its classification was B a/1175. I have been able to consult a copy of the dossier through the courtesy of my friend, Auguste Cornu.

44. Bourgin, *op. cit.*, 65 f. and 77 f.

45. AN, BB³⁰ 487, dossier 5.

46. One of these articles was sent by the Belgian ambassador to his government. AAEB, dossier 1248, Pt. I.

47. Archives du département des Bouches-du-Rhône, M⁶, Liasse 90.

48. AAEB, Correspondance politique, Réfugiés, 1871-86, X, pièce 47. For

the story of this incident, see the letter of Jenny Marx in *Woodhull & Claflin's Weekly*, October 21, 1871.

49. A copy of this long and interesting dispatch from the Portuguese Foreign Minister to his Minister in Madrid was forwarded by the Belgian Minister to his government. AAEB, Correspondance politique, Légations, Portugal, 1871-74, XIII, pièce 128, annexe. See also *ibid.*, pièce 29.

50. *Ibid.*, pièce 87.

51. Sorge Papers: General Council to the local Council in Lisbon, June 20, 1873. State Historical Society, Madison, Wisconsin.

52. AAEB, Correspondance politique, Légations, Portugal, 1871-74, XIII, pièce 137, annexe.

53. *Ibid.*, dossier 1248, Pt. I, letter of June 21, 1871, to the Minister of Foreign Affairs.

54. *Ibid.*, Correspondance politique, Légations, Pays-Bas, XVII, pièce 78 and annexes.

55. *Ibid.*, Correspondance politique, Consulats, 1871-80, XII, pièce 20.

56. The National Library, Paris, has *La Contre-Internationale, première séance du conseil général,* February 15, 1872, a report of the first meeting, and *Projet de statuts de la Contre-Internationale,* containing the principles and rules of the organization. A project for a similar organization was published by Léon Chotteau, *L'Internationale des patrons* (Paris, 1871), 22 f.

57. AAEB, Correspondance politique, Légations, Autriche-Hongrie, 1871, XXXVIII, pièce 72.

58. In 1871 they had received approximately 102,000 votes.

59. AAEB, dossier 1248, Letters of August 28, September 5 and September 13, 1871.

60. *Ibid.*, Correspondance politique, Légations, Allemagne, I, pièce 164.

61. *Ibid.*, Correspondance politique, Légations, Autriche-Hongrie, 1871, XXXVIII, pièce 72; XXXIX, pièce 75.

62. *Ibid.*, Correspondance politique, Légations, Allemagne, I, pièce 164.

63. Bourgin, *op. cit.*, 85 ff.

64. *Underground Russia* (London, 1896), 4th ed., 15 f.

65. AAEB, Correspondance politique, Légations, Russie, 1871-73, XI, pièce 21.

66. See Riazanov, "Marx und Engels über die Polenfrage," *Archiv für die Geschichte des Sozialismus und der Arbeiterbewegung,* Jhrg. VI, 175-221.

67. *Ministère des affaires étrangères: Documents diplomatiques français* (1871-1914), 1er série, I, 55.

68. *Ibid.*, 74.

69. AAEB, Correspondance politique, Légations, Russie, 1871-73, XI, pièce 28.

70. It appeared simultaneously in Brussels and Versailles in 1871.

71. AAEB, Correspondance politique, Légations, Autriche-Hongrie, 1871-72, XXXIX, pièce 92.

72. For the written agreement see Johannes Lepsius and others, eds., *Die grosse Politik der Europäischen Kabinette,* 1871-1914 (Berlin, 1927), I, 206 f.

73. Winifred Taffs, "Conversations between Lord Odo Russell and Andrássy, Bismarck and Gorchakov in September 1872," *Slavonic Review,* 1930, VIII, 705.

74. A. Meyendorff, "Conversations of Gorchakov with Andrássy and Bismarck in 1872," *ibid.*, 1929, VIII, 404 f.

75. AAEB, Correspondance politique, Légations, Russie, 1871-73, XI, pièce 87.

76. See William L. Langer, *European Alliances and Alignments,* 1871-1890 (New York, 1931), 19 f. and *passim.*

77. Archives du département des Bouches-du-Rhône, M⁶ Liasse 1890.

78. AAEB, dossier 1248, Pt. II, January 11, 1879.

INDEX

Adams, John, 66, 69-70
Address on the Civil War in France, 167-8, 179, 181
Alexander II of Russia, 195-6, 198
American Revolution, 39, 42, 48, 63-4, 101
Analyse de la doctrine de Babeuf, 90
Andrássy, Count, 195, 197-8
Antonelle, Marquis d', 87
Assignats, 17, 27, 77-8
Association for Preserving Liberty and Property against Republicans and Levellers, 51
Aubry, Emile, 135, 146, 215n42
Babeuf, François Noël: and Marat, 20, 87; background, 80-2; *Cadastre perpétuel,* 82; program, 59, 82-3, 84-5, 86, 87; French Utopianism, 81; Robespierre, 83; persecution, 83, 84, 87; *Tribun du peuple,* 83-4, 86, 87, 90-1, 92, 97; Babouvist Party, 86, 87-93; *Eclaireur du peuple,* 91; propaganda in armed forces, 93; plan of insurrection, 94-5; transitional authority, 95-6; arrest and trial, 97-8; last letter, 98; neo-Babouvists, 99
Bakunin, Michael, 139, 142, 161, 187-8, 191, 193
Barlow, Joel, 40, 42-4, 45, 49, 203n12, 203-4n15
Barnave, Antoine Joseph, 16, 33-4, 102, 117
Barras, Paul François de, 92, 98
Bastelica, André, 136, 215n42
Beecher, Henry Ward, 179-80
Beust, Count von, 194-5, 197
Bigelow, John, 129
Bismarck, Otto von, 140, 146, 148, 186, 194-5, 197
Blanc, J. J., 123, 125
Blanc, Louis, 115, 154-5
Blanqui, Louis Auguste, 99, 115, 131, 134, 136, 139-40, 142, 147, 148, 151-2, 155, 156, 157, 163, 174, 189
Bodson, Joseph, 85, 86, 89, 92
Boissel, François, 81
Bonaparte, Napoleon, 75, 79, 92, 104, 105, 140, 165
Bright, John, 121, 127
Brissot, Jacques Pierre, 30-1, 34, 35, 36, 68, 81
Büchner, Georg, 113
Buffon, Georges Leclerc de, 63

Buonarroti, Philippe, 38, 69, 80, 85-6, 87, 91, 92, 94, 97-8, 99
Burke, Edmund, 39-41, 43, 45, 50-1, 69
Cabet, Etienne, 118
Carnot, Lazare Nicolas, 97
Cazin, Jean Baptiste, 89, 98
Chartists, 78, 117, 169
Civil War, American, 121, 122-3, 127-8, 129-31, 131-3
Clavière, Etienne, 30
Clemenceau, Georges, 154
Cluseret, Gustave Paul, 162
Cochrane, Baillie, 188, 191
Coleridge, Samuel Taylor, 45, 47
Communist Manifesto, 113, 114, 117-8, 119, 120
Condorcet, Antoine Nicolas de, 64
Considérant, Victor, 113-6, 118
Constitution of 1793, 78, 91, 96
Constitution of 1795, 79, 85
Cordeliers Club, 24
Corot, Jean Baptiste, 160
Courbet, Gustave, 155, 160, 164
Danton, Georges Jacques, 28, 36
Darthé, Augustin, 80, 87, 95, 97, 98
Debon, 86, 87, 94, 95
Declaration of the Rights of Man and of the Citizen, 18
Delescluze, Charles, 147, 156
Democratic internationalism, 52-3, 68-9, 70-1, 92, 169
Deschamps, Dom, 60, 81
Desmoulins, Camille, 14, 23-24, 201n33
Diderot, Denis, 58, 59, 64, 81, 84
Didier, 87, 94, 97
Directory, 79, 80
Dmitrieff, Elisabeth, 161-2, 164-5, 216 n34
Dombrowski, Jaroslaw, 165
Drouet, Jean Baptiste, 96, 97
Eaton, Isaac, 52
Edinburgh Convention, 54-5
Encyclopedists, 111
Engels, Frederick, 100, 104-5, 113-20, 165-6, 191, 220n43
English Revolution, 38, 39, 52
Enragés, 83, 85, 87
Estates General, 10, 11-12, 15, 30, 31, 66, 67
Favre, Jules, 178, 186-8, 191-2, 194-6
Fawcett, Henry, 188
Fion, Jean, 92, 94, 96

Fourier, François Marie, 41, 106, 113
Fourierists, 114-5, 116, 173
Franco-Prussian War, 140, 142, 150-1
Frankel, Léo, 139, 149, 164-5, 174, 178, 215n42
La Fraternité, 115
French labor, 124-5, 135, 138, 141
French Revolution, 12, 13, 16-7, 21, 24, 26-30, 31, 38, 39, 40, 44, 48, 49, 52, 55, 58, 68-9, 72, 89, 101-2, 115
Garibaldi, Giuseppe, 154, 165
Gasparin, Agénor, 127
Genet, Edmond, 72-5
Germain, Charles, 80, 84, 85, 92, 93, 94, 97, 98
Girondins, 30, 31, 33, 35, 36, 73
Godkin, Edwin L., 177
Godwin, William, 40, 45, 46-8, 49, 58
Gorchakov, Prince, 197-8
Government of National Defense, 142, 147-8, 150
Graslin, J. Louis, 59, 84
Grisel, Georges, 94, 96-7, 210n94
Guizot, François, 124, 126
Hardy, Thomas, 41, 48, 49, 54, 55, 56
Harrison, Frederic, 180
Hébert, Jacques René, 23, 83, 85, 86, 87, 94
Hegel, Georg William, 60, 100, 104, 117
Helvetius, Claude Adrien, 46, 58, 81, 84
Historical materialism, 119-20
Hodgskin, Thomas, 116, 117
Holbach, Paul Heinrich d', 45
Holcroft, Thomas, 49
Hugo, Victor, 189-90
International Workingmen's Association (First International): foundation, 123-4, 136, 183; French branch, 132, 136-8, 141-2; principles, 138-9; division, 147-9; opposition to armistice, 148, 151; address of General Council to President Johnson, 132-3; anti-war manifestoes, 142-6; misrepresentation, 175, 183-4, 187, 188; in U.S., 176; defense of Paris Commune, 165-8, 184; literature on, 182, 184; attacks on, 185; hysteria, 186, 199; diplomacy on, 186-9; status in Europe, 191-3; counter-Internationals, 193-5; and Tsarist Russia, 195-6; the *Dreikaiserbund*, 197-8
Jacobin Club, 28, 34, 36, 72
Jaurès, Jean, 29, 102
Jefferson, Thomas: and American Revolution, 57; social philosophy, 13, 58, 59-61, 65; Joel Barlow, 42;

commerce and industry, 60; the common man, 61; American democracy, 61-3, 71, 75; slavery, 63; *Notes on Virginia*, 63; American Bill of Rights, 64, 66; French people, 64, 65; French Revolution, 66-8, 70, 72; internationalism, 70-3; American neutrality, 73-4; Robespierre, 75
Laboulaye, Edouard, 126, 130
Lafargue, Paul, 146, 192
Lafayette, Marquis de, 16, 17, 18, 19, 23, 66, 68
Lambert, Marie Adelaïde, 91
Lapierre, Sophie, 92, 98
Legislative Assembly, 30-1, 33
Le Mel, Nathalie, 160
Léo, André, 160
Le Pelletier, Félix, 87
Leroux, Pierre, 115
Lincoln, Abraham, 76, 127, 129, 130-2
Linguet, Simon Nicolas, 81, 84, 200
Linton, W. J., 181
London Corresponding Society, 41, 49-50, 53-4, 55, 56, 58, 92
London Exhibition of 1862, 123, 124-5
London Revolution Society, 39, 48
London Society of the Friends of the People, 48, 53
Longuet, Charles, 147, 164, 178, 215n42
Louis XVI, 19, 24, 28-9, 37, 73, 96
Lullier, Charles, 154
Mably, Gabriel de, 58, 64, 81, 84, 98
Madison, James, 59, 64
Malon, Benoît, 135, 138, 147-8, 162, 164, 215n42
Manet, Edouard, 160
Manifeste des Egaux, 91, 113
Manifesto of Peaceful Democracy, 113, 114, 116
Manifesto of the Sixty, 125
Marat, Jean Paul: and Robespierre, 9, 13; *Chains of Slavery*, 10-11; *Plan de législation criminelle*, 10; *Offrande à la patrie*, 11-2; *Le moniteur patriote*, 12-3; program, 13, 15; *The Friend of the People*, 14-6, 23, 31; persecution, 15; National Assembly, 14-5, 17-9, 23; isolation, 16-7; Constitution of 1791, 18; disfranchisement, 18-9; Negroes, 20; Nancy Affair, 20; labor policy, 20; Le Chapelier Law, 21; government in a national crisis, 22; popular clubs, 22-3; Camille Desmoulins, 23-4; popularity, 24; view of first stage of Revolution, 26; King's flight, 28-9; opposition to war, 36
Maréchal, Sylvain, 87, 91, 94

Martin, Henri, 126, 132
Marx, Karl, 91, 99, 100, 113, 114-20, 139, 145, 147, 161, 166-8, 178, 188, 189
Mathiez, Albert, 23, 36
Mazzini, Joseph, 110, 173, 178, 188
Michel, Louise, 161
Millet, Jean François, 160
Minck, Paule, 160
Mirabeau, Count, 16, 17, 68
Montalembert, Count, 124, 126
Morelly, 81, 85, 98
Moroy, Juste, 89, 98
Napoleon, Louis, 121, 124-6, 128-30, 131, 134, 137, 140-2, 145
National Assembly, 12, 14, 17, 27, 48
National Guard Federation: rise of, 151; program, 152; central committee after March 18, 1871, 154-5, 157
Neo-Jacobins, 139, 156, 157, 174
Necker, Jacques, 17, 23, 30, 67, 68, 84, 201
Newton, Isaac, 103, 104, 105
O'Brien, James Bronterre, 99, 117
Owen, Robert, 106, 112
Paine, Thomas, 40, 41, 42, 48, 49, 50, 52, 58, 69, 70, 71
Pantheon Club, 80, 87
Paris Commune: rise of, 154; inner resistance to, 155; elections, 155; personnel, 155-6; factions, 156-7; and labor, 157-9; and artists, 159-60; and women, 160-62; and departments, 162-3; government, 163-4, 170; program, 164-5; international character of, 165-7, 170; effect on First International, 168; American press on, 171-8; American pulpits on, 179-80; and communism, 174-5; American defense of, 180-2; effect in Russia, 195
Pecqueur, Constantin, 115
Pelletan, Eugène, 127, 128
Perrachon, 123
Phillips, Wendell, 180-82
Physiocrats, 32, 39, 63, 81, 116-7
Pitt, William, 48, 53, 56
Price, Richard, 39, 42, 48
Proudhon, Pierre Joseph, 30, 91, 116, 118, 125, 138, 156, 157
Proudhonists, 132, 134, 136, 139, 140, 156-7, 174
Pyat, Félix, 147, 156
Reclus, Elisée, 127, 130
Rey, A., 131
Reybaud, Louis, 138
Richard, Albert, 136

Robespierre, Maximilien: and Negroes, 20, 33; labor, 21; King's flight, 28; accusations of, 29, 31, 33; program, 32-3, 36, 59; opposition to war, 34; Camille Desmoulins, 36; a people's war, 37; Jefferson, 68, 75; under Directory, 79, 86, 87, 95
Rochefort, Henri, 141-2
Rossignol, General, 94, 96
Rousseau, Jean Jacques, 13, 58, 81, 84, 98
Sagasta, Praxedes Mateo, 191
Saint-Etienne, Rabaut, 102
Saint-Just, Louis Antoine, 22
Saint-Simon, Henri de: and the United States, 64, 101; view of social classes, 100, 109-10; industry and science, 101, 102-3; property and politics, 102, 106-7, 108-9; view of society, 102, 106; theory of progress, 103-4, 107-8, 111-2; peace, 105; administration of things, 110
Saint-Simonians, 115, 124, 173
Serraillier, Auguste, 146-9, 155-6, 157, 161, 163-4, 173
Seward, William, 129, 131
Shelley, Percy Bysshe, 47
Sismondi, Simonde de, 109, 116
Smith, Adam, 39, 102, 116
Society for Constitutional Information, 49, 53
Sorge, F. A., 165, 192
Southern Confederacy, 125-8
Southey, Robert, 45, 47
Spence, Thomas, 49, 52, 58
Sylvis, William, 174
Thelwall, John, 49, 55
Thermidorian Reaction, 77-9
Thierry, Augustin, 106
Thiers, Adolphe, 152-4, 163, 171, 176, 181, 186, 195, 197, 215-6n12
Tolain, Henri, 123-5, 135-6, 148
Tooke, J. Horne, 39, 55
Vaillant, Edouard, 159, 164
Varlin, Eugène, 135-6, 139, 147-8, 152, 160, 174, 213n4, 215n42
Vésinier, Pierre, 156
Weitling, Wilhelm, 114
Wilkes, George, 180
Wilkes, John, 10, 11, 55, 200n12
Woodhull & Claflin's Weekly, 114, 168, 178, 179
Wollstonecraft, Mary, 42, 45
Workingman's Advocate, 182
Wordsworth, William, 45, 47
Wroblewski, Walery, 165
Young, John Russell, 163, 180